Information for the reader

This edition of European Community environment legislation was compiled on the basis of the official texts in force most of which were published in the Official Journal of the European Communities between 1 October 1991 and 30 June 1994. A number of previous texts, omitted in the preceding edition, have been included in the present edition and are published in German, English, Danish, Spanish, French, Greek, Italian, Dutch and Portuguese.

The laws are presented in chronological order of adoption. If applicable, the principal legislation is directly followed by the amending legislation. Occasionally, technical Annexes have been deleted for reasons of their length and the highly technical information provided for specialists who have access to these texts in other publications. These deletions are indicated at the end of each act concerned.

The EEC Treaty establishes different requirements for each type of Community legislation to become effective:

• Regulations take effect on the date specified in them or, failing this, on the twentieth day following their publication in the Official Journal of the European Communities;

• Directives and decisions must be notified to those they are addressed to and take effect upon their notification. Directives often give a deadline by which the Member State must have implemented them;

• International treaties take effect when they have been ratified by a certain number of States.

Every effort has been taken to assure the completeness and accuracy of the legislation presented herein. Neither the editor nor the institutions of the EC will assume any liability for its usage.

Table of contents

Table of contents

Preface

Legislation has long been the main pillar of the European Union's environment policy. As long ago as 1973, when environmental action first got under way, the Commission adopted a large number of measures aimed at protecting the environment and combating pollution. More often than not these were directives setting limits for emissions and standards for environmental quality, and requiring governments to help implement plans, projects and programmes for safeguarding the environment and for regulating industrial activities and products.

Environmental legislation gathered pace during the 1980s: the completion of the Single Market meant that environmental rules and standards had to be harmonised to allow goods and services to move freely between the Member States.

At the same time, the general approach to environmental problems was changing and the Community introduced new instruments to modernise its action. The Treaty as amended in 1987, and the 1992 Maastricht Treaty, proclaimed the integration of environmental protection into the Community's other policies. Also in 1992, the 5th Action Programme entitled 'Towards Sustainability' was adopted. It provides for the implementation of fiscal, economic and financial instruments and opens up channels of information, communication, education and consultation. Today, more than ever, the Community needs dialogue, cooperation and partnership with national, regional and local authorities, with social and economic agents, associations and citizens, so that everyone can be involved in safeguarding our environment and natural resources.

Nevertheless, legislation remains an important instrument. In several of the spheres in which the European Union is competent, by virtue of the principle of subsidiarity, environmental assessment leads to the introduction of new legislation — as does the carrying out of international obligations.

So it is still very useful to publish these volumes of *Community legislation on the environment*. The first edition was in 1993, and this second edition is the first update. As before, it is being published in all the official languages of the European Union, for use by the growing number of individuals responsible for environmental issues within governments, industry, educational establishments and private organisations. It is hoped that these volumes will provide a useful tool for all those wishing to be involved in the vital task of protecting the environment, safeguarding natural resources and promoting sustainable development.

Ritt Bjerregaard,
Member of the Commission

General introduction

Environment protection in the framework of the Community law

In accordance with the original intentions of the founders, the European Community has developed into a supranational government which — as it approaches its 40th year — is in the process of increasing its membership, thus deepening its democratic structure and strengthening its powers.

Six European states (Belgium, France, Italy, Luxembourg, the Netherlands and the Federal Republic of Germany) — determined to lay the foundations of an ever closer union among the peoples[1] of Europe — joined together on 1 January 1958 to create the European Economic Community[2]. Denmark, the United Kingdom and Ireland joined in 1973, Greece in 1981, and Spain and Portugal in 1985. Finally, in 1995, Austria, Finland and Sweden brought EC Membership to fifteen countries. Today, the list of countries which have declared their intention to seek membership in the European Community would include most of Europe, especially the Central European States which see close ties to the community as a crucial source of economic growth and democratic stability.

Where early post-war proposals for European union failed, Jean Monnet and French Foreign Minister Robert Schuman's pragmatic approach succeeded. 'A united Europe will not emerge overnight or in one grand design. It will be built on practical achievements, creating first a *de facto* interdependence.' Schuman declared.

---

[1] Preamble to the Treaty establishing the European Economic Community, Treaties establishing the European Communities, Office for Official Publications of the European Communities (Luxembourg : 1987), p 217. References in the text to the Treaty mean the EEC Treaty. The EEC Treaty together with the 1951 Treaty establishing the European Coal and Steel Community and the 1957 Treaty establishing the European Atomic Energy Community make up the Constitution of the European Community.

[2] The European Parliament resolved to use the term 'European Community' in 1975 to refer to the supranational political entity created by the founding Treaties. This term is increasingly used in Community documents, e.g. in Article 130r which refers to 'action by the Community relating to the environment'. However, while it is an appropriate designation for the political entity, it occasionally comes into conflict with legal texts under the Treaties, each of which established a separate 'Community', and in formal references to the Community institutions. For example, the formal title of the Commission is : 'Commission of the European Communities', meaning that it is the sole executive authority for the three founding Treaties.

From the outset, the Member States delegated powers to the Community to legislate, implement and enforce the Community's legislation that went beyond the powers of any other international organisation.

The EC is characterised by a number of features which make it unique:

1)   legislative, executive and judicial organs of government;
2)   a transfer of powers from the Member States to the Community by virtue of treaties;
3)   supremacy of Community law over national law, which is subject to exclusive review by the Community's Court of Justice.

Two milestones on the road to a united Europe were the agreement in 1967 to merge the separate organs of government of the three founding treaties which together provide the Community's constitutional framework, and the 1976 Act introducing the direct election of the members of the European Parliament[1].

Another major step forward came on 1 July 1987 when the Single European Act amending the Treaties came into effect[2]. The Single European Act reiterates the objective of economic and monetary union formally declared by the Heads of State at the 1972 Paris Summit, amends and completes the Founding Treaties and contains provisions which codify principles of political cooperation, in particular the endeavour 'to jointly formulate and implement a European foreign policy'[3].

These amendments introduced the aim of achieving an internal market without national frontiers before 31 December 1992. They also introduced for the first time two explicit references to the Community's powers concerning environmental protection: Article 100a stipulates the criteria for environmental protection legislation affecting the internal market and allows legislation to be adopted by qualified majority in the Council. Articles 130r, 130s and 130t lay down the objectives, means and procedures for the adoption of legislation regarding the environment, specifying, however, that these decisions must be taken unanimously.

The Treaty of the European Union, which was signed by the Heads of State and Government of the European Community Member States in Maastricht on 7 February 1992 and which must be ratified by the Member States in 1992, extended the application of the cooperation procedure to environmental legislation generally under Articles 130s. Unanimity is still required in three areas:

---

[1]   Act concerning the election of the representatives of the European Parliament by direct universal suffrage, annexed to Council Decision 76/787/ECSC, EEC, EURATOM (OJ L 278, 8.10.1976).
[2]   Single European Act (OJ L 169, 29.6.1987, p. 1).
[3]   Article 30 (1).

- provisions primarily of a fiscal nature;

- measures concerning town and country planning, land use with the exception of waste management, measures of a general nature and the management of water resources; and

- measures significantly affecting a Member State's choice between different energy sources and the general structure of its energy supply.

The EC's powers regarding the environment

The European Community is an institution with limited powers delegated to it through the Treaties defining both the areas of the Community's exclusive power and the areas where the Community and the Member States jointly decide. Other areas are by definition the competence of the Member States. The environment is one of the areas in which competence is shared and the area of external relations is another. Member States are thus free to adopt legislation in the absence of Community legislation, but where the Community has acted, Community legislation is supreme and binding on both past and future Member State actions.

The European Community can and does actively participate in the preparation of international conventions on the environment and in their implementation. In addition, the Court of Justice has upheld the direct effect of international agreements to which the Community is a part[1.] Community regulations, decisions and directives must be enforced in national courts if the obligation at issue is expressed in a sufficiently precise and unconditional manner.

Types of Community legislation

The European Community can adopt:

- Non-binding **recommendations** and **resolutions**;

- **Regulations** that are binding and directly applicable in all Member States;

- **Decisions** that are directly binding on the persons to whom they are addressed, including Member States, individuals and legal persons.

- **Directives** which must be implemented by the national laws or regulations of the Member States within a designated time limit (normally 18 months to two years).

---

[1] Case 87/75 Bresciani, [1976] ECR 129.

For more than 20 years, the Directive was the main tool of the Community's environmental policy. The Community defines objectives, standards and procedures allowing the Member States some flexibility in integrating them into their national systems of administration and law. Thus, where one Member State may choose to enact a new law virtually reproducing the text of the Directive, another Member State which already has legislation in the sector covered by the Directive may choose to implement it by amending the previous law or by means of administrative regulations.

Because it sometimes takes years to fully implement directives and Member States may differ concerning the transformation of the directives into national law, the Community has recently turned to the adoption of regulations because of their taking effect more rapidly and applying directly throughout the Community.

The EEC Treaty establishes different requirements for the entry into force of each type of Community legislation:

- Regulations must take effect on the date specified in them or, failing that, on the twentieth day following their publication in the Official Journal of the European Communities.

- Directives and decisions must be notified to those they are addressed to and take effect upon their notification. The notification dates are indicated in the footnotes. Directives often give a deadline by which the Member State must have implemented them.

- International treaties take effect when they have been ratified by a certain number of countries. The dates on which these treaties took effect in the Community are indicated in the footnotes.

The institutions of the European Community

The main institutions of the EC include:

- the directly elected **European Parliament**;
- the **Council of Ministers** which has the fundamental power to adopt legislation;
- the **Commission of the European Communities** which has the sole power to propose legislation and which also implements and enforces it; and
- the **Court of Justice** which assures that Community law and the treaties are respected.

The Commission

The European Commission is the executive organ of the European Community. It consists of 20 Commissioners proposed by the Member States and serving a collective 5-year term of office. It employs about 15,000 civil servants. All must swear allegiance to the European Community and declare that they are free from influence by their national governments. Only the Commission has the power to propose legislation. Before doing so, it generally consults with experts from the Member States, from industry and from the groups concerned. Its proposals are published in the *Official Journal of the European Communities*.

Moreover, the Commission is also responsible for implementing, monitoring and controlling the enforcement of Community law and policy. In this respect, it may well bring a Member State before the Court of Justice for not complying with Community law. Finally, it administers the Community budget.

In certain specific cases, the Council can in addition authorise the Commission to adopt complementary legal texts to assure the Community legislation's implementation. This power is generally used to amend the technical Annexes to the original legislation. The Member States participate in the process through one of a series of procedures laid down in Council Decision 87/373/EEC[1].

The Commission consists of 23 Directorates-general, a legal service and a general secretariat. Directorate-General XI (DG-XI) is responsible for environment, nuclear safety and civil protection. Worker protection, industrial technical regulation, regional development and aid to third countries are the responsibility of other DGs. Support for the DGs is provided by a number of other specialised services of the Commission.

The role of the Commission in the law-making process regarding the environment has become increasingly important over the years. Member States must notify the Commission before adopting any legislation that could possibly affect the common market, including most of the environmental legislation aimed at industry and which gives the Community the possibility to adopt Community-wide measures[2]. When the environment is concerned, it is increasingly common for a Member State to take the lead and for other Member States to turn to the Commission to work out a proposal to harmonise the environmental standards within this sector in all Member States rather than adopting their own national policy.

---

[1]   Council Decision 87/373/EEC of 13 July 1987 laying down the procedures for the exercise of implementing powers conferred on the Commission (OJ L 197, 18.7.1987, p. 33).

The Commission also plays an increasing important role in international environmental policy-making. For example, it participates in the work of the Organisation for Economic Cooperation and Development (OECD) and regularly receives mandates from the Council for the negotiation of international treaties on the environment. The European Environmental Agency and its environmental information and observation network were established by the Council to provide the Community, the Member States and other European countries with reliable and comparable information to enable them to take the necessary measures to protect the quality of the environment. The Commission also manages the budget allocated by the Community for aid to Central and Eastern Europe (PHARE) and has been given the task of coordinating all of the aid programmes of the G-24 (OECD) countries.

Once legislation has been adopted, the Commission's fundamental task is to ensure that it is correctly applied by the Member States, formally as well as in practice.

Environmental legislation often provides the Commission with responsibilities that go beyond its duty to monitor and control, for example the development and management of an information system, the defining of guidelines, the organization of technical training, etc. The Commission also convenes regular meetings in Brussels of the national authorities responsible for the implementation of environmental legislation in order to discuss practical problems arising during the implementation of the legislation, needs of information and education or the amendment or adaptation of the legislation to scientific and technical developments.

---

[2]   Council Directive 83/189/EEC of 28 March 1983, laying down a procedure for the provision of information in the field of technical standards and regulations (standstill) (OJ L 109,26.4.1983, p. 8). This Directive stipulates that Member States should notify the Commission well in advance about the adoption of measures liable to affect the Community's or the Member States' policy or the workings of the internal market so as to enable the Commission to propose a harmonised legislation dealing with the subject in question. The Directive 83/189/EEC includes a procedure for Member states to follow in case of creating national standards or technical regulations liable to affect the Common Market by creating non-tariff trade barriers. A large number of national environmental measures is included in this Directive for they impose regulations or define standards applicable to either the process of industrial production or the products, implying a direct or indirect impact on industry and trade.

The Council

The Council is the main legislative organ of the Community and represents the interests of the Member States. It is composed of one representative from each of the governments of the Member States, generally at ministerial level. The foreign affairs minister usually represents the Member State on general matters. The 'Environmental Council' is composed of the ministers responsible for the environment. The presidency of the Council passes from one Member State to another every six months according to an order defined unanimously by the Council. The Member States maintain a permanent representation in Brussels.

The Council is assisted by a standing Committee of Permanent Representations (COREPER) who carry out the day-to-day political work preceding agreements and a Committee of the Regions for consultation.

The European Parliament

The European Parliament represents the interests of the citizens of the European Community but has neither the power to propose legislation nor to adopt it. It does, however, have the power to approve the budget and to dismiss the Commission. Nevertheless, its role has steadily gained importance over the years. The Treaty of the European Union has significantly increased, its powers no longer being merely consultative and controlling. From now on it will exercise " the powers attributed by the present Treaty"[1].

The European Parliament participates in the process of adopting Community Acts both by exercising its powers within the framework of the procedures defined in Articles 189 B and 189 C and by giving either confirming or consultative opinions.

Moreover, it has acquired an official role in the adopted legislation by virtue of the procedures of cooperation and co-decision introduced by the Single European Act and by the Treaty of the European Union respectively. This procedure of cooperation applies, by virtue of Article 130 S (1) of the Treaty, to the actions undertaken by the Community in order to bring about the objectives put forward by the Community's environmental policy.

Members of the European Parliament are elected every five years and are divided into political groups organized at community level.

The Parliament meets for one week a month, usually in Strasbourg (France). Its sessions are open to the public. The commissions usually meet in the pre-

---

[1] Article 137.

ceding week in Brussels. Many commission meetings are open to the public, including those of the Environment, Public Health and Consumer Affairs Commissions.

The legislative procedures

Under the **consultation procedure**, the Commission must send its proposals to the Council, which is usually required to request the opinions of the European Parliament and the Economic and Social Committee. After counselling the European Parliament and the Economic and Social Committee, the proposal is returned to the Council where it will be examined by the COREPER working group concerned. Once the report of this working group has been drawn up, the proposal is studied by COREPER and is then returned to the Council. When COREPER reaches an agreement concerning the Commission's proposal, it is entered into the Council's agenda as item A. Item As are generally adopted by the Council without preliminary discussion. When, on the other hand, no consensus can be reached, the proposal is entered in the Council's agenda as item B implying that the proposal needs to be discussed and negotiated before it is voted or amended by the Council. Whether a simple majority, qualified majority or unanimity is needed depends on the authorizing provision on which the proposal is based.

If the Council is unable to adopt the proposal in accordance with the voting system mentioned in the provision concerned, the proposal is not completely overruled but is merely suspended or, as is increasingly the case, amended or withdrawn by the Commission. Occasionally, an appeal is made to the Council to resolve the deadlock.

This type of consultation applies to the environmental legislation for:

- Provisions primarily of a fiscal nature;

- measures concerning town and country planning, land use with the exception of waste management, measures of a general nature and the management of water resources;

- measures significantly affecting a Member State's choice between different energy sources and the general structure of its energy supply.

The **cooperation procedure** (*figure 1*) was introduced through the Single European Act in order to accomplish two objectives: on the one hand, it was meant to strengthen the role of the Parliament in the law-making process and, on the other hand, to accelerate the legislative process, requiring the Council to adopt a large number of acts by qualified majority and imposing deadlines on the present phase of the procedure's cooperation.

The cooperation procedure also stipulates that the Commission must send its proposals to the Council, which again is obliged to counsel the European Parliament and the Economic and Social Committee. Upon receiving the Parliament's opinion, the Council agrees a common position which is sent back to the Parliament for a second reading. Within three months following this transmission, the European Parliament may approve the common position, not pronounce its opinion, reject it by absolute majority of the constituent members or propose amendments to the Council's common position by the same majority.

If one of the two first-mentioned alternatives is chosen by the Parliament, the Council decides upon the act in accordance with its common position. If the act is rejected, however, the Council can only decide by unanimity. Finally, when the European Parliament opts for to amend the text of the common position, the Commission has three months to re-examine the proposal it based its common position on, starting from the amendments proposed by the European Parliament. Afterwards, the Commission sends not only its re-examined proposal to the Council but also the amendments that have not been accepted, together with the Commission's opinion on them. The Council can adopt these amendments by unanimity and enact the Commission's re-examined proposal by qualified majority of its members. It can also modify the Commission's re-examined proposal by unanimity. The Council is required to decide within three months. If no decision has come through by that time, the proposal is considered not-adopted.

The Treaty of the European Union has significantly enlarged the application of this legislative procedure. Within the framework of the environmental policy, actions to be undertaken by the Community to bring about the objectives mentioned in Article 130R will be decided upon according to the cooperation procedure defined in Article 189c of the Treaty.

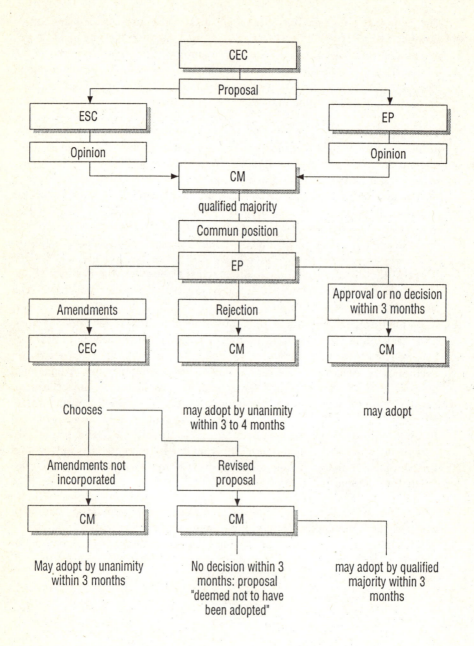

The **co-decision procedure** *(figure 2)* was first introduced by the Treaty of the European Union. This procedure allows the European Parliament to amend or to use its veto regarding certain acts of the Council. Thus, the Parliament is certain to play a more active role in the adoption of Community Legislation. Article 189 B of the Treaty describes the way in which the Parliament exercises its power of co-decision.

Upon submission of a Commission's proposal to the Council and the Parliament, the Council adopts a common position by qualified majority after counselling the Parliament. This common position is subsequently transmitted to the European Parliament. Within a period of three months after this transmission, the European Parliament may approve the common position, not pronounce its opinion, reject it by absolute majority of its constituent members or propose amendments to the common position by the same majority.

If one of the two first-mentioned alternatives is chosen by the Parliament, the Council decides upon the act in accordance with its common position. If the Parliament intends to reject the common position, it is required to inform the Council immediately. The Council can subsequently make an appeal to the Conciliation Committee[1] to fine-tune its position. Subsequently, the European Parliament either confirms the rejection of the common position by absolute majority of its constituent members implying that the act will not be adopted, or proposes amendments. Amendments to the common position need the Parliament's absolute majority of its members after which the amended text is transmitted to the Council and the Commission which have to reach an opinion on it.

If the Council approves the Parliament's amendments by qualified majority within three months, it consequently modifies its position and decrees the act concerned.

If the Council does not decree the act concerned, a meeting of the Conciliation Committee is convened. The Conciliation Committee must reach an agreement on a common project by qualified majority of its members. The Conciliation Committee must approve a common project within six weeks following its convocation. In this case, the Parliament, having decided by absolute majority and the Council, having decided by qualified majority, have another six weeks upon this approval to decree the act concerned in accordance with the common project. If one of the two institutions fails to approve the common project, the act is considered not-adopted which is also the result if the Conciliation Committee has not been able to agree on a common project. However, during the second six-week period starting immediately after the expiry of the six weeks

---

[1]   The Committee of Reconciliation consists of the members of the Council or their representatives and an equal number of representatives of the European Parliament.

granted to the Conciliation Committee, the Council may confirm, by qualified majority, the common position it had agreed upon before the procedure of reconciliation was initiated. This confirmation may possibly include the amendments put forward by the European Parliament. In this case, the act concerned is finally decreed but the European Parliament always has the final word enabling it to reject the text by absolute majority of its members within six weeks following the Council's confirmation, thus causing the act to be considered not-adopted.

Article 130S (3) of the Treaty enables the co-decision procedure to be applicable to the Council's decisions concerning decreeing general action programmes concentrating on environmental priority objectives. The measures needed to implement these programmes are agreed upon according to the procedure of consultation or cooperation, depending on the case.

The legislative procedure also implies numerous direct consultations with the national governments through COREPER and private organisations, both at national and community level. Before expressing their stances regarding proposals for Community legislation, Member States often officially consult their national parliaments and proceed with informally consulting national interest groups.

This complicated consultation process is absolutely necessary to draw up a legislation to:

- assure a 'high level of protection' of public health and the environment;
- harmonise industrial standards and procedures Community-wide;
- be integrated in the various legal systems of the Member States; and
- be implemented by the various administrations and by the various levels of government.

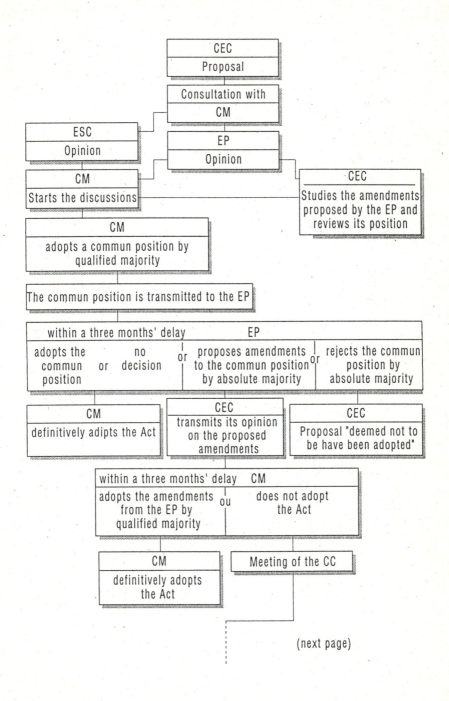

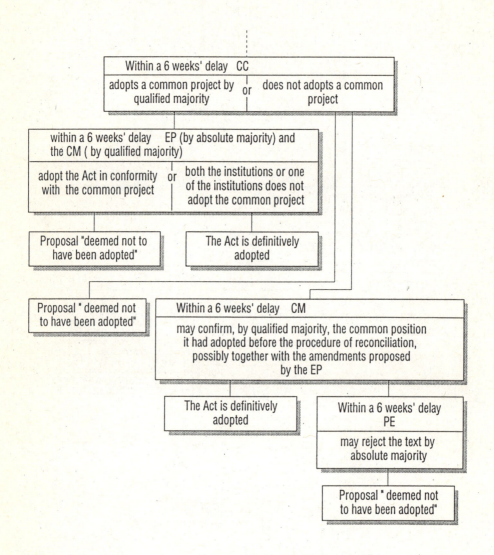

The Court of justice

The Court of Justice is the guardian of the Treaties of Community law. It is composed of judges appointed by agreement with the Member States. The judges are assisted by advocates general, who analyse and propose decisions on the cases before it.

Cases may be brought by the Community institutions against each other, by the Commission against a Member State or vice versa. Cases may also be brought by natural or legal persons against Member States or the Commission under Community law.

Regarding the Court of Justice, the major change introduced by the Treaty of the European Union, is the power granted to the Court to impose fines on Member States[1]. When a Member State fails to take the measures included in the execution of a decree established by the Court of Justice, the Commission may go to Court. The Commission determines the amount of the fine or the penalty to be paid by the Member State, taking into consideration the circumstances. If the Court of Justice finds that a Member State is not complying with its decree, it may impose the payment of the fine or the penalty.

The national courts have the power to review actions taken by their governments for the implementation and enforcement of Community legislation. They may apply to the Court of Justice for a preliminary ruling on an issue of EC law before taking a decision. Moreover, national courts have the power to enforce the decisions of the Court of Justice.

The Court of Justice has rarely ruled on the substance of Community environmental law but several decisions are of fundamental importance in defining the power of the Community to limit the lawmaking authority of the Member States.

The principle of the direct applicability of Community law to individuals was first enunciated in 1963, when the Court stated: 'The Community constitutes a new legal order of international law for the benefit of which the States have limited their sovereign rights, albeit within limited fields", and 'independently of the legislation of Member States, Community law not only imposes obligations on individuals but is intended to confer upon them rights which become part of their legal heritage. These rights arise not only where they are expressly granted by the Treaty but also by reason of obligations which the Treaty imposes in a clearly defined way upon individuals as well as upon the Member States and upon the institutions of the Community"[2].

---

[1]   Article 171 (2).
[2]   Case 26/62 Van Gend & Loos [1963] ECR 10 ; Case 8/81 Becker vs Finanzamt Münster [1982] ECR 50 ; see also Jean-Victor Luis, The Community Legal Order, 2nd ed., Office for Official Publications of the European Community (Luxembourg : 1990).

Hence, in spite of the fact that a Member State has not implemented (or not properly implemented) a Community environmental directive in violation of Article 189 (13) of the Treaty, the Directive may take direct effect. However, the provisions of the Directive regarding the obligations of the Member State must be sufficiently precise and unconditional in order to have the direct effect of national law vis-à-vis the citizen[1]. They must also be capable of being enforced as law by the national courts.

A landmark environmental ruling came in September 1988 when the Court upheld a Danish law requiring all beer and soft drinks to be sold in reusable containers with a deposit. The ensuing trade barrier to non-resident producers (which for reasons of weight and cost prefer to use throw-away containers) was justified because of the 'imperative requirement' to protect the environment in the absence of a Community law covering this issue. The Court nevertheless struck down a clause of the Danish law which limits the quantity of beverages that non-resident manufacturers may import in bottles that do not conform to Danish standards taking the view that this was a significant trade barrier insofar as Danish exporters faced no similar restrictions in other Member States[2].

Evolution of EC Environmental protection policies

In the 1950s, European politicians sought to rebuild European prosperity and secure peace in the future by creating a common trading area. The core objective of the 1957 Treaty of Rome, establishing the European Economic Community, was 'the constant improvement in the living and working conditions' of the European peoples.

Protection of the environment as such did not appear in the EEC Treaty. However, not so many years later, Community lawmakers recognised the need to create common standards to protect consumers in order to assure the free circulation of goods among the Member States. Thus, the first Community environmental legislation dealt with products (dangerous chemicals, motor vehicles and detergents). Product and later industry-related environmental legislation was based on Article 100 of the Treaty, which covered the harmonisation of laws 'in Member States as having a direct impact on the establishment or functioning of the common market.' In addition, environmental legislation was based on Article 235, covering measures which 'prove necessary to attain... one of the objectives of the Community' in the absence of a specific

---

[1] Ludwig Krämer, 'Effet national des directives communautaires en matière d'environnement', 1990 RJE 3, pp. 325 — 349.

[2] Case 302/86 Commission vs Denmark [1988] ECR 4607.

1)   Long-term management of natural resources: soil, water, nature reserves and coastal areas.

2)   The overall fight against pollution and preventive action concerning waste.

3)   Reducing the consumption of non-renewable energy sources.

4)   Improving mobility management, notably by opting for more efficient and environmental-friendly locations and means of transport.

5)   Health and security improvements, particularly regarding the assessment and management of industrial hazards, nuclear safety and protection against radiation.

Tackling these challenges implies adopting new strategies which aim at breaking the tendencies set out by preceding action programmes and turning towards long-term development.

These strategies imply an active commitment of all the major participants and provide access to a wider range of resources including, notably, economic instruments and the improvement of information aimed at contributing to the identifiable and measurable environmental improvements or aim at changing consumer habits which is the principal source of our planet's deterioration.

The Single European Act

The amendments to the Treaty of Rome, which took effect on 1 July 1987, introduced a series of new articles on the environment in the third part of the Treaty which covers the 'foundation and policy of the Community'. Three articles (130r, 130s and 130t) set out the objectives and elements of environmental protection actions by the Community. The objectives of this action are defined as follows:

• to preserve, protect and improve the quality of the environment;

• to contribute towards protecting human health,

• to assure a prudent and rational utilisation of natural resources.

EC environmental protection actions must become integrated into other EC policies, the most important of which are agriculture, regional development and energy and must be based on three principles:

• preventive action;

• environmental damage must be rectified at source;

• the polluter pays.

The integration principle is by far the most significant provision in the new article. Environmental protection is the only area of EC policy that imposes such a sweeping requirement; and the Community must adopt procedures to implement and enforce it[1.]

Article 130s stipulates the requirement of unanimity on the Council[2]. However, the Commission and the Court of Justice have made it clear that Community environmental legislation sets minimum standards, but may not be used to prevent the Member States from going further: 'The protective measures adopted in common pursuant to Article 130s shall not prevent any Member State from introducing more stringent protective measures compatible with this Treaty[3].'

The Single European Act recognised the complicated relationship between the environment and trade in a new Article 100a which states that when the Commission proposes a law concerning health, safety, environmental protection and consumer protection affecting the common market, that proposal must 'take as a base a high level of protection'. Again, Member States are given the opportunity to adopt more stringent standards if they deem it necessary.

The cooperation procedure under Article 100a was first used to break the deadlock on emission limits for medium and large-engine motor vehicles. In April 1987, the Parliament amended the Council text to impose stricter controls on emissions from small-engine cars and managed to convince the Commission to introduce the same standards instead. The Council was forced to agree.

In June 1991, the Court of Justice issued a judgement[4]regarding the legal basis of Directive 89/428/EEC on a progressive phase-out programme for the disposal of titanium dioxide wastes. Through this judgement, the Court cleared the way for the Community to adopt environmental legislation affecting industry by qualified majority instead of unanimity.

The Commission based its proposed Directive on Article 100a of the Treaty (measures furthering the single market) but the Council disagreed and opted for Article 130s on the environment.

---

[1] Pascale Kromarek, 'The Single European Act and the Environment', in European Environment Review 1, 1986, pp. 10 — 12.
[2] It also allows the Council to define matters on which decisions will be taken by majority opinion.
[3] Article 130t.
[4] Case 300/89 Commission vs Council [1991].

Under Article 100a, the European Parliament would have two readings of a proposal which could be adopted by qualified majority. In practice, basing legislation on Article 100a gives the more environmentally progressive forces in Parliament and the Council greater influence over the final text, but this practice has been strongly fought against by some Member States which are concerned about the Parliament's increased power and the loss of national legislative authority to the Community.

Under the terms of Article 130s, the Parliament has only one "consultative" reading and the Council must decide by unanimity (which is sometimes difficult to achieve).

The Court struck down the Directive, accepting the Commission's argument that since national environmental laws regulating this industry could lead to distortions in competition, Article 100a was the correct legal basis for creating a harmonised Community system. Since Article 100a (3) states that such laws affecting the environment must achieve 'a high level of protection', it is clear that, according to the Court, 'the objectives of environmental protection cited in Article 130r can be efficiently pursued through harmonisation measures based on Article 100a'.

This decision cleared up a knotty problem that had been pending since July 1987 when the amendments to the Treaty took effect. It means that the Commission is free to base other environmental proposals on Article 100a without fear of upset in the Council.

The Treaty of the European Union

The Treaty of the European Union significantly modifies the 'environment' sector of the EEC Treaty adding a fourth objective of the environmental policy to Article 130r. Community policy should 'contribute to promoting on an international scale measures taken to deal with regional or global environmental problems.'

Concerning the environment, the Treaty also implies a policy of high-level protection, taking into account the diversity of the Community's regions.

The new Article 130r (2) strengthens the existing provision that environmental needs must be integrated in the definition and implementation of all other Community policies. Measures of harmonisation dealing with these needs may include a safeguard clause, authorising Member States to take temporary measures based on non-economic environmental reasons, under a Community procedure of supervision.

The Treaty deletes the fourth paragraph of Article 130r which stipulates that "the Community acts in environmental matters whose objectives can easier be achieved at Community level than at national level". Nevertheless, the environmental policy generally remains submitted to the subsidiary principle in Article 3 B of the Treaty. It also stipulates that Decisions are to be made as close to citizen-level as possible[1].

Article 130s stipulates that concerning its contents, the Council must decide by qualified majority[2] in accordance with the procedure of cooperation determined in Article 189c in order to attain the objectives stipulated in Article 130r. Unanimity, however, is required for:

• provisions primarily of a fiscal nature;

• measures concerning town and country planning, land use with the exception of waste management, measures of a general nature and the management of water resources;

• measures significantly affecting the choice of a Member State between different energy sources and the general structure of its energy supply.

Action programmes of a general nature regarding priority objectives are adopted by the Council in accordance with the cooperation procedure established in Article 189 B of the Treaty.

The Member States have to assure the funding and execution of the Community's environmental policy. If the policy's implementation implies funds going beyond the Member State's means, the Council includes in the act containing the measure taken in order to achieve the objectives set out in Article 130r (1) the appropriate provisions by means of a temporary derogation and/or financial support from the Cohesion Fund.

Financial instruments for the environment

On 26 May 1994, the Cohesion fund[3] replaced the financial instrument of cohesion[4], introducing a financial backing to both environmental projects and transeuropean networks of transport in the Member States whose Gross

---

[1]   Article A.
[2]   The Council is authorised by Article 130s to determine the matters to be voted by qualified majority.
[3]   The Council's Regulation (EEC) 1164/94 from 16 May 1994 establishing the Cohesion Fund (OJ L 130,25.05.1994, p.1).
[4]   The Council's Regulation (EEC) 792/93 from 30 March 1993 establishing a funding instrument of cohesion (OJ L 97, 01.04.1993, p. 74).

National Product per capita is less than 90% of the Community's average: i.e. Greece, Spain, Portugal and Ireland.

In order to be eligible, environmental projects must contribute to the completion of the objectives mentioned in Article 130r of the Treaty, including the measures taken in conformity with Article 130s and the objectives which have priority within the Community's environmental policy. A project's funding by the Cohesion Fund is agreed upon by the Commission consonant with the Member State in question. The funding rate is between 80 and 85% of public spending and is in line with the interventions to be made. In order to make sure that the projects financed by the Cohesion Fund are correctly carried out and in order to avoid any irregularity whatsoever, a control system was introduced by the Member States.

The financial instrument for the environment (Life) introduces a financial backing to actions contributing to the implementation of the Community's environmental policy based on the principle of "the polluter pays". Also eligible are projects of technical support to third countries around the Mediterranean and the Baltic sea and, more exceptionally, to regional and global actions regarding environmental problems as established international agreements.

Financial backing is either agreed upon as co-financing, the level of which varies between 30 and 100% according to the kind of action or as an interest reduction.

Proposals of actions to be financed must be submitted to the Commission by the Member State concerned. These proposals are then studied by a committee made up of representatives from the Member States and the Commission and are adopted, in most cases, by the Commission.

The Commission is also responsible for the success of the projects financially supported by the Community. If any irregularities are found, it has the right to decrease, suspend or reclaim the funds awarded.

Communication 94/C 139/03[1] defines the priority actions to be implemented in 1995 within the framework of LIFE.

Finally, the new provisions included in the modified regulations concerning the Structural Funds, adopted in July 1993[2], increased the attention given to

---

[1] The Commission's communication 94/C 139/03 in conformity with the Council's regulation (EEC) 1973/92 containing the creation of a funding instrument for the environment (Life) regarding the priority actions to be carried out in 1995 (OJ C 139, 21.05.1994, p. 3).

[2] OJ L 215, 30.07.1992, p. 85.

environmental problems. These provisions want these national and regional funding programmes to bring about a revaluation of the national and regional environmental situation as well as the results of the actions aimed at. It also specifies that these programmes must specify the provisions agreed upon with the authorities concerned.

Citizen rights under Community Law

The Treaty of the European Union introduces a European citizenship. "Every person with the nationality of a Member State is a citizen of the Union'.

Citizens of the Union have five general rights:

1) The right to travel and reside unconditionally on the territory of a Member State;

2) The right to vote as well as the eligibility in both municipal elections and elections for the European Parliament in the Member State in which they reside under the same conditions as the nationals;

3) The right to protection from the diplomatic and consular authorities of every Member State on the territory of a third country where his country is not represented;

4) The right to petition the European Parliament about a matter within the Community's competence which directly concerns him; and

5) The right to complain to the ombudsman, appointed by the European Parliament, regarding wrong administration of the Community's institutions or organs except for the Court of Justice and the Court of First Instance concerning the exercise of their judicial powers.

In addition to these rights directly related to Union citizenship, citizens also have the right to formally complain to the Commission about a violation of Community law; this may form the basis of an infringement proceeding by the Commission against the Member State concerned.

European citizens only have the right to bring a complaint directly before the Court of Justice under decisions or regulations addressed directly and individually to them. Since directives are addressed to the Member States, no standing arises for citizens or citizen groups. However, citizen groups have the right to appear before the Court of Justice in support of a case already before the Court, if the Court agrees that the group has a legal interest in supporting the case (e.g. a consumer organisation in a consumer protection case).

Introduction

Cost of the fight against pollution

The "polluter pays" principle

Environmental protection applies the principle of the "polluter pays"[1], implying that the legal or natural persons in private or public law who are responsible for pollution must pay the cost of the measures necessary to avoid or reduce pollution so as to meet quality standards and objectives. When there are no such standards and objectives, it is the standards imposed by the public authorities that have to be met. Charging the cost of fighting pollution to the polluters incites them to reduce pollution and to research less-polluting products and technologies as well as enabling more efficient use of environmental resources. Every Member State applies the "polluter pays" principle to any kind of pollution in its territory without making a difference between pollution affecting the country concerned and pollution affecting a neighbouring country.

The "Green Paper" on responsibility for environmental damage[2], recommends the implementation of the "polluter pays" principle as well as provoking a debate on repairing the damage to the environment caused by major environmental disasters. That is why the "Green Paper" puts the mechanism of liability forward as the most suitable legal instrument. However, the difficulties involved in the implementation of liability are emphasised: it is difficult to prove the transgression and the causal connection between the transgression and the damage done in case of liability and it is difficult to determine the activities which involve an increased risk for the environment and to which a system of no-fault liability applies.

The proposed alternative consists of different systems of common compensations or collective indemnification mechanisms.

---

[1] Council Recommendation 75/436/Euratom,ECSC,EEC, of 3 March 1975, regarding cost allocation and action by public authorities on environmental matters (OJ L 194, 25.07.1975, p. 1). See also Community Legislation concerning the environment, volume 1, General Policy, first edition, p. 5 and xxv.

[2] Green Paper on remedying environmental damage (93/C 149/08) (OJ C 149, 29.05.1993, p. 12).

Assessing the cost of battling pollution

Council Recommendation 79/3/EEC[1] determines the principles, definitions and methods of assessment with regard to the cost of battling pollution in the industrial sector. It aims at harmonising the assessment procedures of the costs of battling pollution which are implemented in the different Member States so as to enable the implementation of a common policy in this field.

Assessment of the impact of certain public and private projects on the environment

Directive 85/337/EEC[2] concerns the assessment of the environmental impact of public and private projects which are likely to have a significant impact on the environment. The Member States are required to take the necessary measures to submit projects which are likely to have a significant impact on the environment, to an assessment regarding their effects. The assessment concerns the nature, size and location of the project. The aforementioned assessment is based upon the principle that the best environmental policy consists in avoiding, at source, the creation of pollution and nuisances rather than combating their effects at a later date. Assessing environmental effects involves the identification and the description of the direct and indirect effects of a project on man, fauna and flora, soil, water, air, climate, landscape, material assets and cultural heritage.

Since 3 July 1988 onwards, the Member States have been taking the necessary measures to apply this Directive. Beyond this date, the Member States who have been late in implementing the Directive, are no longer authorised, through a transitional provision, to impose the obligation to assess the impact on the environment of projects of which the authorisation procedures started before the Directive became national law but after the deadline of 3 July 1988. This is dealt with in the verdict of the Court of Justice in the case of Bund Naturschutz in Bayern versus Richard Stahnsdorf and 40 other people[3].

---

[1] Council Recommendation 79/3/EEC, of 19 December 1978, to the Member States regarding methods of evaluating the cost of pollution control to industry (OJ L 5, 09.01.1979, p. 29). See also Community Legislation concerning the environment, volume 1, General Policy, first edition, p. 13 and xxvi.

[2] Council Directive 85/337/EEC, of 27 June 1985, on the assessment of the effects of certain public and private projects on the environment (OJ L 175, 05.07.1985, p. 40). See also Community Legislation concerning the environment, volume 1, General Policy, first edition, p. 30 and xxvii.

[3] Case C 396/92, Bund Naturschutz in Bayern vs. Richard Stahnsdorf and 40 other people, 09.08.1994, Rec. 1994, I -3717.

Most infringements on Community environmental law relate to Directive 85/337/EEC: the majority of the complaints regarding the environment concern the lack of impact studies within the framework of practical projects. Even though many States have only just started the formal and practical implementation of Directive 85/337, experience shows that the planning, concept and authorisation of projects are gradually being influenced by the process of assessing environmental effects.[1] However, experience also shows that the Directive is not yet completely successful: aforementioned often starts too late; adequate quality control on studies concerning environmental effects and on the assessment of the effects is sometimes lacking; larger extenuating measures are rarely and erroneously being included in the planning and the concept of projects; the availability of studies on effects and the consultation procedure often leave much to be desired; both the contribution of the assessment process of effects to the final decision and the monitoring of the implementation of a project are neither as clear nor as efficient as they should be. Nevertheless, it is clear that environmental protection in the Member States has benefited from the Directive as it provides the authorities with the necessary environmental information to assess proposed individual projects; the environment also benefits from the Directive as it stipulates extenuating measures for the environmental effects of the project which must be added to the proposed project before it has started. Even though the formal participation of the environmental authorities in the analysis of projects has not been totally satisfactory it has nonetheless fostered greater awareness of the impact of projects on important biotopes in the Community.

Financial instruments

Various financial support mechanisms encourage the environmental policy.

LIFE is a financial instrument for the environment instituted by Regulation (EEC) n° 1973/92[2] and in force since 23 July 1992.

Article 130 D of the Treaty on the European Union institutes a Cohesion Fund for four Member States: Spain, Portugal, Greece and Ireland. This Fund concerns environmental investments and investments concerning transeuropean transport networks.

---

[1]   See Commission Report on the implementation of Directive 85/337/EEC on the assessment of environmental effects of certain public and private projects concerning the environment, COM (93), 28 final, 2 April 1993.

[2]   Council Regulation (EEC) N° 1973/92, of 21 May 1992, establishing a financial instrument for the environment (LIFE) (OJ L 206, 22.07.1992, p. 1).

The Community adopted Regulation (EEC) n° 792/93[1], which institutes a financial cohesion instrument, in anticipation of the Treaty's ratification. Regulation (EEC) n° 792/93 was subsequently replaced by Regulation (EEC) n° 1164/94[2] which institutes the Cohesion Fund.

The Altener programme[3] determines that any study or action in favour of the use of renewable energy sources, thus inciting the Member States to reduce carbon dioxide emissions, is eligible for the Community's financial aid. 40 million ECUs have been earmarked for the duration of the programme (1993/1997). Funding varies between 30 and 50% of the total cost depending on the type of activities carried out. The cost of technical research and assessments to define standards or technical specifications are refunded in full.

Environmental information

The European Environmental Agency

Regulation (EEC) n° 1210/90[4] institutes the European Environmental Agency and the European environment information and observation network. The European Environmental Agency aims at providing the Community and the Member States with objective, reliable and comparable information at Community level. This information allows the Community and the Member States to take the necessary measures to protect the environment, to assess their implementation, to provide the public with information on the state of the environment and to provide the required technical and scientific support. Thus, the task of the Agency is therefore not so much to monitor the correct application of Community Environmental Legislation but rather to gather information on the basis of which the present and foreseeable state of the environment can be determined. The Agency also provides information which can be directly applied to the implementation of the Community's Environmental Policy.

---

[1] Council Regulation (EEC) N° 792/93, of 30 March 1993, establishing a cohesion financial instrument (OJ L 79, 01.04.1993, p. 74).

[2] Council Regulation (EC) N° 1164/94, of 16 May 1994, establishing a Cohesion Fund (OJ L 130, 25.05.1994, p. 1).

[3] Council Decision 93/500/EEC, of 13 September 1993, concerning the promotion of renewable energy sources in the Community (Altener programme) (OJ L 235, 18.09.1993, p. 41).

[4] Council Regulation (EEC) N° 1210/90, of 7 May 1990, on the establishment of the European Environment Agency and the European environment information and observation network (OJ L 120, 11.05.1990, p. 1).
See also Community Legislation concerning the environment, volume 1, General Policy, first edition, p. 151 and xxx.

Access to information on the environment

In 1990, the Council adopted a Directive[1] on freedom of access to information on the environment. Directive 90/313 aims at assuring freedom of access to information on the environment held by the public authorities as well as the distribution of information and the definition of the basic conditions under which this information should be made accessible. The Directive applies to all national, regional and local bodies with responsibility for the environment and with environmental information, except for public bodies acting within the framework of their legal or legislative powers.

These public authorities provide information relating to the environment to any natural or legal person at his request without his having to prove an interest. A request for such information may be refused where it affects public security; the confidentiality of the proceedings of public authorities, international relations; the confidentiality of national defence; matters which are under legal inquiry; commercial and industrial confidentiality and the confidentiality of personal data. The request may also be refused when it is manifestly unreasonable or formulated in too general a manner. A person who deems that his request has been unreasonably refused or that his request has been inadequately answered may seek a judicial or administrative review of the decision in accordance with the relevant national legal system.

General access to information

Following a comparative inquiry[2] carried out by the Commission on the existing policies in the Member States and in certain third countries regarding access to information, it became clear that access to Community documents must be developed. A framework on general access to documents needs to be instituted and the principle of access to information needs to be shared by all Community institutions and the Member States.

By virtue of the Code of Conduct concerning public access to documents of Council and of the Commission[3], these two institutions agree on the principles governing public access to their documents. Access to documents of the Council and of the Commission is to be as broad as possible. A request from

---

[1] Council Directive 90/313/EEC, of 7 June 1990, on the freedom of access to information on the environment (OJ L 158, 23.06.1990, p. 56).
See also Community Legislation concerning the environment, volume 1, General Policy, first edition, p. 164 and xxxi.

[2] Communication 93/C 156/05 to the Council, the Parliament and the Economic and Social Committee, Public access to the institutions' documents (OJ C 156, 08.06.1993, p. 5).

[3] Code of Conduct concerning public access to Council and Commission documents (93/730/EC) (OJ L 340, 31.12.1993, p. 41).

the public must be sufficiently specific, does not need to be justified and must be answered as rapidly as possible. The Council and the Commission each ensure the implementation of aforementioned principles to their respective documents in Decisions 93/731/EEC[1] and 94/90/ECSC/EC/EURATOM[2].

The Community eco-label

Regulation (EEC) n° 880/92[3] institutes a Community eco-label award scheme which aims at encouraging the design, production, marketing and use of products which have less impact on the environment during their entire life-cycle. The Directive also aims at improving consumer information on the effects of the products on the environment.

The conditions for the eco-label award are defined per product category. The eco-label may be awarded to non-dangerous products which comply with the Community requirements on health, safety and the environment, except for foodstuffs, beverages and pharmaceutical products. The specific ecological criteria which apply to each product category must ensure a high level of environmental protection and must be based upon the use of environmentally-friendly technologies. The Commission consults with the main interest groups in order to define the product categories and the ecological criteria.

The application for the awarding of the eco-label must be transmitted to the competent body, which is instituted in every Member State. This body assesses the ecological performance of the product. When the eco-label may be awarded, the competent body notifies its decision to the Commission. Decision 94/10/EC[4] establishes a standard summary form for the notification of the decisions to award the Community eco-label. The Commission subsequently informs the competent bodies of the other Member States. If no objection has been raised by a certain time, the body awards the eco-label. However, when there are objections which cannot be withdrawn, the Commission is authorised to decide upon the awarding of the eco-label in each case.

---

[1] Council Decision 93/731/EC, of 20 December 1993, on public access to Council documents (OJ L 340, 31.12.1993, p. 43).

[2] Commission Decision 94/90/ECSC,EC,Euratom, of 8 February 1994, on public access to Commission documents (OJ L 46, 18.02.1994, p. 58).

[3] Council Regulation (EEC) N° 880/92, of 23 March 1992, on a Community eco-label award scheme (OJ L 99, 11.04.1992, p. 1).

[4] Commission Decision 94/10/EC, of 21 December 1993, on a standard summary form for the notification of a decision to award the Community eco-label (OJ L 7, 11.01.1994, p. 17).

The use of the label is included in a contract between the competent body and the user. Decision 93/51/EEC[1] adopts a standard contract relating to the conditions of the use of the label. Moreover, the conditions of the label's use include, inter alia, the payment of administrative costs for the dossier and a fee for the use of the label by the applicant. The guidelines for establishing these costs and fees are defined in Decision 93/326/EEC[2].

Decisions 93/430/EEC[3] and 93/431/EEC[4] establish the ecological criteria for the award of the eco-label to washing machines and dishwashers, respectively.

The Community eco-management and audit scheme

Council Regulation (EEC) n° 1836/93 [5] establishes a Community eco-management and audit scheme in which companies in the industrial sector may voluntarily participate.

This scheme aims at ensuring a constant improvement in environmental results, obtained by industrial activities, in accordance with the means of the company. It also aims at the companies' implementing environmental policies, programmes and management schemes on their premises. The scheme also envisages a systematic, objective and periodic assessment of the efficiency of these elements, and information to the public on the environmental results that have been achieved.

The general consultative Forum on the environment

Decision 93/701/EEC[6] institutes a general consultative Forum on the environment. The Forum is composed of representatives of the public authorities and of the private sector with a specific environmental competence. The Forum may be consulted by the Commission regarding all problems of the Commu-

---

[1] Commission Decision 93/517/EEC, of 15 September 1993, on a standard contract covering the terms of use of the Community eco-label (OJ L 243, 29.09.1993, p. 13).

[2] Commission Decision 93/326/EEC, of 13 May 1993, establishing indicative guidelines for the fixing of costs and fees in connection with the Community eco-label (OJ L 129, 27.05.1993, p. 23).

[3] Commission Decision 93/430/EEC, of 28 June 1993, establishing the ecological criteria for the award of the Community eco-label to washing machines (OJ L 198, 07.08.1993, p. 35).

[4] Commission Decision 93/431/EEC, of 28 June 1993, establishing the ecological criteria for the award of the Community eco-label to dishwashers (OJ L 198, 07.08.1993, p. 38).

[5] Council Regulation (EEC) N° 1836/93, of 29 June 1993, allowing voluntary participation by companies in the industrial sector in a Community eco-management and audit scheme (OJ L 168, 10.07.1993, p. 1).

[6] Commission Decision 93/701/EC, of 7 December 1993, on the setting-up of a general consultative forum on the environment (OJ L 328, 29.12.1993, p. 53).

nity's environmental policy. No votes are made on the Forum's opinions and they are included in a report which is transmitted to the Commission.

Protection of experimental animals

In 1986, the Council adopted a Directive[1] which aims at ensuring that where animals are used for experimental or other scientific purposes, the provisions laid down by law, regulation or administrative provisions in the Member States for their protection are approximated so as to avoid affecting the establishment and functioning of the common market by competitive distortions or trade barriers. Directive 86/609/EEC requires the number of experimental animals used to test medicines, foodstuffs and other substances or products as well as to protect the natural environment to be reduced to a minimum. These experimental animals should be treated with adequate care and no useless pain, suffering, distress or lasting harm should be inflicted upon them. If such tests cannot be avoided, they should be reduced to an absolute minimum. The experiments must be carried out by a qualified person who has been authorised to carry them out. In order to avoid duplication of experiments, the Member States recognise the validity of the results generated by experiments carried out in the territory of another Member State.

Protection of the environment in the Mediterranean region

In 1991, a Community action on the protection of the environment in the Mediterranean region was adopted within the framework of Regulation (EEC) n° 563/91[2]. This Regulation aims at intensifying efforts to protect and improve the quality of the environment and to help to increase the integration of the environmental policy in other Community policies. The Regulation also concerns the increase of cooperation and coordination concerning the environment in the Mediterranean basin by integrating Community action in operations carried out at regional, national an international level. Finally, it encourages the transfer of the appropriate technologies to protect the environment.

---

[1] Council Directive 86/609/EEC, of 24 November 1986, on the approximation of laws, regulations and administrative provisions of the Member States regarding the protection of animals used for experimental and other scientific purposes (OJ L 358, 18.12.1986, p.1). See also Community Legislation concerning the environment, volume 1, General Policy, first edition, p. 47 and xxviii.

[2] Council Regulation (EEC) N° 563/91, of 4 March 1991, on action by the Community for the protection of the environment in the Mediterranean region (MEDSPA) (OJ L 63, 09.03.1991, p. 1).

In the Community, financial aid will be allocated to natural and legal persons as well as to organisations which deal with the collection, storage and treatment of waste in coastal cities with fewer than one million inhabitants and in small islands. Aid will also be awarded to the disposal of sludge and toxic and dangerous waste, to the treatment of water from ships' tanks, to the integrated management of biotopes of Community interest and to the protection of soil.

In non-Community Mediterranean countries, technical assistance required for the establishment of environmental policies and action programmes, and help with the establishment of administrative structures will also be allocated.

The efficient implementation of MEDSPA will be monitored by the Commission notably by means of regular reports, drawn up in accordance with procedures agreed jointly between the Commission and the beneficiary of the operation, and by sampling checks.

Standardising and rationalising reports relating to the implementation of Directives on the environment

Directive 91/692/EEC[1] rationalises and improves, on a sectorial basis, the stipulations on transmitting information and publishing reports regarding certain Community Directives on environmental protection. These reports are established every three years with a year's interval per sector concerned, except for the report stipulated in Directive 76/160/EEC[2] concerning the quality of bathing water, which is to appear every year.

Integrating the environmental policy in other policies

Industrial competitiveness and the environment

Council Resolution 92/C 331/03[3] invites the Commission to consult with the industrial sector before adopting any proposal of legislative provisions or any other instrument to implement the environmental policy. The aforementioned

---

[1] Council Directive 91/692/EEC, of 23 December 1991, standardizing and rationalizing reports on the implementation of certain Directives relating to the environment (OJ L 377, 31.12.1991, p. 48).

[2] Council Directive 76/160/EEC, of 8 December 1975, concerning the quality of bathing water (OJ L 31, 05.02.1976, p. 1).
See also Community Legislation concerning the environment, volume 7, Water, first edition, p. 36 and xxix.

[3] Council Resolution 92/C 331/03, of 3 December 1992, concerning the relationship between industrial competitiveness and environmental protection (OJ C 331, 16.12.1992, p. 5).

instruments will take particular care to maintain a balance between the cost which they represent for industry and the benefits for industry and for the environment.

Health and environment

Council Resolution 91/C 304/06[1] invites the Commission to draw up an inventory on the available knowledge and experience relating to the relationship between health and the environment. This knowledge may be improved, and will be used within the framework of national health policies.

Education and the environment

Citizens play a paramount role in environmental protection. That is why environmental education needs to be strengthened on every level of the educational system so as to make students become aware of both local environmental problems and the diversity of their region and its particularities[2].

Relations with other third countries

The Lomé convention

Within the framework of the fourth Lomé Convention[3], the Community and its Member States, on the one hand, and the ACP countries, on the other hand, recognise the priority given to environmental protection and conservation of natural resources. These are essential preconditions for sustainable and balanced development at an economic and human level. Consequently, cooperation actions between the Community and the ACP States in all areas are invariably based upon the need to achieve compatibility between economic growth and development while maintaining natural equilibria.

The Community supports the environmental policy of the ACP States, the major objectives of which are the protection and the proper use of the environment and natural resources, the halting of the deterioration of land and forests,

---

[1]   Resolution 91/C 304/06 of the Council and the Ministers for health, meeting within the Council, of 11 November 1991, on health and the Environment (OJ C 304, 23.11.1991, p. 6).

[2]   Conclusions 92/C 151/02 of the Council and the Ministers of education meeting within the Council, of 1 June 1992, on the development of environmental education (OJ C 151, 16.06.1992, p. 2).

[3]   The fourth ACP-EEC Convention, signed in Lomé on 15 December 1989 (OJ L 229, 17.08.1991, p. 3).

the restoration of ecological equilibria and the preservation of natural resources as well as their rational exploitation. To this end, three types of approach are given priority: a preventive approach aimed at avoiding harmful effects on the environment as a result of any programme or operation; a systematic approach that will ensure ecological viability at all stages, from identification to implementation; and a trans-sectoral approach that takes into account not only the direct but also the indirect consequences of the actions undertaken. The achievement of these objectives aims at an immediate improvement in the living conditions of the populations concerned and at the preservation of those of future generations.

The European Economic Area

The contracting parties agree to extend the implementation of the principles governing the protection and improvement of the environment in the Community, to the entire European Economic Area, as well as a whole range of Community Directives on the different environmental sectors. The European Economic Area comprises the Member States of the Community, Austria, Finland, Iceland, Liechtenstein, Norway, Sweden and Switzerland[1].

---

[1] Decision 94/1/EC, ECSC of the Council and the Commission, of 13 December 1993, on the conclusion of the agreement on the European Economic Area between the European Communities, their Member States and the Republic of Austria, the Republic of Finland, the Republic of Iceland, the Principality of Liechtenstein, the Kingdom of Norway, the Kingdom of Sweden and the Swiss Confederation (OJ L 1, 03.01.1994, p. 1).

Summary of the Legislation

Council Resolution 91/C 304/06[1] — Health and environment

This Resolution which considers the relationship between health and environment, incited the Council and the Ministers for health, meeting within the
Council, to invite the Commission to draw up an inventory on the available
knowledge and experience relating to the aforementioned relationship. This
inventory serves as a basis for the Commission to study how this knowledge
can be gathered, exchanged and improved and how it may be useful within the
framework of national health policies.

Periodically, the Commission must report to the Council about the progress of
the works. This reporting is required to take place for the first time before
1994.

Council Directive 91/692/EEC[2] — Standardising and rationalising reports relating to the implementation of Directives on the environment

This Directive rationalises and improves, on a sectorial basis, the stipulations
on transmitting information and publishing reports on certain Community
directives concerning environmental protection.

The Member States are required to establish these reports and subsequently
transmit them to the Commission every three years with a year's interval per
sector concerned. These reports are drawn up on the basis of a questionnaire
established by the Commission which is assisted by a committee. The questionnaire is transmitted to the Member States six months before the start of the
period covered by the report.

The Commission publishes a summarised report per sector within nine months
following the transmission of the reports by the Member States.

---

[1] Resolution 91/C 304/06, of the Council and the Ministers for health, meeting within the
Council, of 11 November 1991, on health and the environment (OJ C 304, 23.11.1991,
p. 6).

[2] Council Directive 91/692/EEC, of 23 December 1991, standardising and rationalising
reports on the implementation of certain Directives relating to the environment (OJ L
377, 31.12.1991, p. 48).

Concerning the implementation of Directive 76/160/EEC[1] on the quality of bathing water, the report is published on an annual basis and early enough to inform the public on the quality of bathing water during the most recent period. The Commission publishes its report within four months upon receipt of the reports of the Member States.

Council Resolution 92/C 59/01[2] — The future Community policy on the European coastal zone

Through this Resolution, the Council invites the Commission to propose a Community strategy of an integrated management of the coastal zone based on the principles of durability and good ecological and environmental practices.

Council Regulation (EEC) No 880/92[3] — The Community eco-label award scheme

This Regulation institutes a Community eco-label award scheme which aims at encouraging the design, production, marketing and use of products which have less impact on the environment during their entire life-cycle. The Directive also aims at improving consumer information on the impact of the products on the environment. The eco-label may be awarded to non-hazardous products which comply with the Community requirements on health, safety and the environment, except for foodstuffs, beverages and pharmaceutical products.

The conditions for the eco-label award are established per product category. The specific ecological criteria which apply to each product category are defined in accordance with the general approach which is based upon the afore-mentioned general principles and the parameters of the assessment matrix in Annexe I. These criteria are to ensure a high level of environmental protection. They are to be based upon the use of environmental-friendly technologies and they are to present the opportunity to optimise the length of the product's life.

The Commission consults with the main interest groups which meet in a consultation forum to define the product categories and the ecological criteria. The

---

[1] Council Directive 76/160/EEC, of 8 December 1975, concerning the quality of bathing water (OJ L 31, 05.02.1976, p. 1). See also Community Legislation concerning the environment, volume 7, Water, first edition, p. 36 and xxix.

[2] Council Resolution 92/C 59/01, of 25 February 1992, on the future Community policy concerning the European coastal zone (OJ L 59, 06.03.1992, p. 1).

[3] Council Regulation (EEC) No 880/92, of 23 March 1992, on a Community eco-label award scheme (OJ L 99, 11.04.1992, p. 1).

consultation results are transmitted to the committee and are accompanied by the project of measures to be taken.

The committee subsequently states its opinion and when the measures aimed at meet the committee's opinion, the Commission definitively adopts them. However, when they do not meet the committee's opinion or when the committee does not state its opinion, the measures are immediately submitted to the Council which decides by qualified majority. If the Council does not give its opinion within a three-month period, the Commission adopts the proposed measures.

The eco-label includes the logo given in Annexe II.

For the awarding of an eco-label, the manufacturers or importers must address the competent body instituted by the Member State in which the product is manufactured or marketed for the first time or imported from a third country. This body assesses the ecological performance of the product on the basis of which the product is awarded or refused the eco-label. When the eco-label may be awarded, the competent body informs the Commission on its decision. The Commission subsequently informs the competent bodies of the other Member States. If noobjection has been stated within 30 days following the notification of the decision to the Commission, the body is allowed to proceed with the awarding of an eco-label. However, when objections are raised or cannot be lifted, the Commission, in consultation with the committee, decides on the proposed award in each case. When the awarding of the label is refused, the competent body informs both the Commission and the applicant of the grounds for the refusal.

Concerning the use of the label, each competent body draws up a contract relating to the conditions of the label's use including, inter alia, clauses on the withdrawal of the authorisation to use the label.

All information transmitted during the assessment process of a product for the awarding of a label must remain confidential. However, when it has been decided to award the label, the name of the product, its manufacturer or importer as well as the grounds of and the relevant information on the awarding of the label must be divulged.

The product categories and ecological criteria related to them are published in the Official Journal of the European Communities.

Regulation (EEC) No 1973/92[1] — The financial instrument for the environment (LIFE)

This Regulation institutes a financial instrument for the environment (LIFE) and was adopted to encourage the development and implementation of the Community environmental policy by funding certain priority actions in the Community. LIFE is also meant to finance technical assistance actions in third countries around the Mediterranean and the Baltic sea and, more exceptionally, actions concerning regional and global environmental problems laid down in international agreements. The maximum amount of resources which can be allocated to the aforementioned actions is maximum 5%.

Actions are only eligible for financial aid if they are of Community interest, significantly contribute to the implementation of the Community's environmental policy and respect the "polluter pays" principle.

Financial aid is awarded by means of co-funding of actions or an interest rate reduction with reference to the type of action to be carried out. The ceiling for the contribution of the Community varies between 30 and 100% of the costs depending on the type of action.

LIFE will be implemented in different phases, the first one of which ends on 31 December 1995. In the first phase, 400 million ECUs will be available. The Member States and, in certain cases, third countries, must submit proposals of actions to be funded to the Commission. The Commission may invite natural and legal persons to submit applications for aid.

The actions under LIFE are submitted to a committee which is composed of representatives from the Member States and which is presided by a representative of the Commission. These actions, except for certain cases, are adopted by the Commission. The actions take either the form of a decision with the Commission's approval of the action concerned or the form of a contract or agreement stipulating the rights and obligations of the parties, agreed upon with the beneficiaries responsible for the implementation of the action.

The Commission is required to ensure the success of the actions carried out by means of the European Community's financial aid. The Commission is allowed to reduce, suspend or reclaim financial aid when it finds irregularities or when major modifications have been introduced which are not coherent with or conducive to the conditions of the action.

---

[1] Council Regulation (EEC) No 1973/92 of 21 May 1992, establishing a financial instrument for the environment (LIFE) (OJ L 206, 22.07.1992, p. 1).

Council Conclusions 92/C 151/02[1] — Development of environmental education

Since the adoption of the Resolution on environmental education of 24 May 1988, it is clear that environmental protection on every level of society is acute. In this respect, citizens play a paramount role: they must realise that environmental conservation is a common duty, that they are directly responsible for pollution, that they produce waste and that they consume goods and services. That is why environmental education must be considered as an integrated and essential part of the education of each European citizen. Therefore, environmental education must be strengthened at every level of the educational system and be considered as an important means to establish links between educational institutions and the Community in which they are located by making the students realise both local environmental problems and the diversity of their region and its particularities. Thus, training and retraining of teachers in this matter must be developed.

Council Resolution 92/C 331/03[2] — The relationship between industrial competitiveness and environmental protection

Through this Resolution, the Council invites the Commission to encourage a dialogue with the industrial sector and in particular with small and medium-sized companies as well as to inform them on every proposal of legislative provisions or other instruments geared towards the implementation of the Community's environmental policy. When opting for instruments and methods to protect and improve the environment, the Commission chooses the best possible balance between, on the one hand, the cost for the industry, and in particular for small and medium-sized companies and, on the other hand, the benefits for the industry and the environment. The Commission also makes sure that the environmental protection measures offer maximum flexibility for the industry to adopt the most suitable and economically feasible technologies and techniques to comply with the environmental objectives.

The Member States are invited to cooperate with the Commission to encourage the elaboration of environment-friendly technologies and their distribution in all the regions of the Community. During this process it is required to maintain the integrity of the internal market by encouraging high-level environmental

---

[1] Conclusions 92/C 151/02 of the Council and the Ministers of education meeting within the Council, of 1 June 1992, on the development of environmental education (OJ C 151, 16.06.1992, p. 2).

[2] Council Resolution 92/C 331/03, of 3 December 1992, concerning the relationship between industrial competitiveness and environmental protection (OJ C 331, 16.12.1992, p. 5).

protection. Standardisation organisations must give the required attention to considerations relating to the environment in the process of elaborating industrial standards. The awarding of an eco-label to inform the consumers about a product's environmental characteristics will be encouraged and the compatibility between an open commercial policy and environmental protection will be ensured.

Resolution 93/C 138/01[1] of the Council and the Representatives of the Governments of the Member States — Fifth environmental action programme

On 1 February 1993, the Council of Ministers of the Environment adopted a resolution which approves the proposal of the European Commission on a fifth Community programme of policy and action concerning environment and sustainable development. This programme is in line with the extension of the fourth environmental action programme which expired at the end of 1992. It adopts a new approach regarding environmental problems. This new approach, which is based on the principle of sustainable development, does not only concern the authorities but also every economic agent and, in particular, the citizens who also share environmental responsibilities.

This programme is based upon the principles of sustainable development, resorting to preventive measures and shared responsibility which are mentioned in the Treaty of the European Union signed in Maastricht on 7 February 1992. The programme aims at designing a structure for the implementation of Agenda 21 which has been ratified by the Community and the Member States upon the United Nations Conference on the Environment and Development (UNCED).

Regulation (EEC) No 792/93[2] — The cohesion financial instrument

This Regulation was adopted to strengthen economic and social cohesion within the Community. However, the economic and social cohesion requires a Community action which complements the action of the Structural Funds, the

---

[1] Resolution 93/C 138/01 of the Council and the Representatives of the Governments of the Member States meeting within the Council, of 1 February 1993, on a Community programme of policy and action in relation to the environment and sustainable development (OJ C 138, 17.05.1993, p. 1).

[2] Council Regulation (EEC) No 792/93, of 30 March 1993, establishing a cohesion financial instrument (OJ L 79, 01.04.1993, p. 74).

European Investment Bank and other financial instruments relating to the environment and to transport infrastructure of common interest.

The Community awards its financial aid to projects relating to the environment and transeuropean networks of transport infrastructure to the Member States whose GNP per capita is lower than 90% of the Community's average: Greece, Spain, Ireland and Portugal.

In order to be eligible, environmental projects have to contribute to the achievement of the objectives mentioned in Article 130r of the Treaty, including the projects resulting from the actions that have been carried out in application of Article 130s of the Treaty. The projects of common interest regarding transport infrastructure must be in line with the guidelines on transeuropean networks. Preparatory studies and, in particular, preliminary evaluations, cost-benefit analyses as well as measures of technical support to eligible projects, may also funded.

The projects to be funded by means of the financial instrument are adopted by the Commission in consultation with the Member State concerned. A balance must be established between environmental projects and projects regarding transport infrastructure. The high quality of the projects submitted to the Commission will be assessed on the basis of their economic and social benefits, their contribution to the implementation of Community policies on the environment and transeuropean networks, their compatibility with Community policies and their coherence with other structural measures of the Community as well as on the basis of priorities set by the Member States benefiting from the aid.

The rate of funding awarded by the financial instrument is between 80 and 85% of the public or similar spending and is in line with the nature of the interventions to be made. Preparatory studies may be funded, in exceptional cases, up to 100% of their total cost, which must not exceed 0.5% of the resources of the financial instrument.

In order to ensure the efficiency of Community aid, the Commission and the Member States benefiting from the aid institute a systematic assessment of the projects and evaluate, in particular, whether the initial objectives have been achieved or not.

This Financial instrument remains in force until the implementation of a regulation which institutes a Cohesion Fund or until 1 April 1994 at the latest. Regulation (EEC) No 566/94[1] extends Regulation (EEC) No 792/93 until 31 January 1994.

---

[1] Council Regulation (EC) No 566/94, of 10 March 1994, extending Regulation (EEC) No 792/93 establishing a cohesion financial instrument (OJ L 72, 16.03.1994, p. 1).

Commission Decision 93/326/EEC[1] — Costs and fees in connection with the Community eco-label

This Decision defines the guidelines relating to the setting of costs and fees in connection with the Community eco-label. The application for the awarding of a label involves the payment of fees whose amount covers the handling of the dossier. The reference sum amounts to 500 ECUs. The applicants who received an eco-label are required to pay a fee for its use once a year. The amount of this annual fee is determined on the basis of a percentage (0.15%) of the turnover of the product bearing the eco-label obtained in the Community. However, the competent governmental bodies are allowed to set fees of which the amount is lower or higher than 20% of the reference amounts established in this Decision. In this case, they observe the same deviation from the reference amounts for all the fees they receive.

The Annexe defines additional guidelines which are to be observed by both the establishment of introduction fees for applications for the eco-label and the establishment of the annual fees.

Commission Communication 93/C 149/08[2] — "Green Paper" on the responsibility for environmental damage

The "Green Paper" aims to provoke a debate on repairing the damage caused by major ecological disasters so as to provide the Community with action resources to deal with them.

The legal mechanism of civil liability appears to be very useful in this respect. First, it provides a means of designating the person responsible and having him indemnify the victim thus complying with the principle of "the polluter pays". Subsequently, the mechanism also works preventively as a means of dissuading future damage.

Nevertheless, the implementation of civil liability faces a number of difficulties. It is not always easy to prove a transgression and the causal connection between the transgression and the damage done. Moreover, it is difficult to determine the activities which imply an increased risk for the environment and for which a system of no-fault liability applies. When the responsible party has

---

[1] Commission Decision 93/326/EEC, of 13 May 1993, establishing indicative guidelines for the fixing of costs and fees in connection with the Community eco-label (OJ L 129, 27.05.1993, p. 23).

[2] Green paper on remedying environmental damage (93/C 149/08) (OJ C 149, 29.05.1993, p. 12).

been identified, it is still necessary to determine the damage done to the environment, the suitable remedy, the insurability of the risks.

The alternative consists of different systems of common compensations or joint indemnification mechanisms, even when other restrictions are imposed.

Commission Communication 93/C 156/05[1] — Public access to the institutions' documents

The implementation of the declaration given in the Treaty of Maastricht relating to improving public access to information incited the Commission to draw up a comparative inquiry on the existing policies in the Member States and in certain third countries regarding public access to information. This inquiry had to unveil that access to information consisted of two essential elements. First, the public authorities adopt measures to inform the public on their actions. Second, information is put at the citizen's disposal upon request. Information is only distributed when it does not affect public or private interests and when it safeguards the good functioning of the public authorities concerned.

Taking into account the results of the inquiry, access to information at Community level is yet to be developed. A framework to grant general access to documents must be instituted and the principle of access to information must be shared by all Community institutions and Member States. These operations are based upon principles which determine that access to information will only be granted for documents of which a specific definition is given. The request from the public must be sufficiently specific, does not need to be motivated and must receive a reply as rapidly as possible. The request for information may be rejected in order to protect privacy, industrial and financial confidentiality, public security, including international relations and monetary stability as well as confidential information which is communicated to the institutions.

---

[1] Communication 93/C 156/05 to the Council, the Parliament and the Economic and Social Committee, Public access to the institutions' documents (OJ C 156, 08.06.1993, p. 5).

Commission Decision 93/430/EEC[1] — Ecological criteria for the awarding of the Community eco-label to washing machines

This Decision applies to washing machines with a frontal or vertical loading device sold to the public excluding twin-tub washing machines for washing and draining, and washing/drying machines. A washing machine's ecological performance essentially depends on its energy consumption as well as on its water and detergent consumption based on the most significant impact of these machines on the environment; the optimum utilisation criteria relating to the functions of a washing machine which provide a means of reducing its impact on the environment and the performance criteria for washing and rinsing.

The definition of the type of washing machine in the present Decision and the specific ecological criteria for this type of machine is only valid until 30 June 1996.

Commission Decision 93/431/EEC[2] — The Community eco-label for dishwashers

This Decision applies to dishwashers sold to the public. Their ecological performance depends on the essential ecological criteria for energy and water consumption based on the most significant impact of these machines on the environment; optimum utilisation criteria relating to the functions of a dishwasher which provide a means of reducing its impact on the environment and the performance criteria for washing and drying.

The definition of the type of dishwasher in the present Decision and the specific ecological criteria for this type of machine is only valid until 30 June 1996.

---

[1]   Commission Decision 93/430/EEC, of 28 June 1993, establishing the ecological criteria for the award of the Community eco-label to washing machines (OJ L 198, 07.08.1993, p. 35).

[2]   Commission Decision 93/431/EEC, of 28 June 1993, establishing the ecological criteria for the award of the Community eco-label to dishwashers (OJ L 198, 07.08.1993, p. 38).

Council Regulation (EEC) No 1836/93[1] — Voluntary participation by companies in the industrial sector in a Community eco-management and audit scheme

This Regulation establishes a Community eco-management and audit scheme in which companies in the industrial sector may voluntary participate. The objectives of this scheme involve the constant improvement of environmental results, obtained by industrial activities, in accordance with the means of the company and the companies' implementing environmental policies, programmes and management schemes on their premises. The scheme also envisages a systematic, objective and periodic assessment of the efficiency of these elements, as well as information being made available to the public on the environmental results that have been achieved.

Entering a plant in the scheme requires the company which exploits it to adopt a company environmental policy which complies with the stipulations of the present Regulation and which includes the commitment to constantly improve environmental results. The company must also carry out an environmental analysis of the plant concerning the items mentioned in Annexe I, point C. Subsequently, on the basis of the environmental analysis, the company implements an environmental programme regarding the company environmental policy as well as an environmental management scheme which applies to all activities in the plant. Environmental audits must be carried out on the sites concerned on the basis of which objectives for constant environmental improvement are being established as well as a specific environmental declaration regarding the audited site. Afterwards, the environmental audit needs to be rendered valid, transmitted to the competent body of the Member State and distributed to the public.

The environmental audit of a site is carried out by auditors belonging to the company or by external auditors working on the company's account. The audit is carried out in accordance with the criteria mentioned in Annexe I, point C and Annexe II.

An official and independent inspector studies the policies, programmes and management systems, environmental audit analyses and procedures as well as the environmental declarations so as to verify their compliance with the Regulation. He also renders the environmental declarations valid on the basis of Annexe III. The information obtained within the framework of the audit and

---

[1]   Council Regulation (EEC) No 1836/93, of 29 June 1993, allowing voluntary participation by companies in the industrial sector in a Community eco-management and audit scheme (OJ L 168, 10.07.1993, p. 1).

verification activities cannot be disclosed without the authorisation of the company's management.

An environmental declaration is drawn up for each site following the initial environmental analysis and upon each future audit. The declaration includes, inter alia, a description of the company's activities on the site concerned; an assessment of all the major environmental problems related to the activities concerned; a summary of the numeric data on polluting emissions, waste production, consumption of raw material, energy and water, and noise; a presentation of the environmental policy, programme and management scheme which the company has implemented on the site concerned.

Each Member State is required to establish an approval system of independent environmental inspectors and the supervision of their activities. These approval systems are to be instituted so as to ensure the independence and neutrality of the inspectors with reference to their assignment. The approval of the environmental inspectors and the monitoring of their activities must comply with the stipulations of Annexe III. A list of approved inspectors is transmitted to the Commission and is revised every six months.

When a plant meets all the requirements of the Regulation and when the environmental declaration has been rendered valid, the competent public authority can register the plant upon receipt of the registration fees mentioned in Article 11. The list of registered plants and its updates are transmitted to the Commission.

The Member States encourage the participation of small and medium-sized companies in the Community scheme of environmental management and audit and are allowed to experiment with the implementation of analogous stipulations in other sectors such as distribution or public services...

The Commission is assisted by a committee which gives its opinion on proposals and decisions.

This Regulation will be revised at the latest five years following its coming into force.

Council Decision 93/500/EEC[1] — Renewable energy sources

This Decision aims at promoting the use of renewable energy sources by inciting the Member States to limit carbon dioxide emissions which are mainly due to the consumption of fossil fuels. The Community institutes a financial contribution, within the framework of the Altener programme, to technical research and assessments which aim at establishing standards or technical specifications; to measures for maintaining the initiatives of the Member States to expand or create infrastructures regarding renewable energy sources; to the creation of an information network which aims at improving the coordination between local and general activities; to research, assessments and other appropriate actions which aim at evaluating the technical possibility and economic and environmental benefits of exploiting the biomass for energy usage.

40 million ECUs have been earmarked for the period 1993/1997 and funding varies between 30 and 50%, exceptionally 60%, of the total cost depending on the kind of activities that have been carried out. The cost of technical research and assessments for defining standards or technical specifications are entirely funded by the Community.

Within the framework of its activities, the Commission is assisted by an consultative committee which gives its opinion on the measures to be taken.

In 1995, the Commission must transmit a report to the European Parliament and the Council on the results achieved by the implementation of the Directive and, if necessary, propose a revision of the latter. The Directive is applicable from 1 January 1993 to 31 December 1997.

Commission Decision 93/517/EEC[2] — The standard contract covering the terms of use of the Community eco-label

This Decision adopts a format for the contract mentioned in Article 12 of Regulation (EEC) No 880/92 which stipulates that the competent public body must sign a contract covering the use of the eco-label with each applicant for a Community eco-label. The competent public body can insert additional stipulations to those concerning the rights and duties of the holder, advertising, conformity control, confidentiality, suspension or withdrawal of the awarding of the label, the limitation of responsibilities, fees, complaints, duration of the contract, as well as the laws which apply, provided that they comply with Regulation (EEC) No 880/92.

---

[1] Council Decision 93/500/EEC, of 13 September 1993, concerning the promotion of renewable energy sources in the Community (Altener program) (OJ L 235, 18.09.1993, p. 41).

[2] Commission Decision 93/517/EEC, of 15 September 1993, on a standard contract covering the terms of use of the Community eco-label (OJ L 243, 29.09.1993, p. 13).

Commission Directive 93/80/EEC[1] — Transitional measures for Germany

This Directive authorises the prolongation until 31 December 1995 of the implementation delays of certain Community Regulations relating to the disposal of hazardous substances in the former Democratic Republic of Germany as set out in Directive 90/656/EEC.

The environmental problems in the former Democratic Republic of Germany are significantly greater than the estimations on which the implementation date, 31 December 1992, of the Community Regulations was based. These problems are certainly due to the obsolete production units located in the Democratic Republic of Germany emitting hazardous substances into surface waters. Directive 93/80/EEC subsequently extends the implementation date till 31 December 1995 taking into account the time required to modify the aforementioned production units in order to meet the stipulations of the Directives mentioned in Article 3 of Directive 90/656/EEC.

Decision 93/C 323/01[2] of the representatives of the governments of the Member States — The location of the seats of certain bodies and departments of the European Communities and of Europol

Through this Decision, the location of the seats of several European bodies and departments are determined by the representatives of the governments of the Member States. Among these bodies, the seat of the European Environment Agency has been established in the Copenhagen region.

---

[1] Commission Directive 93/80/EEC, of 23 September 1993, amending Council Directive 90/656/EEC on the transitional measures applicable in Germany with regard to certain Community provisions relating to the protection of the environment (OJ L 256, 14.10.1993, p. 32).

[2] Decision 93/C 323/01 taken by common agreement between the representatives of the governments of the Member States, meeting at head-of-state and government level, on the location of the seats of certain bodies and departments of the European Communities and of Europol (OJ L C 323, 30.11.1993, p. 1).

Commission Decision 93/701/EC[1] — The general consultative Forum on the environment

This Decision aims at instituting a general consultative forum on the environment. This Forum is composed of 32 members from the production sector, local and regional authorities, consumer and environmental protection organisations, trade unions and people with a specific environmental competence. The Forum may be consulted by the Commission regarding problems of the Community's environmental policy. The Members of the Forum are designated by the Commission and serve a renewable three-year mandate. The Forum is presided by a representative of the Commission. Two vice-presidents are elected among the Forum's members for an 18-month term which is renewable once. The president and the two vice-presidents constitute the bureau which prepares and organises the Forum's activities.

The proceedings of the Forum deal with the requests for information put forward by the Commission. The Forum's opinion is not voted but is included in a report which is transmitted to the Commission. The information that the Forum's members are required to know within the framework of their activities is not to be disclosed when the Commission states that the requested opinion or the question put forward concerns a confidential issue.

Code of Conduct concerning public access to Council and Commission documents[2]

This Code of Conduct concerns the common agreement of the Council and the Commission on the principles governing public access to Council or Commission documents which contain existing data adopted by either the Council or the Commission. This agreement concerns the access to documents on any support whatsoever.

The request to access a document must be stated in writing and must be sufficiently specific so as to enable the identification of the document concerned. The access to the document concerns either consultation on the spot or by the transmission of a copy of which the cost is borne by the applicant. However, the fee is not to exceed a reasonable amount. The institution concerned informs the applicant in writing whether the request will be granted or not within one month.

---

[1] Commission Decision 93/701/EC, of 7 December 1993, on the setting-up of a general consultative forum on the environment (OJ L 328, 29.12.1993, p. 53).

[2] Code of Conduct concerning public access to Council and Commission documents (93/730/EC) (OJ L 340, 31.12.1993, p. 41).

If the request has not been granted, the·applicant is allowed one month to request the institution to revise its position. If the applicant fails to do so, he is considered to have abandoned his initial request. Should the institution concerned still refuse access to the document, it must communicate its decision, duly motivated, to the applicant as rapidly as possible. This written decision must also indicate the possible remedies — legal remedies and complaints to the ombudsman.

The institutions prohibit the access to documents whose disclosure could adversely affect public interests, the protection of the individual and privacy, the protection of commercial and industrial confidentiality and the financial interests of the Community. A request may also be refused to ensure the institution's interests concerning the confidentiality of its proceedings.

This Code of Conduct will be revised after two years of being operative following the reports from the secretary-generals of the Council and the Commission.

Council Decision 93/731/EC[1] — Public access to Council documents

Through this Decision, the Council assures the implementation of the principles governing public access to its documents as stipulated in the Code of Conduct concerning public access to Council and Commission documents.

Council and Commission Decision 94/1/ECSC, EC[2] — The European Economic Area

The contracting parties agree to preserve, protect and improve the quality of the environment and to contribute to the protection of human health and to ensure a rational and economical use of natural resources. In this respect a whole range of Community directives concerning the environment apply to the entire European Economic Area. These measures of protection, however, do not obstruct the participants to maintain or stipulate reinforced measures of protection in line with the present agreement.

---

[1] Council Decision 93/731/EC, of 20 December 1993, on public access to Council documents (OJ L 340, 31.12.1993, p. 43).

[2] Decision 94/1/EC, ECSC of the Council and the Commission, of 13 December 1993, on the conclusion of the agreement on the European Economic Area between the European Communities, their Member States and the Republic of Austria, the Republic of Finland, the Republic of Iceland, the Principality of Liechtenstein, the Kingdom of Norway, the Kingdom of Sweden and the Swiss Confederation (OJ L 1, 03.01.1994, p. 1).

Their action with respect to the environment is based on the principles of preventive action, tackling environmental problems, preferably at source, and the principle of "the pollutant pays". The stipulations concerning the environment must be inserted in the other policies of the contracting parties.

Commission Decision 94/10/EC[1] — The standard summary form for the notification of a decision to award the Community eco-label

This Decision establishes a standard summary form, stipulated in Article 10 paragraph 3 of Regulation (EEC) No 880/92, for the notification of a decision to award the Community eco-label.

Commission Decision 94/90/ECSC/EC/EURATOM[2] — Public access to Commission documents

Through this Decision, the Commission adopts and assures the implementation of the principles governing public access to its documents as stipulated in the Code of Conduct concerning public access to Council and Commission documents.

Regulation (EC) No 1164/94[3] — the Cohesion Fund

In accordance with Article 130 D of the Treaty of the European Union, Regulation (EEC) No 1164/94 institutes the Cohesion Fund which is intended to replace Regulation (EEC) No 729/93[4] from 26 May 1994 onwards. This Fund contributes to strengthening the economic and social cohesion in the Community by funding Community actions which are complementary to those of the Structural Funds, European Investment Bank and other financial instruments for the environment and transport infrastructures of common interest.

The Fund awards its financial aid to projects in support of the achievement of the objectives, established in the Treaty of the European Union, regarding the

---

[1] Commission Decision 94/10/EC, of 21 December 1993, on a standard summary form for the notification of a decision to award the Community eco-label (OJ L 7, 11.01.1994, p. 17).

[2] Commission Decision 94/90/ECSC,EC,Euratom, of 8 February 1994, on public access to Commission documents (OJ L 46, 18.02.1994, p. 58).

[3] Council Regulation (EC) No 1164/94 of 16 May 1994, establishing a Cohesion Fund (OJ L 130, 25.05.1994, p. 1).

[4] See above.

environment and transeuropean transport infrastructure networks in Member States whose GNP is lower than 90% of the Community's average and which have implemented a programme to meet the conditions of economic convergence, stipulated in Article 104 C of the Treaty. At present, only Greece, Spain, Ireland and Portugal comply with these criteria.

In order to be eligible for financial aid, environmental projects are to concern the achievement of the objectives mentioned in Article 130r of the Treaty, including projects which result from the measures taken in accordance with Article 130s, the objectives which have priority within in the Community's environmental protection policy and the common interest projects of transport infrastructure within the framework of Article 129 C of the Treaty. Transport infrastructure projects aimed at the implementation of Article 129 B of the Treaty, may be financed until the Council has adopted suitable guidelines. Preparatory studies, in particular those necessary to implement projects, as well as technical support measures may also be financed.

A project's funding by the Cohesion Fund is agreed upon by the Commission consonant with the Member State benefiting from the aid. It is required to establish a balance between environmental projects and projects regarding transport infrastructure. Moreover, the projects are to have a significant impact on either of the two areas. The quality of the projects submitted to the Commission will be assessed on the basis of their economic and social benefits, their contribution to the implementation of Community policies on the environment and transeuropean networks, their compatibility with Community policies and their connection to other structural measures of the Community as well as on the basis of priorities set by the Member States benefiting from the aid.

The funding rate awarded by the Cohesion Fund is between 80 and 85% of the public or similar spending and is in line with the nature of the interventions to be made. When aid has been awarded to a revenue-generating project, the Commission establishes the amount of the costs which serves as the basis for the Fund to determine the aid by taking into account the net revenues of the initiator. Preparatory studies may exceptionally be funded up to 100% of their total cost without, however, exceeding 0.5% of the total resources of the Fund.

In order to make sure that the projects financed by the Cohesion Fund are correctly carried out, the Member States must establish a monitoring system and take the necessary measures in order to avoid any irregularity whatsoever and to reclaim the funds awarded when an irregularity or negligence has been found.

In order to ensure the efficiency of Community aid, the Commission and the Member States adopt a systematic assessment of the projects and verify, in particular, whether or not the initial objectives have been achieved.

The Commission transmits an annual report on the activities of the Fund to the other Community institutions, and also ensures to inform the Member States. The publicity of the projects benefiting from financial aid from the Fund is ensured by the States which are responsible for the implementation of these actions.

Annexe II describes the implementation of this Regulation.

Commission Communication 94/C 139/03[1] — The financial instrument for the environment (LIFE)

This Communication defines the priority actions to be implemented within the framework of LIFE in 1995.

In 1995, the Community will witness the implementation of actions promoting both sustainable development and environmental quality as well as the elaboration of new measurement techniques and new monitoring techniques for environmental quality, clean technologies, and techniques for the collection, storage, recycling and elimination of waste. 1995 will also see the establishment of models which aim at the integration of the environment into the organisation and management of the territories as well as the improvement in environmental quality of inner-city areas.

Priority is also given to projects on the protection of habitats and the conservation of nature as well as to projects encouraging wider co-operation between the governments of the Member States. The latter item particularly concerns the tackling of transboundary and global environmental problems and the institution of different administrative and professional centres for the environment.

The technical assistance required for the establishment of environmental action policies and programmes beyond the Community's boundaries will be awarded.

---

1   Commission Communication 94/C 139/03 in accordance with Council Regulation (EEC) No 1973/92 of 21 May 1992, establishing a financial instrument for the environment (LIFE), relating to priority actions to be implemented in 1995 (OJ C 139, 21.05.1994, p. 3).

Commission Communication[1] — The annual report on the monitoring of the implementation of Community law

The part of the report dealing with the environment provides information relating to the implementation in the Member States of the different Community Directives that have been adopted concerning the environment. The results obtained by the Member States in 1993 are satisfactory: the rate of Directives for which national implementation measures have been communicated to the Commission generally exceeds 90%. Statistics reveal that the rate of implementation of the Directives is considerably lower in Italy (81%), Greece (84%) and Ireland (88%). These countries must undertake additional efforts to comply with their obligations.

Regarding the erroneous implementation of Directives, most difficulties concern Directives relating to waste, discharges of hazardous substances in water, the protection of wild birds and the assessment of impact on the environment.

Belgium has the greatest difficulty in implementing Directives relating to water problems.

The implementation of Directives in Denmark is generally satisfactory.

Germany's major problems in connection with the implementation of Directives concern waste and the quality of water in the new Länder.

Greece is still tackling problems concerning the protection of wild birds, waste and the quality of the air. There is an ever-increasing number of complaints concerning environmental impact.

Spain's problems concerning the implementation of Directives mainly relate to nature, the assessment of environmental impact, water and waste.

Complaints in France mainly concern the conservation of wild birds and the assessment of environmental impact.

Ireland and the United Kingdom have difficulty in implementing Directives relating to waters (bathing waters, shellfish waters, drinking-water...).

---

[1] Commission Communication 94/C 154/0, Eleventh annual report to the European Parliament on monitoring the application of Community law -1993 (OJ C 154, 06.06.1994, p. 1).

There are difficulties in Italy with regard to the implementation of Directives relating to the protection of wild birds and the assessment of the impact of public and private projects on the environment.

The problems of Luxembourg relating to waters and waste may well be justified as the majority of the Directives impose obligations on the smallest Member State which are similar to those imposed on the larger Member States that have great difficulty in complying with aforementioned obligations.

In the Netherlands, attention is mainly given to the difficulties relating to the implementation of Directives on the protection of wild birds, particularly concerning the designation and observance of special and wetland areas.

Finally, Portugal has difficulty implementing the Directives on waste and waters.

Legislation concerning General Policy

RESOLUTION 91/C 304/06[1] OF THE COUNCIL AND THE MINISTERS FOR HEALTH, MEETING WITHIN THE COUNCIL
of 11 November 1991
on health and the environment

THE COUNCIL OF THE EUROPEAN COMMUNITIES AND THE MINIS-TERS FOR HEALTH OF THE MEMBER STATES, MEETING WITHIN THE COUNCIL,

Having regard to the Treaties establishing the European Communities,

Whereas the quality of life is largely determined by one's state of health;

Recognizing that health and wellæbeing are dependent on a number of factors, including the quality of the environment;

Considering the transfrontier nature of health issues related to the environment and the interdependence of countries in finding solutions; whereas the Member States, the Community and neighbouring countries should cooperate in that respect;

Whereas a knowledge of, and information concerning, the effects of environmental factors on health are matters to be taken into account in drawing up a health policy;

Taking account of national, Community, international and, in particular, World Health Organization projects under way in this field;

Emphasizing that it is important to ensure that healthæpolicy aims are taken into account in Community policies;

INVITE the Commission, in close cooperation with the competent authorities of the Member States, to take stock of the knowledge and experience available in the Member States, the Community and international organizations regarding the relationship between health and the environment;

---

[1] OJ No C 304, 23. 11. 1991, p. 6.

On that basis, the Commission will be able to examine:

— how to gather and exchange such knowledge and experience,

— how the available knowledge can be improved and how it can be made accessible and usable in all the Member States, within the framework of their health policies,

— how to promote efforts to clarify the links between health and environment;

INVITE the Commission to report to the Council on the progress of activities at regular intervals, and for the first time, including a report on the abovementioned stocktaking, before 1994.

COUNCIL DIRECTIVE 91/692/EEC[1]
of 23 December 1991
standardizing and rationalizing reports on the implementation of certain Directives relating to the environment

THE COUNCIL OF THE EUROPEAN COMMUNITIES,

Having regard to the Treaty establishing the European Economic Community, and in particular Article 130s thereof,

Having regard to the proposal from the Commission[2],

Having regard to the opinion of the European Parliament[3],

Having regard to the opinion of the Economic and Social Committee[4],

Whereas some Community Directives relating to the environment require the Member States to establish a report on the measures taken to implement them; whereas the Commission drafts a consolidated report; whereas other Community Directives relating to the environment call for no such reports;

Whereas the existing provisions on the establishment of reports stipulate different intervals between reports and set different requirements for their content;

Whereas such an obligation should be introduced to enable the Member States and the Commission alike to assess the progress made in implementing these Directives throughout the Community's territory and, at the same time, to provide the general public with a source of information on this subject;

Whereas the existing provisions should therefore be harmonized to make them more consistent and more complete on a sectoral basis;

Whereas the interval at which the Member States submit these reports to the Commission should be fixed at three years, with a one-year interval between sectors; whereas the reports are to be drawn up on the basis of a questionnaire produced by the Commission with the assistance of a committee and sent to

---

[1] OJ No L 377, 31. 12. 1991, p. 48.
[2] OJ No C 214, 29. 8. 1990, p. 6.
[3] OJ No C 19, 28. 1. 1991, p. 587.
[4] OJ No C 60, 8. 3. 1991, p. 15.

Member States six months before the start of the period referred to by the report; whereas the Commission is to publish a consolidated report on the sector concerned within nine months of Member States' submission of their respective reports;

Whereas, in particular, the report on the implementation of Council Directive 76/160/EEC of 8 December 1975 concerning the quality of bathing water[1], as last amended by the 1985 Act of Accession, should appear annually and in sufficient time to inform the public of the quality of bathing water for the most recent period.

Whereas the measures which need to be taken by Member States do not entail the adoption of legislation or regulations since the drawing-up of reports on the implementation of Community Directives does not at present require the adoption of such provisions by Member States,

HAS ADOPTED THIS DIRECTIVE:

Article 1

The purpose of this Directive is to rationalize and improve on a sectoral basis the provisions on the transmission of information and the publication of reports concerning certain Community Directives on the protection of the environment, without prejudice to the provisions of the first indent of Article 155 of the Treaty.

Article 2

1)   The provisions listed in Annex I shall be replaced by the following:

'At intervals of three years the Member States shall send information to the Commission on the implementation of this Directive, in the form of a sectoral report which shall also cover other pertinent Community Directives. This report shall be drawn up on the basis of a questionnaire or outline drafted by the Commission in accordance with the procedure laid down in Article 6 of Directive 91/692/EEC[(*)]. The questionaire or outline shall be sent to the Member States six months before the start of the period covered by the report. The report shall be sent to the Commission within nine months of the end of the three-year period covered by it.

---

[1]   OJ No L 31, 5. 2. 1976, p. 1.
See also Community Legislation concerning the environment, volume 7, Water, first edition.

The first report shall cover the period from 1993 to 1995 inclusive.

The Commission shall publish a Community report on the implementation of the Directive within nine months of receiving the reports from the Member States.

(*)   OJ No L 377, 31. 12. 1991, p. 48.'

2.   The text set out in paragraph 1 shall be inserted into the Directives listed in Annex II as there indicated.

Article 3

Article 13 of Directive 76/160/EEC shall be replaced by the following:

'Article 13

Every year, and for the first time by 31 December 1993, the Member States shall send to the Commission a report on the implementation of this Directive in the current year. The report shall be drawn up on the basis of a questionnaire or outline drafted by the Commission in accordance with the procedure laid down in Article 6 of Directive 91/692/EEC[*]. The questionnaire or outline shall be sent to the Member States six months before the start of the period covered by the report. The report shall be made to the Commission before the end of the year in question.

The Commission shall publish a Community report on the implementation of the Directive within four months of receiving the reports from the Member States.

(*)   OJ No L 377, 31. 12. 1991, p. 48.'

Article 4

1.   The provisions listed in Annex III shall be replaced by the following:

'At intervals of three years the Member States shall send information to the Commission on the implementation of this Directive, in the form of a sectoral report which shall also cover other pertinent Community Directives. This report shall be drawn up on the basis of a questionnaire or outline drafted by the Commission in accordance with the procedure laid down in Article 6 of Directive 91/692/EEC[*]. The questionnaire or outline shall be sent to the Member States six months before the start of the period covered by the report.

The report shall be sent to the Commission within nine months of the end of the three-year period covered by it.

The first report shall cover the period from 1994 to 1996 inclusive.

The Commission shall publish a Community report on the implementation of the Directive within nine months of receiving the reports from the Member States.

(*)   OJ No L 377, 31. 12. 1991, p. 48.'

2.   The text set out in paragraph 1 shall be inserted into the Directive listed in Annex IV as there indicated.

3.   The following text shall be inserted into the Directives listed in Annex V as there indicated:

'The Commission shall each year communicate to the Member States the information it has received pursuant to this Article.'

Article 5

The provisions listed in Annex VI shall be replaced by the following:

'At intervals of three years Member States shall send information to the Commission on the implementation of this Directive, in the form of a sectoral report which shall also cover other pertinent Community Directives. The report shall be drawn up on the basis other of a questionnaire or outline drafted by the Commission in accordance with the procedure laid down in Article 6 of Directive 91/692/EEC(*). The questionnaire or outline shall be sent to the Member States six months before the start of the period covered by the report. The report shall be made to the Commission within nine months of the end of the three-year period covered by it.

The first report shall cover the period 1995 to 1997 inclusive.

The Commission shall publish a Community report on the implementation of the Directive within nine months of receiving the reports from the Member States.

(*)   OJ No L 377, 31. 12. 1991, p. 48.'

Article 6

The Commission shall be assisted by a committee composed of the representatives of the Member States and chaired by the representatives of the Commission.

The representative of the Commission shall submit to the committee a draft of measures to be taken. The committee shall deliver its opinion on the draft within a time limit which the chairman may lay down according to the urgency of the matter. The opinion shall be delivered by the majority laid down in Article 148 (2) of the Treaty in the case of decisions which the Council is required to adopt on a proposal from the Commission. The votes of the representatives of the Member States within the committee shall be weighted in the manner set out in that Article. The chairman shall not vote.

The Commission shall adopt measures which shall apply immediately. However, if these measures are not in accordance with the opinion of the committee, they shall be communicated by the Commission to the Council forthwith. In that event:

— the Commission may defer applications of the measures which it has decided for a period of not more than one month from the date of such communication,

— the Council, acting by a qualified majority, may take a different decision within the time limit referred to in the first indent.

Article 7

1. The Member States shall take such measures as are needed to comply with the provisions of:

— Articles 2 and 3 by 1 January 1993 at the latest,

— Article 4 by 1 January 1994 at the latest,

— Article 5 by 1 January 1995 at the latest.

They shall immediately notify the Commission of the measures taken.

2. The existing provisions of the various Directives which have been amended by new provisions shall remain in force until the dates mentioned in the first subparagraph 1.

3. When Member States adopt the measures referred to in paragraph 1, they shall contain a reference to this Directive or shall be accompanied by such

reference on the occasion of their official publication. The methods of making such a reference shall be laid down by the Member States.

Article 8

This Directive is addressed to the Member States.

Done at Brussels, 23 December 1991.

For the Council

The President

V. VAN ROOY

ANNEX I

Directives amended in accordance with Article 2 (1) of this Directive

a) Article 13 (1) of Council Directive 76/464/EEC of 4 May 1976 on pollution caused by certain dangerous substances discharged into the aquatic environment of the Community[1].

b) Article 14 of Council Directive 78/176/EEC of 20 February 1978 on waste from the titanium oxide industry[2], as amended by Directive 83/29/EEC[3].

c) Article 16 of Council Directive 78/659/EEC of 18 July 1978 on the quality of fresh waters needing protection or improvement in order to support fish life[4], as last amended by the 1985 Act of Accession.

d) Article 8 of Council Directive 79/869/EEC of 9 October 1979 concerning the methods of measurement and frequencies of sampling and analysis of surface water intended for the abstraction of drinking water in the Member States[5], as last amended by Directive 81/855/EEC[6].

e) Article 14 of Council Directive 79/923/EEC of 30 October 1979 on the quality required of shellfish waters[7].

---

[1] OJ No L 129, 18. 5. 1976, p. 23.
See also Community Legislation concerning the environment, volume 7, Water, first edition.

[2] OJ No L 54, 25. 2. 1978, p. 19.
See also Community Legislation concerning the environment, volume 6, Waste, first edition.

[3] OJ No L 32, 3. 2. 1983, p. 28.
See also Community Legislation concerning the environment, volume 6, Waste, first edition.

[4] OJ No L 222, 14. 8. 1978, p. 1.
See also Community Legislation concerning the environment, volume 7, Water, first edition.

[5] OJ No L 271, 29. 10. 1979, p. 44.
See also Community Legislation concerning the environment, volume 7, Water, first edition.

[6] OJ No L 319, 7. 11. 1981, p. 16.
See also Community Legislation concerning the environment, volume 7, Water, first edition.

[7] OJ No L 281, 10. 11. 1979, p. 47.
See also Community Legislation concerning the environment, volume 7, Water, first edition.

f) Article 16 (1) of Council Directive 80/68/EEC of 17 December 1979 on the protection of groundwater against pollution caused by certain dangerous substances[1].

g) Article 5 (1) and (2) (1) first subparagraph of Council Directive 82/176/EEC of 22 March 1982 on limit values and quality objectives for mercury discharges by the chlor-alkali electrolysis industry[2].

h) Article 5 (1) and (2) of Council Directive 83/513/EEC of 26 September 1983 on limit values and quality objectives for cadmium discharges [3].

i) Article 6 (1) of Council Directive 84/156/EEC of 8 March 1984 on limit values and quality objectives for mercury discharges by sectors other than the chlor-alkali electrolysis industry[4].

j) Article 5 (1) and (2) of Council Directive 84/491/EEC of 9 October 1982 on limit values and quality objectives for discharges of hexachlorcyclohexane[5].

k) Article 6 (1) and (2) of Council Directive 86/280/EEC of 12 June 1986 on limit values and quality objectives for discharge of certain dangerous substances included in list I of the Annex to Directive 76/464/EEC[6], as last amended by Directive 90/415/EEC[7].

---

[1] OJ No L 20, 26. 1. 1980, p. 43.
See also Community Legislation concerning the environment, volume 7, Water, first edition.

[2] OJ No L 81, 27. 3. 1982, p. 29.
See also Community Legislation concerning the environment, volume 7, Water, first edition.

[3] OJ No L 291, 24. 10. 1983, p. 2.
See also Community Legislation concerning the environment, volume 7, Water, first edition.

[4] OJ No L 74, 17. 3. 1984, p. 49.
See also Community Legislation concerning the environment, volume 7, Water, first edition.

[5] OJ No L 274, 17. 10. 1984, p. 11.
See also Community Legislation concerning the environment, volume 7, Water, first edition.

[6] OJ No L 181, 4. 7. 1986, p. 16.
See also Community Legislation concerning the environment, volume 7, Water, first edition.

[7] OJ No L 219, 14. 8. 1990, p. 49.
See also Community Legislation concerning the environment, volume 7, Water, first edition.

ANNEX II

Directives supplemented in accordance with Article 2 (2) of this Directive

a) Council Directive 75/440/EEC of 16 June 1975 concerning the quality required of surface water intended for the abstraction of drinking water in the Member States[1], as last amended by Directive 79/869/EEC[2].

The text of Article 2 (1) of this Directive is incorporated as Article 9a.

b) Council Directive 80/778/EEC of 15 July 1980 relating to the quality of water intended for human consumption[3], as last amended by Directive 81/858/EEC[4].

The text of Article 2 (1) of this Directive is incorporated as Article 17a.

---

[1] OJ NO L 194, 25. 7. 1975, p. 26.
See also Community Legislation concerning the environment, volume 7, Water, first edition.

[2] OJ NO L 271, 29. 10. 1979, p. 44.
See also Community Legislation concerning the environment, volume 7, Water, first edition.

[3] OJ NO L 229, 30. 8. 1980, p. 11.

[4] OJ NO L 319, 7. 11. 1981, p. 19.

ANNEX III

Directives amended in accordance with Article 4 (1) of this Directive

a) Article 8 of Council Directive 80/779/EEC of 15 July on air quality limit values and guide values for sulphur dioxide and suspended particulates[1], as last amended by Directive 89/427/EEC[2].

b) Article 18 of Council Directive 82/501/EEC of 24 June 1982 on the major-accident hazards of certain industrial activities[3], as last amended by Directive 88/610/EEC[4].

c) Article 6 of Council Directive 82/884/EEC of 3 December 1982 on a limit value for lead in the air[5].

d) Article 8 of Council Directive 85/203/EEC of 7 March 1985 on air quality standards for nitrogen dioxide[6], as amended by Directive 85/580/EEC[7].

e) Article 13 (1) of Council Directive 87/217/EEC of 19 March 1987 on the prevention and reduction of environmental pollution by asbestos [8].

---

[1] OJ No L 229, 30. 8. 1980, p. 30.
    See also Community Legislation concerning the environment, volume 2, Air, first edition.

[2] OJ No L 201, 14. 7. 1989, p. 53.
    See also Community Legislation concerning the environment, volume 2, Air, first edition.

[3] OJ No L 230, 5. 8. 1982, p. 1.
    See also Community Legislation concerning the environment, volume 3, Chemicals, Industrial Risks and Biotechnology, first edition.

[4] OJ No L 336, 7. 12. 1988, p. 14.
    See also Community Legislation concerning the environment, volume 3, Chemicals, Industrial Risks and Biotechnology, first edition.

[5] OJ No L 378, 31. 12. 1982, p. 15.
    See also Community Legislation concerning the environment, volume 2, Air, first edition.

[6] OJ No L 87, 27. 3. 1985, p. 1.
    See also Community Legislation concerning the environment, volume 2, Air, first edition.

[7] OJ No L 372, 31. 12. 1985, p. 36.
    See also Community Legislation concerning the environment, volume 2, Air, first edition.

[8] OJ No L 85, 28. 3. 1987, p. 40.
    See also Community Legislation concerning the environment, volume 3, Chemicals, Industrial Risks and Biotechnology, first edition.

ANNEX IV

Directives amended in accordance with Article 4 (2) of this Directive

a) Council Directive 75/716/EEC of 24 November 1975 on the approximation of the laws of the Member States relating to the sulphur content of certain liquid fuels[1], as last amended by Directive 87/219/EEC[2].

The text of Article 4 (2) of this Directive is incorporated in Article 7a.

b) Council Directive 84/360/EEC of 28 June 1984 on the combating of air pollution from industrial plants[3].

The text of Article 4 (2) of this Directive is incorporated as Article 15a.

---

[1] OJ No L 307, 27. 11. 1975. p. 22.
See also Community Legislation concerning the environment, volume 2, Air, first edition.

[2] OJ No L 91, 3. 4. 1987, p. 19.
See also Community Legislation concerning the environment, volume 2, Air, first edition.

[3] OJ No L 188, 16. 7. 1984, p. 20.
See also Community Legislation concerning the environment, volume 2, Air, first edition.

ANNEX V

Directives amended in accordance with Article 4 (3) of this Directive

a) Council Directive 80/779/EEC of 15 July 1980 on air quality limit values and guide values for sulphur dioxide and suspended particulates, as amended by Directive 89/427/EEC.

The text of Article 4 (3) of this Directive is incorporated as Article 7 (4).

b) Council Directive 82/884/EEC of 3 December 1982 on a limit value for lead in the air.

The text of Article 4 (3) of this Directive is incorporated as Article 5 (4).

c) Council Directive 85/203/EEC of 7 March 1985 on air quality standards for nitrogen dioxide, as amended by Directive 85/580/EEC.

The text of Article 4 (3) of this Directive is incorporated as Article 7 (4).

ANNEX VI

Directives amended in accordance with Article 5 of this Directive

a) Article 18 of Council Directive 74/439/EEC of 16 June 1975 on the disposal of waste oils[1], as amended by Directive 87/101/EEC[2].

b) Article 12 of Council Directive 75/442/EEC of 15 July 1975 on waste[3], as amended by Directive 91/156/EEC[4].

c) Article 10 of Council Directive 76/403/EEC of 6 April 1976 on the disposal of polychlorinated biphenyls and polychlorinated terphenyls [5].

d) Article 16 of Council Directive 78/319/EEC of 20 March 1978 on toxic and dangerous waste[6], as last amended by the 1985 Act of Accession.

e) Article 13 (1) of Council Directive 84/631/EEC of 6 December 1984 on the supervision and control within the European Community of the trans-frontier shipment of hazardous waste[7], as last amended by Commission Directive 87/112/EEC[8].

f) Article 6 of Council Directive 85/339/EEC of 27 June 1985 on containers of liquids for human consumption[9].

---

[1] OJ No L 194, 25. 7. 1975, p. 23.
See also Community Legislation concerning the environment, volume 6, Waste, first edition.

[2] OJ No L 42, 12. 2. 1987, p. 43.
See also Community Legislation concerning the environment, volume 6, Waste, first edition.

[3] OJ No L 194, 25. 7. 1975, p. 39.
See also Community Legislation concerning the environment, volume 6, Waste, first edition.

[4] OJ No L 78, 26. 3. 1991, p. 32.
See also Community Legislation concerning the environment, volume 6, Waste, first edition.

[5] OJ No L 108, 26. 4. 1976, p. 41.
See also Community Legislation concerning the environment, volume 6, Waste, first edition.

[6] OJ No L 84, 31. 3. 1978, p. 43.
See also Community Legislation concerning the environment, volume 6, Waste, first edition.

[7] OJ No L 236, 13. 12. 1984, p. 31.
See also Community Legislation concerning the environment, volume 6, Waste, first edition.

[8] OJ No L 48, 17. 2. 1987, p. 31.
See also Community Legislation concerning the environment, volume 6, Waste, first edition.

g) Article 17 of Council Directive 86/278/EEC of 12 June 1986 on the protection of the environment, and in particular of the soil, when sewage sludge is used in agriculture[1].

---

[9] OJ No L 176, 6. 7. 1985, p. 18.
See also Community Legislation concerning the environment, volume 6, Waste, first edition.

[1] OJ No L 181, 4. 7. 1986. p. 6.
See also Community Legislation concerning the environment, volume 6, Waste, first edition.

COUNCIL RESOLUTION 92/C 59/01[1]
of 25 February 1992
on the future Community policy concerning the European coastal zone

THE COUNCIL OF THE EUROPEAN COMMUNITIES,

RECOGNIZING that the European coastal zone, including islands, is a fragile and vital common heritage, and that it is essential that its biological diversity, landscape value, ecological quality and its capacity to sustain life, health, economic activities and social well-being are safeguarded;

EMPHASIZING that a key to sustainable use and development of coastal zones lies in the full integration of economic, physical planning and environmental policies;

ACKNOWLEDGING that the vulnerabilities of the environment, including the natural and cultural heritage, in coastal areas should explicitly be taken into account in developing coastal policies;

TAKES NOTE of the final declaration of the European Coastal Conservation Conference, held in The Hague, the Netherlands, from 19 to 21 November 1991 about the future policy with regard to the European coastal zone;

CONCLUDES that, taking into account the subsidiarity principle, there is a clear need for a Community strategy for integrated planning and management of the coastal zones based on the principles of sustainability and sound ecological and environmental practice;

CONCLUDES that conservation and sustainable use of coastal zones is one of the fundamental aspects of such a strategy and that accordingly high priority should be given to specific action in this field;

INVITES THE COMMISSION:

— to propose for consideration a Community strategy for integrated coastal zone management which will provide a framework for conservation and sustainable use,

— to incorporate this initiative into the Fifth Environmental Action Programme.

---

[1] OJ No C 59, 6. 3. 1992, p. 1.

COUNCIL REGULATION (EEC) No 880/92[1]
of 23 March 1992
on a Community eco-label award scheme

THE COUNCIL OF THE EUROPEAN COMMUNITIES,

Having regard to the Treaty establishing the European Economic Community, and in particular Article 130s thereof,

Having regard to the proposal from the Commission[2],

Having regard to the opinion of the European Parliament[3],

Having regard to the opinion of the Economic and Social Committee[4],

Whereas the objectives and principles of the Community's environment policy, as set out in the European Communities' action programme on the environment[5], aim, in particular, at preventing, reducing and as far as possible eliminating pollution, as a priority at source, and ensuring sound management of raw materials resources, on the basis also of the 'polluter pays' principle; whereas the Fourth European Community action programme on the environment (1987 to 1992)[6] highlights the importance of developing a policy towards clean products;

Whereas the Council resolution of 7 May 1990[7], invited the Commission to submit as soon as possible a proposal for a Community-wide eco-labelling scheme covering the environmental impact during the entire life cycle of the product;

---

[1] OJ No L 99, 11. 4. 1992, p. 1.
[2] OJ No C 75, 20. 3. 1991, p. 23,
    and OJ No C 12, 18. 1. 1992, p. 16.
[3] OJ No C 13, 20. 1. 1992, p. 37.
[4] OJ No C 339, 31. 12. 1991, p. 29.
[5] OJ No C 112, 20. 12. 1973, p. 1;
    OJ No C 139, 13. 6. 1977, p. 1;
    OJ No C 46, 17. 2. 1983, p. 1;
    OJ No C 70, 18. 3. 1987, p. 3.
[6] OJ No C 328, 7. 12. 1987, p. 1.
[7] OJ No C 122, 18. 5. 1990, p. 2.

Whereas the European Parliament, in its resolution of 19 June 1987 on the waste disposal industry and old waste dumps[1], supported a European label for clean products;

Whereas there is increased public interest in information about products with reduced environmental impact; whereas some Member States have already an award scheme for such products and several other Member States are considering the setting up of such a scheme;

Whereas a system to award an eco-label for products with reduced environmental impact will highlight more benign alternatives and therefore provide consumers and users with guidance;

Whereas such guidance can best be achieved by establishing uniform criteria for the award scheme to apply throughout the Community;

Whereas, while existing or future independent award schemes can continue to exist, the aim of this Regulation is to create the conditions for ultimately establishing an effective single environmental label in the Community;

Whereas the award scheme should be based on voluntary application; whereas such an approach, in relying on market forces, will also contribute to research and the development, in particular, of clean technologies, and thereby lead to innovation;

Whereas uniform application of criteria and compliance with procedures should be ensured throughout the Community;

Whereas the award scheme for the eco-label will take into account the interests of the principal groups concerned and therefore should provide for appropriate involvement of these groups in the definition of product groups and specific ecological criteria for each product group;

Whereas consumers and undertakings should be informed by appropriate means about the eco-label award scheme;

Whereas this label should complement other existing or future Community labelling systems,

HAS ADOPTED THIS REGULATION:

---

[1]   OJ No C 190, 20. 7. 1987, p. 154.

Article 1 Objectives

This Regulation establishes a Community eco-label award scheme which is intended to:

— promote the design, production, marketing and use of products which have a reduced environmental impact during their entire life cycle,

and

— provide consumers with better information on the environmental impact of products,

without, however, compromising product or workers' safety or significantly affecting the properties which make a product fit for use.

Article 2 Scope

This Regulation shall not apply to food, drink or pharmaceuticals.

Article 3 Definitions

For the purpose of this Regulation:

a) 'substance' means chemical elements and their compounds as defined in Article 2 of Council Directive 67/548/EEC of 27 June 1967 on the approximation of the laws, regulations and administrative provisions relating to the classification, packaging and labelling of dangerous substances[1];

b) 'preparation' means mixtures or solutions as defined in Article 2 of Council Directive 67/548/EEC;

c) 'product group' means products which serve similar purposes and which have equivalence of use;

d) 'cradle to grave' means the life cycle of a product from manufacturing, including the choice of raw materials, distribution, consumption and use to disposal after use.

---

[1] OJ No L 196, 16. 8. 1967, p. 1. Directive as last amended by Directive 91/410/EEC (OJ No L 228, 17. 8. 1991, p. 67).

Article 4   General principles

1.   The eco-label can be awarded to products which meet the objectives set out in Article 1 and which are in conformity with Community health, safety and environmental requirements.

2.   The eco-label shall in no case be awarded:

   a) to products which are substances or preparations classified as dangerous in accordance with Directives 67/548/EEC and 88/379/EEC[1].

   The label may be awarded to products containing a substance or preparation classified as dangerous in accordance with that Directive in so far as the products meet the objectives set out in Article 1;

   b) to products manufactured by processes which are likely to harm significantly man and/or the environment.

3)   Products imported into the Community, for which the award of an eco-label in accordance with this Regulation has been requested, must at least meet the same strict criteria as products manufactured in the Community.

Article 5   Product groups and ecological criteria

1.   The conditions for awarding the label shall be defined by product groups.

Product groups, the specific ecological criteria for each group and their respective periods of validity shall be established in accordance with the procedure laid down in Article 7 following the consultation procedure provided for in Article 6.

2.   The Commission shall begin these procedures at the request of the competent body or bodies referred to in Article 9, or on its own initiative. A competent body may act on its own initiative or at the request of any interested organization or individual; in the latter case it shall decide whether such a request is appropriate. Before submitting a request to the Commission the competent body shall conduct appropriate consultation of interest groups and inform the Commission of the results thereof.

3.   Each product group shall be defined in such a way as to ensure that all competing products which serve similar purposes and which have equivalence of use are included in the same group.

---

[1]   OJ No L 187, 16. 7. 1988, p. 14.

4.   The specific ecological criteria for each product group shall be established using a 'cradle-to-grave' approach based on the objectives set out in Article 1, the general principles set out in Article 4 and the parameters of the indicative assessment matrix shown in Annex I. The criteria must be precise, clear and objective so as to ensure uniformity of application by the competent bodies. They must ensure a high level of environmental protection, be based as far as possible on the use of clean technology and, where appropriate, reflect the desirablility of maximizing product life.

Should it prove necessary to adapt the indicative assessment matrix to technical progress, such adaptation shall be made in accordance with the procedure laid down in Article 7.

5.   The period of validity of product groups shall be about three years. The period of validity of a criterion may not exceed the period of validity of the product groups to which it relates.

Article 6   Consultation of interest groups

1.   With a view to the definition of the products groups and the specific ecological criteria referred to in Article 5 and before submitting a draft to the Committee referred to in Article 7, the Commission shall consult the principal interest groups who shall meet for this purpose within a consultation forum. In so doing, the Commission shall take account of the results of national consultations.

2.   The forum should involve at least the Community-level representatives of the following interest groups:

—   industry[1],
—   commerce[1],
—   consumer organizations,
—   environmental organizations.

Each of them may be represented by having a maximum of three seats.

The participating interest groups should ensure appropriate representation according to the product groups concerned and having regard to the need to ensure continuity in the work of the consultation forum.

---

[1] Including trade unions as appropriate.

3.   The rules of procedure of the forum shall be established by the Commission in accordance with the procedure laid down in Article 7.

4.   The period allowed for the consultation of the forum may not exceed six weeks in any one case.

5.   The Commission shall forward the outcome of the consultations to the committee referred to in Article 7 together with the draft measures to be adopted.

Article 7   Committee

1.   The Commission shall be assisted by a committee composed of the representatives of the Member States and chaired by the representative of the Commission.

2.   The representative of the Commission shall submit to the committee a draft of the measures to be taken. The committee shall deliver its opinion on the draft within a time limit which the chairman may lay down according to the urgency of the matter. The opinion shall be delivered by the majority laid down in Article 148 (2) of the Treaty in the case of decisions which the Council is required to adopt on a proposal from the Commission. The votes of the representatives of the Member States within the committee shall be weighted in the manner set out in that Article. The chairman shall not vote.

3.   The Commission shall adopt the measures envisaged if they are in accordance with the opinion of the committee.

4.   If the measures envisaged are not in accordance with the opinion of the committee, or if no opinion is delivered, the Commission shall, without delay, submit to the Council a proposal relating to the measures to be taken. The Council shall act by a qualified majority.

5.   If the Council has not acted within three months from the date of referral to it, the proposed measures shall be adopted by the Commission.

Article 8   The eco-label

1.   The eco-label shall bear the logo shown in Annex II.

2.   Applications for the award of the label shall be made in accordance with the procedures laid down in Article 10.

3.   The decision to award a label to individual products which fulfil the criteria referred to in Articles 4 and 5 shall be taken by the competent bodies referred to in Article 9 in accordance with the procedure laid down in Article 10.

4.   In accordance with the procedure laid down in Article 7, the Commission shall decide on a case-by-case basis whether it is possible to state on the label the principal reasons for awarding the eco-label and establish rules for this purpose.

5.   The label shall be awarded for a fixed production period which may in no circumstances exceed the period of validity of the criteria.

Where the criteria relating to products are extended without change, the validity of the label may be extended for the same period.

6.   The eco-label shall under no circumstances be used before the conclusion of a contract covering the conditions of use as provided for in Article 12.

Article 9   Designation of competent bodies

1.   Within six months from the entry into force of this Regulation each Member State shall designate the body or bodies, hereinafter referred to as the 'competent body (bodies)', responsible for carrying out the tasks provided for in this Regulation, particularly in Article 10, and shall inform the Commission thereof.

2.   The Member States shall ensure that the composition of the competent bodies is such as to guarantee their independence and neutrality and that the competent bodies apply the provisions of this Regulation in a consistent manner.

Article 10   Applications for the award of an eco-label

1.   Manufacturers or importers in the Community may apply for the award of an eco-label only to the competent body or bodies designated by the Member State in which the product is manufactured or first marketed or into which the product is imported from a third country.

2.   Before proceeding to an assessment of applications, the competent body shall consult the registers referred to in paragraph 9. The competent body shall assess the environmental performance of the product by reference to the principles in Article 4 and the specific criteria for the product groups in Article 5.

For this purpose, all required certification and documents (including the results of independent testing) shall be presented to the competent body.

3.   After the product assessment, the competent body shall decide whether to award a label. If it decides that a label should be awarded, it shall notify the Commission of its decision and enclose the full results of the assessment together with a summary thereof. A standard summary form shall be established by the Commission in accordance with the procedure laid down in Article 7.

Within five days following notification the Commission shall forward to the competent bodies of the other Member States a copy of the aforesaid decision and summary as well as, at their request, a copy of the full results of the assessment.

4.   After a period of 30 days following the dispatch of this notification to the Commission the competent body may implement the award unless the Commission has by that time informed the competent body of reasoned objections to the award. If such objections are raised and cannot be resolved by informal consultations, the Commission shall take a decision on the proposed award in accordance with the procedure laid down in Article 7.

5.   If the competent body decides to award a label to a product already rejected by the competent body of another Member State, it shall draw the Commission's attention to this fact when notifying its decision under paragraph 3. The Commission shall in all such cases take a decision on the proposed award in accordance with the procedure laid down in Article 7.

6.   In the cases referred to in paragraphs 4 and 5, the Commission shall, within 45 days after the receipt of the decision of the competent body to award a label, submit a draft of the measures to be taken to the committee referred to in Article 7.

7.   If an application for the award of an eco-label is rejected, the competent body shall immediately inform the Commission and advise the applicant of the reasons for the rejection.

8.   On receiving an application for a label, the competent body may conclude that the product does not fall within a product group for which criteria have already been agreed. In these cases, the competent body shall decide if a proposal for the establishment of a new product group should be forwarded to the Commission for adoption in line with the procedures laid down in Articles 6 and 7.

9. The Commission shall maintain separate registers of all applications received, all applications approved and all applications rejected. Those showing the received and rejected applications shall be accessible only to the competent bodies of Member States.

10. A manufacturer or importer who intends to withdraw an application for the award of a label or to cease to use a label shall notify the appropriate competent body.

Article 11   Costs and fees

1. Every application for the award of a label shall be subject to the payment of the costs of processing the application.

2. The conditions governing the use of the label shall include payment of a fee by the applicant for the use of the label.

3. The sums referred to in paragraphs 1 and 2 shall be fixed by the competent bodies referred to in Article 9 and may vary from Member State to Member State. Indicative guidelines for this purpose shall be established in accordance with the procedure laid down in Article 7.

Article 12   Terms of use

1. The competent body shall conclude a contract, covering the terms of use of the label, with each applicant. To this end a standard contract shall be adopted in accordance with the procedure laid down in Article 7.

2. The terms of use shall also include provisions for withdrawing the authorization to use the label.

Article 13   Confidentiality

Competent bodies, the Commission and all other persons concerned may not disclose to third parties information to which they have gained access in the course of assessing a product with a view to the award of the label.

Once a decision has been taken to award the label, however, the following information may not in any circumstances be kept confidential:

— the name of the product,

— the manufacturer or importer of the product,

— the reasons and relevant information for awarding the label.

Article 14   Publication

The Commission shall publish in the *Official Journal of the European Communities*:

a) the product groups, the relevant specific ecological criteria and their respective periods of validity;

b) a list of products for which an eco-label has been awarded, the names of the relevant manufacturers or importers and the expiration dates of the labels. Such publication shall take place at least once a year.

c) the names and addresses of the competent bodies.

The Commission shall also publish from time to time for the information of consumers and undertakings a consolidated list of the products for which an eco-label has been awarded.

Article 15   Information

Each Member State shall ensure that consumers and undertakings are informed by appropriate means of the following:

a) the objectives of the eco-label award scheme;

b) the product groups which have been selected;

c) the ecological criteria for each product group;

d) the procedures to be followed for applying for a label;

e) the competent body or bodies in the Member State.

Article 16   Advertising

1.   References to the eco-label in advertising may not be made until a label has been awarded and then only in relation to the specific product for which it was awarded.

2.   Any false or misleading advertising or the use of any label or logo which leads to confusion with the Community eco-label introduced by this Regulation is hereby prohibited.

Article 17   Implementation

Member States shall within six months of the entry into force of this Regulation inform the Commission of measures taken to ensure compliance with this Regulation.

Article 18   Review

1.   Within five years of the entry into force of this Regulation the Commission shall review the scheme in the light of the experience gained during its operation.

2.   The Commission shall propose any appropriate amendments to this Regulation.

This Regulation shall be binding in its entirety and directly applicable in all Member States.

Done at Brussels, 23 March 1992.

For the Council

The President

Carlos BORREGO

ANNEX I

INDICATIVE ASSESSMENT MATRIX

Environmental fields	Product life-cycle				
	Pre-production	Production	Distribution (including packaging)	Utilization	Disposal
Waste relevance					
Soil pollution and degradation					
Water contamination					
Air contamination					
Noise					
Consumption of energy					
Consumption of natural resources					
Effects on eco-systems					

ANNEX II

LOGO

The logo shall be printed either:

—   in two colours (Pantone 347 green and Pantone 279 blue), or

—   in black on white, or

—   in white on black.

COUNCIL REGULATION (EEC) No 1973/92[1]
of 21 May 1992
establishing a financial instrument for the environment (LIFE)

THE COUNCIL OF THE EUROPEAN COMMUNITIES,

Having regard to the Treaty establishing the European Economic Community, and in particular Article 130s thereof,

Having regard to the proposal from the Commission[2],

Having regard to the opinion of the European Parliament[3],

Having regard to the opinion of the Economic and Social Committee[4],

Whereas the Treaty establishing the European Economic Community provides for the development and implementation of a Community environment policy and sets out the objectives and principles which should guide that policy;

Whereas, pursuant to Article 130r of the Treaty, action by the Community relating to the environment aims, in particular, to preserve, protect and improve the quality of the environment; whereas, in preparing its action, the Community is to take account, inter alia, of environmental conditions in the various regions of the Community;

Whereas Article 130r (4) of the Treaty provides that the Commission shall take action relating to the environment to the extent to which the objectives referred to can be attained better at Community level than at the level of the individual Member States; whereas, without prejudice to certain measures of a Community nature, the Member States shall finance and implement the other measures;

Whereas a unified financial instrument for the environment (LIFE) should be established to contribute to the development and implementation of Community policy and legislation regarding the environment;

Whereas it is important to define the eligible areas of action which LIFE might support while complying with the 'polluter pays' and subsidiarity principles;

---

[1] OJ No L 206, 22. 7. 1992, p. 1.
[2] OJ No C 44, 20. 2. 1991, p. 4.
[3] OJ No C 267, 14. 10. 1991, p. 211.
[4] OJ No C 191, 22. 7. 1991, p. 7.

Whereas priority actions for implementation in eligible fields of action should be established at the latest by 30 September of each year for the following year;

Whereas it is necessary to specify the detailed rules for LIFE assistance;

Whereas provision should be made for an instrument the first phase of which will end on 31 December 1995;

Whereas an amount of ECU 400 million is deemed necessary for the implementation of this instrument over the period 1991 to 1995; whereas for the period 1991 to 1992 under the current financial perspective, the amount deemed necessary is ECU 140 million;

Whereas mechanisms should be established so that Community assistance may be adapted to the particular features of the measures to be supported;

Wheres it is necessary to establish effective methods of monitoring, assessment and evaluation as well as to ensure adequate information for potential beneficiaries and for the public;

Whereas a Committee should be set up to assist the Commission in implementing the Regulation;

Whereas, in the light of the experience gained during the first three years of implementation, the Council should re-examine LIFE's provisions on the basis of a Commission proposal to be submitted no later than 31 December 1994,

HAS ADOPTED THIS REGULATION:

Article 1

A financial instrument for the environment, hereinafter referred to as 'LIFE', is hereby established.

The general objective of LIFE shall be to contribute to the development and implementation of Community environmental policy and legislation by financing:

a) priority environmental actions in the Community;

b)
    i) technical assistance actions with third countries from the Mediterranean region or bordering on the Baltic Sea;

    ii) in exceptional circumstances, actions concerning regional or global environmental problems provided for in international agreements.

Financing of these actions from LIFE shall be the subject of a specific Decision by the Council, acting on a proposal from the Commission.

The maximum amount of resources which can be allocated to the actions referred to in (i) and (ii) shall be 5 %.

Article 2

1.   The fields of action eligible for Community financial assistance are defined in the Annex.

2.   Community financial assistance may be provided for actions which are of Community interest, contribute significantly to the implementation of Community environmental policy and meet the conditions for implementing the 'polluter pays' principle.

This assistance will cover, in particular, preparatory measures, demonstration schemes, awareness campaigns and actions providing incentives or technical assistance.

In addition, for the protection of habitats and nature this assistance must in particular contribute to the co-financing of measures necessary for the maintenance or restoration, at a favourable conservation status, of priority natural habitat types and priority species on the sites concerned as listed in Annex I and Annex II respectively to Council Directive 92/43/EEC of 21 May 1992 on the conservation of natural and semi-natural habitats and of wild fauna and flora[1].

Article 3

Without prejudice to the procedure laid down in Article 21 of Directive 92/43/EEC:

—   by 30 September each year, the Commission shall establish, in accordance with the procedure laid down in Article 13, the priority actions to be implemented within the fields of action defined in the Annex and the corresponding allocation of resources,

—   the Commission shall, in accordance with the procedure laid down in Article 13, specify the additional criteria to be used for selecting the actions to be financed.

---

[1]   See page 7 of this Official Journal (OJ No L 206, 22. 7. 1992).

Article 4

Financial assistance shall be provided in one of the following forms, depending on the nature of the operations to be carried out:

a)   co-financing of actions;

b)   interest rebates.

Article 5

Actions receiving aid provided for under the structural funds or other Community budget instruments shall not be eligible for financial assistance under this Regulation.

Article 6

The Commission shall ensure that actions undertaken in the framework of this Regulation are consistent with those undertaken under the Structural Funds or other Community financial instruments.

Article 7

1.   LIFE shall be implemented in phases. The first phase shall end on 31 December 1995.

2.   The Community financial resources estimated as necessary for implementation of the first phase amount to ECU 400 million, of which ECU 140 million are available for the period 1991 to 1992 in the framework of the 1988 to 1992 financial perspective.

For the subsequent period of implementation of LIFE, the amount shall fall within the Community financial framework in force.

3.   The budget authority shall determine the appropriations available for each financial year, taking into account the principles of sound financial management referred to in Article 2 of the Financial Regulation applicable to the general budget of the European Communities.

4.   The Annex contains an indication of the percentage of Community resources which may be allocated to each field of action.

Article 8

1.   Except as provided for in paragraph 2, the rate of Community assistance shall be subject to the following ceilings:

—   30 % of the cost in the case of actions involving the financing of income-generating investments.

The operator's contribution to the financing must be at least as much as the Community assistance,

—   100 % of the cost of measures designed to provide the information necessary for the execution of an action and of technical assistance measures implemented on the Commission's initiative,

—   50 % of the cost of other actions.

2.   The rate of Community assistance for actions concerning the conservation of priority biotopes or habitats of Community interest may be:

i)   normally, a maximum of 50 % of the cost of the actions;

ii) by way of exception, a maximum of 75 % of the cost provided the actions concern;

-    biotopes or habitats hosting species in danger of extinction in the Community, or

-    habitats at risk of disappearing from the Community, or

-    populations of species in danger of extinction in the Community.

Article 9

1.   Proposals for actions to be financed shall be submitted to the Commission by the Member States. In the case of actions involving more than one Member State, consultation shall take place between the Commission and the interested parties prior to the submission of proposals.

2.   However, the Commission may ask any legal or natural persons established in the Community to submit applications for assistance in respect of measures of particular interest to the Community by means of a notice published in the *Official Journal of the European Communities*.

3.   Applications from third countries shall be submitted to the Commission by the relevant national authorities.

4.   The Commission shall forward to the Member States proposals received in the framework of such expressions of interest and applications submitted by third countries.

5.   Actions under LIFE shall be approved under the procedure in Article 13 and shall give rise:

a) either to a Commission decision approving the action concerned, addressed to the Member States;

b) or to a contract or agreement governing the rights and obligations of the parties, concluded with the beneficiaries responsible for implementation.

c) The amount of financial assistance, financial procedures and controls, as well as all the technical conditions necessary for giving the assistance shall be determined on the basis of the nature and form of the approved action and shall be laid down either in the Commission decision or in the contract or agreement concluded with the beneficiaries.

Article 10

1.   'In order to ensure the success of the actions carried out by those receiving Community financial assistance, the Commission shall take the necessary measures to:

— verify that actions financed by the Community have been carried out properly,

— prevent and take action against irregularities,

— recover sums improperly received owing to abuse or negligence.

2.   Without prejudice to the audits carried out by the Court of Auditors in liaison with the national audit bodies or the competent national departments pursuant to Article 206a of the Treaty, or any inspection carried out pursuant to Article 209 (c) of the Treaty, officials and other staff of the Commission may carry out on-the-spot checks, including sample checks, on actions financed under LIFE.

The Commission shall inform the beneficiary in advance of an on-the-spot check unless there are good reasons to suspect fraud and/or improper use.

3.   For a period of five years following the last payment in respect of any action, the beneficiary of financial assistance shall keep available for the Commission all the supporting documents regarding expenditure on the action.

Article 11

1.   The Commission may reduce, suspend or recover the amount of financial assistance granted for an action if it finds irregularities or if it transpires that, without Commission approval having been sought, the action has been subjected to a major change which conflicts with the nature or implementing conditions of the action.

2.   If the deadlines have not been observed or if only part of the allocated financial assistance is justified by the progress in implementation of an action, the Commission shall request the beneficiary to submit its observations within a specified period. If the beneficiary does not give a satisfactory answer, the Commission may cancel the remaining financial assistance and demand repayment of sums already paid.

3.   Any undue payment must be repaid to the Commission. Interest may be added to any sums not repaid in good time. The Commission shall lay down detailed rules for the implementation of this paragraph.

Article 12

1.   The Commission shall ensure effective monitoring of the implementation of Community-financed actions. This monitoring shall take place on the basis of reports drawn up using the procedures agreed by the Commission and the beneficiary and shall also involve sample checks.

2.   For each multiannual action the beneficiary shall submit progress reports to the Commission within six months of the end of each full year of implementation. Within six months of completion of the action a final report shall also be forwarded to the Commission. For each action lasting less than two years the beneficiary shall submit a report to the Commission within six months of completion of the action. The Commission shall determine the form and content of these reports.

3.   On the basis of the monitoring procedures and reports referred to in paragraphs 1 and 2 the Commission shall, if necessary, adjust the scale or the conditions of allocation of the financial assistance originally approved and also the timetable for payments.

4.   A list of actions financed by LIFE shall be published each year in the *Official Journal of the European Communities*. Every two years, after consulting the Committee referred to in Article 13, the Commission shall submit a progress report to the European Parliament and the Council on the implementation of LIFE, and in particular on the use of appropriations.

Article 13

The Commission shall be assisted by a committee composed of the representatives of the Member States and chaired by the representative of the Commission.

Without prejudice to Article 8 of Directive 92/43/EEC, the representative of the Commission shall submit to the committee a draft of the measures to be taken. The committee shall deliver its opinion on the draft within a time limit which the chairman may lay down according to the urgency of the matter. The opinion shall be delivered by the majority laid down in Article 148(2) of the Treaty in the case of decisions which the Council is required to adopt on a proposal from the Commission. The votes of the representatives of the Member States within the committee shall be weighted in the manner set out in that Article. The chairman shall not vote.

The Commission shall adopt the measures envisaged if they are in accordance with the opinion of the committee.

If the measures envisaged are not in accordance with the opinion of the committee, or if no opinion is delivered, the Commission shall, without delay, submit to the Council a proposal relating to the measures to be taken. The Council shall act by a qualified majority.

If, on the expiry of a period of one month from the date of referral to the Council, the Council has not acted, the proposed measures shall be adopted by the Commission.

Article 14

No later than 31 December 1994, the Commission shall submit a report to the European Parliament and the Council on the implementation of this Regulation and shall make proposals for any adjustment to be made with a view to continuing the action beyond the first phase.

The Council, acting by a qualified majority on a proposal from the Commission, shall decide on the implementation of the second phase as from 1 January 1996.

Article 15

This Regulation shall not affect the continuation of actions decided on and coming into operation on the basis of the Regulations referred to in Article 16 before the entry into force of this Regulation.

Article 16

Regulation (EEC) No 563/91 (Medspa)[1], (EEC) No 3907/91 (Acnat)[2] and (EEC) No 3908/91 (Norspa)[3] are hereby repealed.

Article 17

This Regulation shall enter into force on the day following that of its publication in the *Official Journal of the European Communities*.

This Regulation shall be binding in its entirety and directly applicable in all Member States.

Done at Brussels, 21 May 1992.

For the Council

The President

Arlindo MARQUES CUNHA

---

[1] OJ No L 63, 9. 3. 1991, p. 1.
See also Community Legislation concerning the environment, volume 1, General Policy, first edition.
[2] OJ No L 370, 31. 12. 1991, p. 17.
[3] OJ No C 370, 31. 12. 1991, p. 28.

ANNEX

FIELDS OF ACTION REFERRED TO IN ARTICLE 2 (1) AND INDICATIVE ALLOCATION OF RESOURCES REFERRED TO IN ARTICLE 7 (4)

Field of action	Indicative allocation of resources
A. ACTIONS IN THE COMMUNITY	
1. Promotion of sustainable development and the quality of the environment Actions:	40 %
– to establish and develop new techniques and methods of measuring and monitoring the quality of the environment;	
– to establish and develop new clean technologies, i.e. which create little or no pollution and make fewer demands on resources;	
– to establish and develop techniques for the collection, storage, recycling and disposal of waste, particularly toxic and dangerous waste and waste water;	
– to establish and develop techniques for locating and restoring sites contaminated by hazardous waste and/or hazardous substances;	
– to establish and develop models to integrate environmental actors into land use planning and management and socio-economic activities;	
– to reduce the discharge into the aquatic environment of nutritive substances and potentially bio-accumulative toxic, persistent pollutants;	
– to improve the quality of the urban environment both in central and peripheral areas.	
2. Protection of habitats and of nature Actions:	45 %
– taken pursuant to Directive 79/409/EEC[1] to maintain or re-establish biotopes which are the habitat of endangered species or seriously threatened habitats which are of particular importance to the Community, or to implement measures to conserve or re-establish endangered species;	
– to maintain or re-establish types of natural habitats of Community interest and the animal and plant species of Community interest referred to in the third subparagraph of Article 2 (2);	
– to protect soil threatened or damaged by fire, desertification, coastal erosion or the disappearance of the dune belt;	
– to promote the conservation of marine life;	
– to protect and conserve areas of fresh ground water and fresh surface water.	

Field of action	Indicative allocation of resources
3. Administrative structures and environment services Actions:	5 %
– to foster greater cooperation between the authorities of the Member States particularly with regard to the control of transboundary and global environmental problems;	
– to equip, modernize or develop monitoring networks in the context of a strengthening of environmental legislation.	
4. Education, training and information Actions:	5 %
– to promote environmental training in administrative and professional circles;	
– to promote environmental education, in particular through the provision of information, exchanges of experience, training and educational research;	
– to foster better understanding of problems and hence encourage behaviour models consistent with environmental objectives;	
– to disseminate knowledge concerning sound management of the environment.	
B. ACTIONS OUTSIDE COMMUNITY TERRITORY Actions:	5 %
– to promote the establishment of the necessary administrative structures in the environmental field;	
– to provide the technical assistance needed for the establishment of environment policies and action programmes;	
– to promote the transfer of appropriate environment-friendly technologies and to foster sustainable development;	
– to provide assistance for third countries faced with ecological emergencies.	

[1] OJ No L 103, 25. 4. 1979, p. 1. Directive as last amended by Directive 91/244/EEC (OJ No L 115, 8. 5. 1991, p. 41).

CONCLUSIONS 92/C 151/02[1] OF THE COUNCIL AND THE MINISTERS OF EDUCATION MEETING WITHIN THE COUNCIL
of 1 June 1992
on the development of environmental education

The Council and the Ministers of Education have taken note of a report presented to them by the Education Committee on the implementation of their resolution of 24 May 1988 on environmental education. They recognize that many positive actions to intensify environmental education have been carried out by the Member States and the Commission.

Since the resolution was adopted in 1988 the urgency of protecting the environment at all levels has been thrown into even greater relief. There is now wider recognition, both by society and by individuals, of the importance of protecting the environment within the Community in order to bring about better living conditions and balanced and harmonious growth.

Members of the public have a number of crucial roles to play:

—   as individuals concerned with the common duty of maintaining, protecting and improving the quality of the environment, as a contribution to the protection of human health and the safeguarding of the ecological balance,

—   as direct producers of pollution and waste,

—   as consumers of goods and services.

The Dublin European Council of 1990, in its statement on environmental issues, emphasized the vital need to improve information to the public and in particular to respond to the interest of young people who are acutely aware of environmental issues.

Education is of major importance in regard to environmental issues. The lines of action for environmental education set out in the 1988 resolution of the Council and the Ministers of Education continue to be relevant; these lines should be pursued and intensified.

In line with the objective and the guiding principles set out in the 1988 resolution, environmental education:

---

[1]   OJ No C 151, 16. 6. 1992, p. 2.

—   should be considered an integral and essential part of every European citizen's upbringing,

—   should be strengthened as soon as possible at all educational levels,

—   should have an interdisciplinary perspective,

—   should be considered an important vehicle for linking education institutions to their surrounding community, enhancing pupils' and students' awareness of local environmental issues and of their region's diversity and special features.

Special attention should be given to the intensification of initial and in-service training of teachers in this area.

The Council and Ministers of Education take note with satisfaction that the Commission's fifth action programme refers to the need for better provision of environmental information and education.

They request the Education Committee to make a further report to them on activities in implementation of the 1988 resolution by the end of 1994.

COUNCIL RESOLUTION 92/C 331/03[1]
of 3 December 1992
concerning the relationship between industrial
competitiveness and environmental protection

THE COUNCIL OF THE EUROPEAN COMMUNITIES,

Having regard to the Treaty establishing the European Economic Community,

Having regard to the Communication 'Industrial policy in an open and competitive environment: guidelines for a Community' presented by the Commission on 20 November 1990,

Having regard to the programme 'Towards Sustainability' presented by the Commission on 29 April 1992,

Having regard to relevant international agreements, and in particular the Rio Declaration and Agenda 21, adopted by the United Nations Conference on Environment and Development (UNCED) in Rio de Janeiro, 3 to 14 June 1992,

Whereas the Community and its Member States subscribed to the Rio Declaration and Agenda 21 which are aimed at achieving sustainable patterns of development worldwide and which recognise the importance of major groups and in particular the role of industry in achieving sustainable growth;

Whereas Article 130r of the Treaty establishing the European Economic Community sets out the objectives of the Community relating to the environment and the principles and factors which shall be taken into account in preparing action to achieve those objectives; and whereas the Community shall take action to the extent that the objectives can be achieved better at Community level than at the level of the individual Member States;

Acknowledging that environmental protection requirements must be integrated into the definitions and implementation of other Community policies;

Acknowledging the contribution which healthy and sustainable growth can make to providing the resources and know-how needed to improve the environment and the central importance of industry and industrial competitiveness to achieving such growth;

---

[1] OJ No C 331, 16. 12. 1992, p. 5.

Acknowledging that small and medium-sized enterprises as well as large enterprises must play a part in protecting and improving the environment in order to achieve sustainable development;

Acknowledging that policies to protect and improve the environment can stimulate the development and use of more efficient processes and can create markets for new products and processes as well as adding to the costs of industry;

Acknowledging the existence of growing public pressure for improvement in industry's environmental performance and of a desire for products which have less adverse impact on the environment;

Acknowledging that the development and implementation of measures to protect and improve the environment should take into account the nature of the problem to be addressed, the efficiency of the measures and the potential benefits and costs of action or lack of action;

Acknowledging that measures shall also seek to improve the competitive position of Community industry in world markets;

Acknowledging that such measures which distort competition within the Community or restrict trade must nonetheless be avoided in accordance with the provisions of the Treaty;

Acknowledging that the Community's policy for the environment must take account of the balanced development of its regions and recognizing that the Cohesion Fund to be established can make a clear contribution to improving environmental protection and industrial competitiveness in the less developed regions and regions undergoing reconversion,

HAS ADOPTED THIS RESOLUTION:

THE COUNCIL:

1.   WELCOMES the Communication on industrial competitiveness and environmental protection adopted by the Commission on 4 November 1992 and agrees that close coordination between policies for industry and the environment is essential;

2.   AFFIRMS its commitment to integrating environmental objectives into policies affecting industry; considers that industry should take into account environmental considerations into its own strategies and calls on it to develop and adopt clean or cleaner available processes and products and to develop appropriate internal management systems;

3.   CONSIDERS that a preventative and market-based approach to environmental protection can be beneficial to industrial competitiveness and should be adopted whenever possible;

4.   AFFIRMS its commitment to enhanced industrial competitiveness coupled with a high level of environmental protection and declares that it will consider further how this is to be achieved;

5.   WELCOMES the Commission's intention, as indicated by the programme 'Towards Sustainability_, to establish clear, long term environmental objectives for industry, and considers that to play its full part in achieving sustainable development, industry, particularly small and medium-sized enterprises must be closely involved from the outset in a dialogue on the development of policies to achieve those objectives,

6.   RECOGNIZES that economic instruments to provide incentives for improved environmental performance and voluntary action by industry, including agreements between industry and Government provided they are implemented effectively and are compatible with the competition rules of the EEC Treaty, may achieve progress towards the Community's environmental objectives more cost-effectively than compulsory environmental provisions; it considers that such alternative approaches should always be examined as an option to achieve the most appropriate mix of instruments;

7.   CONSIDERS that measures to achieve the Community's environmental objectives should be coherent, predictable, and practicable for industry, taking into particular account the specific needs of small and medium-sized enterprises and the environmental conditions of the various regions of the Community and must be enforced consistently in all parts of the Community;

8.   CONSIDERS that there is a need for improved and systematic methods of assessing the benefit of measures to protect and improve the environment and their costs and benefits to industry,

9.   CONSIDERS that, as proposals aimed at improving and protecting the environment are of such importance to industry, general procedures concerning the preparation and publication of impact assessments should be followed in most cases;

10.   CONSIDERS that there is a need for more intensified information to industry on the potential benefits to its competitiveness of the development and use of cleaner technologies;

11.   CONSIDERS it important that the relationship between trade policy and the environment should be clarified, affirms its intention to cooperate with

the work in this area in the OECD, GATT and other international fora, and agrees to intensify its examination of this issue;

12.   CONSIDERS that competition within the Community will be improved if industrial and private consumers are provided with more reliable and consistent information on the environmental performance of firms and products;

13.   AFFIRMS its commitment to the 'polluter pays_ principle;

14.   CONSIDERS that in certain areas there is a need also for an improved statistical framework and for clarification of the scope and size of the Community market for environmental technologies;

15.   INVITES THE COMMISSION TO:

i) promote an effective dialogue with industry and ensure that general procedures concerning consultation with interested parties, particularly small and medium-sized enterprises, are followed in relation to its new proposals for legislation or other instruments to implement environmental policy;

ii) have regard to the most cost-effective instruments to achieve the Community's environmental policy objectives, taking into account, in particular, the scope for voluntary action by industry and the advantages of economic instruments as an alternative or complement to regulation;

iii) have regard to the balance between the costs to industry, including small and medium-sized enterprises, of measures to protect and improve the environment and their benefits to industry and the environment;

iv) develop, as a matter of urgency, in consultation with Member States and other interested parties, improved and systematic methods for determining the best instrument or mix of instruments to give effect to environmental policies and for assessing the costs to industry and benefits to the environment of those policies;

v) ensure that measures to protect and improve the environment provide maximum flexibility for industry to develop and adopt the most appropriate and economically feasible technologies and techniques for achieving environmental targets based on effective and clean technology;

vi) consider further and, insofar as necessary, how the statistical framework required to inform the Community's policies towards the environment and the environmental technology industry might be improved;

16.   INVITES THE COMMISSION AND MEMBER STATES TO:

a)   cooperate to encourage the development of environmental technologies, including cleaner technologies and their diffusion to industry, including to small and medium-sized enterprises in all regions of the Community;

b)   give greater emphasis to the development of environmental technologies including cleaner technologies within existing or planned programmes for the support of research and development relevant to industrial processes;

c)   cooperate to maintain the integrity of the internal market whilst promoting protection of the environment at a high level by avoiding the creation of new trade barriers at national level;

d)   encourage standards-making bodies at national and international level to give adequate weight to environmental considerations in the development of industry standards;

e)   give greater priority to ensuring, for example by ecolabelling, that consumers receive information on the environmental performance of products which is reliable and consistent throughout the Community;

f)   cooperate to ensure compatibility between an open trade policy and protection of the environment and to avoid unilateral trade measures.

17.   DECLARES its intention to consider these issues further in the first half of 1993.

RESOLUTION 93/C 138/01[1] OF THE COUNCIL AND THE REPRESENTATIVES OF THE GOVERNMENTS OF THE MEMBER STATES, MEETING WITHIN THE COUNCIL
of 1 February 1993
on a Community programme of policy and action in relation to the environment and sustainable development

THE COUNCIL OF THE EUROPEAN COMMUNITIES AND THE REPRE-SENTATIVES OF THE GOVERNMENTS OF THE MEMBER STATES OF THE EUROPEAN COMMUNITIES, MEETING WITHIN THE COUNCIL,

Having regard to the Treaty establishing the European Coal and Steel Community,

Having regard to the Treaty establishing the European Economic Community,

Having regard to the Treaty establishing the European Atomic Energy Community,

Having regard to the draft from the Commission,

Having regard to the opinion of the European Parliament[2],

Having regard to the opinion of the Economic and Social Committee[3],

Whereas the Treaty establishing the European Economic Community, as amended by the Single European Act, explicitly provides for the development and implementation of a Community policy on the environment; whereas the Treaty on European Union signed at Maastricht on 7 February 1992 has as a principal objective the promotion of sustainable growth respecting the environment, and specifies the objectives and guiding principles of that policy and the factors which must be taken into account in its preparation;

Whereas the Declaration of the Heads of State and Government, meeting in Council on 26 June 1990, calls inter alia for a further action programme for the environment to be elaborated on the basis of the principles of sustainable development, preventive and precautionary action and shared responsibility;

---

[1] OJ No C 138, 17. 5. 1993, p. 1.
[2] Opinion delivered on 17 November 1992 (not yet published in the Official Journal).
[3] OJ No C 287, 4. 11. 1992, p. 27.

Whereas the Community and its Member States have acquired considerable experience in the development and implementation of environmental policy and legislation and have thereby enhanced protection of the environment;

Whereas the United Nations Conference on Environment and Development (UNCED) meeting in Rio de Janeiro, 3 to 14 June 1992, adopted the Rio Declaration and Agenda 21 which are aimed at achieving sustainable patterns of development worldwide as well as a declaration of forest principles; whereas important Conventions on climate change and biodiversity were opened for signature and were signed by the Community and its Member States; whereas the Community and its Member States also subscribed to Agenda 21 and the said Declarations;

Whereas at the European Council meeting in Lisbon on 27 June 1992 the Community and its Member States committed themselves to the rapid implementation of the principal measures agreed at UNCED;

Whereas the European Council meetings in Lisbon on 27 June 1992 and in Birmingham on 16 October 1992 invited the Commission and the Council to undertake work relating to the implementation of the principle of subsidiarity and the European Council meeting in Edinburgh on 11 and 12 December 1992 approved principles, guidelines and procedures for its practical application; whereas in accordance with the principle of subsidiarity, some aspects of the policy and specific actions embodied in the programme 'Towards sustainability'[1], hereafter referred to as the 'programme' fall to be carried out at levels other than those involving the competencies of the European Communities;

Whereas the strategy advanced in the programme relies on the satisfactory integration of environment and other relevant policies,

ACKNOWLEDGE that the programme presented by the Commission has been designed to reflect the objectives and principles of sustainable development, preventive and precautionary action and shared responsibility set out in the declaration of the Heads of State and the Government of the Community meeting in Council on 26 June 1990 and in the Treaty on European Union signed at Maastricht on 7 February 1992;

CONSIDER that in so far as it provides a comprehensive framework as well as a strategic approach to sustainable development the programme constitutes an appropriate point of departure for the implementation of Agenda 21 by the Community and the Member States;

---

[1] See page 5 of this Official Journal. (OJ No C 138, 17. 5. 1993.)

NOTE that many current forms of activity and development are not environmentally sustainable and ENDORSE, accordingly, the general objective of progressively orientating human activity and development towards sustainable forms;

AGREE that the achievement of sustainable development calls for significant changes in current patterns of development, production, consumption and behaviour;

DECLARE that such changes imply a sharing of responsibility at global, Community, regional, national, local and even personal levels;

ACKNOWLEDGE that the programme when implemented will take into account the diversity of the various regions of the Community, and will be consistent with the objectives of strengthening economic and social cohesion, and will aim at a high level of protection of the environment;

NOTE that the conclusions of the European Councils at Birmingham on 16 October 1992 and Edinburgh on 11 and 12 December 1992 will guide the Community's work in relation to the principle of subsidiarity;

CALL on the Commission to ensure that all proposals it makes relating to the environment fully reflect that principle, and UNDERTAKE to consider those proposals on a case-by-case basis to ensure consistency with the principle;

ACKNOWLEDGE that, pursuant to the principle of subsidiarity and the concept of shared responsibility, some aspects of the policy and specific actions indicated in the programme fall to be implemented at levels other than that of the Community;

NOTE that the application of the principle of subsidiarity will not lead to a step backwards in Community policy or hinder its effective development in the future; NOTE however that the policy will be made more effective if actions are taken at the appropriate level;

In so far as environment and development within the European Communities are concerned:

NOTE the report on the state of the environment which the Commission has published in conjunction with the programme; NOTE the generally positive impact that previous action programmes have made on certain environmental problems; NOTE that the end of the time-frame of the current action programme on the environment coincides with the completion of the Internal Market; NOTE that, during the fifth programme, the environmental dimension of the Internal Market should be reinforced;

CONSIDER, however, that the current measures do not appear to be sufficient to meet the increased pressures on the environment likely to arise in consequence of current and anticipated trends in economic and social activity within the Community and developments in neighbouring regions, especially central and eastern Europe and at a wider international level;

AGREE that more progressive, coherent and better coordinated policies and strategies for the environment and development involving all levels of society are called for;

ADVOCATE in order, inter alia, to reduce wasteful consumption of natural resources and to prevent pollution, the elaboration of the concept of life‾cycle management of products and processes, particularly in relation to waste management, the use of clean or cleaner technology and the substitution of certain hazardous processes and substances with less hazardous processes and substances in the most cost‾effective way;

ENDORSE the strategy of giving increased and appropriate attention to certain key sectors in a coordinated and comprehensive manner including through a strengthening of dialogue with the main actors in the sectors identified in the programme;

ACKNOWLEDGE the need for consideration of a comprehensive Community strategy and action plan for nature conservation and protection, especially in relation to biodiversity and forests;

REAFFIRM the crucial importance of ensuring that environmental concerns are taken fully into account from the outset in the development of other policies and in the implementation of those policies, and the need for appropriate mechanisms within the Member States, the Council and the Commission to help achieve this integration, upon which the strategy advanced in the programme relies;

INVITE the Commission to consider developing initiatives to this end, including examination of the possibilities for the following areas, and to report on its conclusions in due course:

— new mechanisms within the Commission to increase cooperation between policy areas in the development of proposed legislation including organizational aspects,

— the incorporation, in regular progress reports on the implementation of the programme and of Agenda 21, of specific assessments, sector by sector, of the contribution of other policy areas to the achievement of environmental objectives,

— the inclusion in new legislative proposals of a section dealing with the likely implications for the environment,

— the environmental dimension in the granting of community funds;

UNDERTAKE to consider at the national level, and at the level of the Council in its various formations, the introduction of comparable measures to achieve the same aims;

RECOGNIZE that the involvement of all levels of society in a spirit of shared responsibility requires a deepening and broadening of the range of instruments to complement normative legislation including, where appropriate,

— market-based and other economic instruments,

— research and development, information, education and training,

— financial support mechanisms,

— voluntary schemes;

NOTE the objectives, targets, actions and time-frames indicated in the programme, and consider that these constitute a useful start in moving towards sustainable development;

ACKNOWLEDGE the programme's contribution to efforts to fulfil the objective specified in the Treaty establishing the European Economic Community that the Community's environmental policy should take account of the potential benefits and costs of action or lack of action; INVITE the Commission to develop appropriate proposals in the light of such further study as may be necessary;

NOTE that sustainability of activity and development will not be attained within the life-span of this programme and, consequently, that further, still more progressive, measures will probably be necessary beyond the year 2000 in order to hand on the environment to the next generation in a fit state to maintain public health and social and economic welfare at a high level;

NOTE, also, that while many of the measures and actions are set within a time-frame which extends to 2000, and even beyond, it is intended to undertake a review of the programme before the end of 1995; in the meantime INVITE the Environmental Policy Review Group proposed in the programme, once it be established, to keep the implementation of the programme under review on the basis of regular reports from the Commission summarizing progress under the programme; as part of the review process consideration should be given to the relationship between trade and the environment;

CALL on the Commission in its reviews of the programme to give special attention to any necessary revision of objectives and priorities, after adequate consultation, especially with the Member States;

CONSIDER that in order to ensure that community measures on the environment are more effectively implemented, cooperation procedures between the Commission and the Member States should be further improved;

EMPHASIZE the importance of effective implementation and enforcement of Community legislation in all Member States; STRESS that due regard should be given both at the stage when legislation is proposed and when it is adopted to the quality of the drafting of the legislation, in particular in terms of the practicability of implementing and enforcing it; UNDERTAKE to discuss in Council the Commission's annual report on the state of implementation and enforcement of Community legislation in the Member States;

NOTE that, while Member States are responsible for the implementation and enforcement of measures agreed by the Council, the Commission will continue to be the appropriate body for the monitoring of that implementation and enforcement; CALL on the Commission to consider bringing forward proposals for helping to improve the functioning of enforcement agencies within the Member States and encouraging the spread of best practice;

STRESS the urgency of the European Environment Agency beginning work as soon as possible;

NOTE the proposal in the programme for the establishment of a consultative forum and an Environmental Policy Review Group and a network of enforcement agencies from the Member States; WELCOME the principle of wider and more systematic consultation with interested bodies;

In so far as environment and development at the wider international level are concerned,

ASSERT that the Community and the Member States will contribute positively to the implementation of effective strategies to deal with such problems as climate change, deforestation, desertification, depletion of the ozone layer and loss of biodiversity and to fulfil as early as possible the commitments to which they have agreed upon ratification of relevant international Conventions;

UNDERTAKE to play a positive role in the formulation of programmes of sustainable development including in the developing countries and in the countries of central and eastern Europe within the framework of the Community's cooperation and association agreements;

NOTE that many of the internal Community measures in the programme are designed to reduce wasteful consumption of resources and, thereby, will contribute to greater efficiency in resource management at the wider international level;

REAFFIRM their commitment to implement the eight point plan for follow‾up to UNCED agreed at the Lisbon European Council. Tasks for the Community and its Member States which need to be addressed include:

— to establish the basis for ratification of the climate change and biodiversity Conventions with the aim of ratification by the end of 1993, and to prepare the relevant national strategies by the same time,

— to integrate the Rio Declaration, Agenda 21 and Statement of Forest Principles into appropriate policies of the Community and its Member States as soon as possible,

— to work to review, under the aegis of the Commission on Sustainable Development (CSD), the implementation of the forest principles, and to work towards the preparation of a possible forest convention,

— to participate positively in negotiations on a future desertification convention,

— to fulfil the commitments to strengthen assistance to developing countries in the field of sustainable development and to increase funding for Agenda 21 by identifying financial support to be given to developing countries including significant new and additional resources;

in this regard, to put into concrete form the ECU 3 billion commitment which the European Community and its Member States made in Rio as an initial contribution to the prompt and effective implementation of Agenda 21 with priority being given to technology transfer, institutional capacity building, and poverty reduction;

— to work for the restructuring and replenishment of the global environment facility so that it can become the permanent financial mechanism for relevant new global environmental Conventions, in particular the climate change and biodiversity Conventions,

— to continue to give consideration to an earth increment to the International Development Association (IDA) for environment purposes;

NOTE that the implementation of the programme will make a major contribution to the follow‾up to Agenda 21 by the European Community and its Member States;

STRESS the need to promote the participation of non-governmental organizations (NGOs) and other major groups in the follow-up to UNCED at the national and CSD levels;

STRESS the importance of establishing the CSD and the need for full participation of the Community in the work of the CSD in line with the conclusions agreed by the Council on 23 November 1992 and NOTE that the Community and the Member States will submit regular progress reports on the implementation of Agenda 21 to the CSD;

and, in the light of the foregoing,

SUBSCRIBE to the necessity for a programme of policy and action in relation to the environment designed to achieve a sustainable development path;

APPROVE the general approach and strategy of the programme 'Towards sustainability' presented by the Commission;

INVITE the Commission to come forward with appropriate proposals to give effect to the programme in so far as it pertains to action at Community level;

UNDERTAKE to decide on proposals submitted by the Commission as expeditiously as possible taking account of the relevant indicative objectives, targets and time-frames set out in the programme which will be discussed in the context of those proposals;

CALL on all Community institutions, Member States, enterprises and citizens to accept their relative responsibilities to protect the environment for this and future generations and to play their full part in implementing this programme.

TOWARDS SUSTAINABILITY

A European Community programme of policy and action in relation to the environment and sustainable development[1]

---

[1] Only the programme summary is included in the present volume. The complete version is published in OJ No C 138, 17. 5. 1993, p. 5.

EXECUTIVE SUMMARY

Introduction

1.   Over the past two decades four Community action programmes on the environment have given rise to about 200 pieces of legislation covering pollution of the atmosphere, water and soil, waste management, safeguards in relation to chemicals and biotechnology, product standards, environmental impact assessments and protection of nature. The Community's 4th Action Programme on the Environment has not been completed — it runs up to the end of 1992 — and its impact will not be known for some years to come. While a great deal has been achieved under these programmes and measures, a combination of factors calls for a more far-reaching policy and more effective strategy at this juncture:

> i)   a new *Report on the State of the Environment* published in conjunction with this Programme[1] indicates a slow but relentless deterioration of the general state of the environment of the Community notwithstanding the measures taken over the past two decades, particularly as respects the issues referred to in para 16 below; the Report also shows up significant deficiencies in the quantity, quality and comparability of data which are crucial for environment-related policies and decisions. In this context it is of the utmost importance that the European Environment Agency become operational;

> ii) the present approach and existing measures are not geared to deal with the expected growth in international competition and the upward trends in Community activity and development which will impose even greater burdens on natural resources, the environment and, ultimately, the quality of life;

> iii) global concerns about the climate change/deforestation/energy crisis, the seriousness and persistence of problems of underdevelopment and the progress of political and economic change in Central and Eastern Europe add to the responsibility of the European Community in the international field.

2.   The new Treaty on European Union, signed by all Member States on 7 February 1992 has introduced as a principal objective the promotion of sustainable growth respecting the environment (Article 2). It includes among the activities of the Union a policy in the sphere of the environment (Article 3k), specifies that this policy must aim at a high level of protection and that environmental protection requirements must be integrated into the definition and

---

[1]   This is not published here. See COM(92) 23 final — Vol. III.

implementation of other Community policies (Article 130r (2)). The new Treaty also attaches special value to the principle of subsidiarity (Article 3b), and states that decisions should be taken as closely as possible to the citizens (Article A). Furthermore, the Community policy on the environment is required to contribute to promoting measures at international level to deal with regional or worldwide environmental problems (Article 130r (1)). In this latter context the Community will endeavour to find solutions in the field of development and environment at the United Nations Conference on Environment and Development (UNCED) in Rio de Janeiro in June 1992.

3.   All human activity has an impact on the biophysical world and is, in turn, affected by it. The capacity to control this interrelationship conditions the continuity, over time, of different forms of activity and the potential for economic and social development. Within the Community, the long-term success of the more important initiatives such as the Internal Market and economic and monetary union will be dependent upon the sustainability of the policies pursued in the fields of industry, energy, transport, agriculture and regional development; but each of these policies, whether viewed separately or as it interfaces with others, is dependent on the carrying capacity of the environment.

4.   The achievement of the desired balance between human activity and development and protection of the environment requires a sharing of responsibilities which is both equitable and clearly defined by reference to consumption of and behaviour towards the environment and natural resources. This implies integration of environment considerations in the formulation and implementation of economic and sectoral policies, in the decisions of public authorities, in the conduct and development of production processes and in individual behaviour and choice. It also implies effective dialogue and concerted action among partners who may have differing short-term priorities; such dialogue must be supported by objective and reliable information.

5.   As used in the Programme, the word 'sustainable' is intended to reflect a policy and strategy for continued economic and social development without detriment to the environment and the natural resources on the quality of which continued human activity and further development depend. The Report of the World Commission on Environment and Development (Brundtland) defined sustainable development as *development which meets the needs of the present without compromising the ability of future generations to meet their own needs*. It entails preserving the overall balance and value of the natural capital stock, redefinition of short, medium and long-term cost/benefit evaluation criteria and instruments to reflect the real socio-economic effects and values of consumption and conservation, and the equitable distribution and use of resources between nations and regions over the world as a whole. In the latter context, the Brundtland Report pointed out that the developed countries, with

only 26 % of the world population, are responsible for about 80 % of world consumption of energy, steel and other metals, and paper and about 40 % of the food.

6.   Following are some of the practical requirements for achieving sustainable development:

—   since the reservoir of raw materials is finite, the flow of substances through the various stages of processing, consumption and use should be so managed as to facilitate or encourage optimum reuse and recycling, thereby avoiding wastage and preventing depletion of the natural resource stock;

—   production and consumption of energy should be rationalized; and

—   consumption and behaviour patterns of society itself should be altered.

7.   It is clear that sustainable development is not something which will be achieved over a period as short as that covered by this Programme. 'Towards Sustainability' should be seen, accordingly, as an important step only in a longer-term campaign to safeguard the environment and the quality of life of the Community and, ultimately, our planet.

The Community's rôle in the wider international arena

8.   In the early stages, Community policy and action on the environment were mainly focussed on the solution of particularly acute problems within the Community. Later there was a clearer recognition that pollution did not stop at its frontiers and that it was necessary, therefore, to intensify co-operation with third countries. In recent years, the evolution has gone a step further and it is now generally accepted that issues of a global nature — climate change, ozone depletion, diminution of biodiversity, etc. — are seriously threatening the ecological balance of our planet as a whole.

9.   These issues are to be addressed at the highest level at the United Nations Conference on Environment and Development (UNCED). Just as the 1972 UN Conference in Stockholm created a new awareness and concern about the environment at broad international level, so too can UNCED bring global political will and commitment to effective action into a new dimension. Apart from the expected adoption of framework conventions on climate change and biodiversity and of principles on conservation and development of forests, UNCED should pave the way forward by adopting:

—   an 'Earth Charter' or Declaration of basic rights and obligations with respect to environment and development;

— an agenda for action, '*Agenda 21*', which will constitute an agreed work programme of the international community for the period beyond 1992 and into the 21st century.

10.   In the declaration on the environment made in Dublin in June 1990 the European Council stressed the special responsibility of the Community and its constituent Member States in the wider international arena when it stated that '*the Community must use more effectively its position of moral, economic and political authority to advance international efforts to solve global problems and to promote sustainable development and respect for the global commons*'. In conformity with the said declaration, the Community and the Member States must increase their efforts to promote international action to protect the environment and to meet the specific needs and requirements of its partners in the developing world and in Central and Eastern Europe.

The credibility of the industrialised world, including the Community, from the viewpoint of developing countries will be commensurate with the extent to which it puts its own house in order. In adopting and implementing this Programme, the Community will be in a position to offer the leadership foreseen in the Dublin Declaration.

The new strategy for environment and development

11.   The approach adopted in drawing up this new policy programme differs from that which applied in previous environmental action programmes:

— it focuses on the agents and activities which deplete natural resources and otherwise damage the environment, rather than wait for problems to emerge;

— it endeavours to initiate changes in current trends and practices which are detrimental to the environment, so as to provide optimal conditions for socio-economic well-being and growth for the present and future generations;

— it aims to achieve such changes in society's patterns of behaviour through the optimum involvement of all sectors of society in a spirit of shared responsibility, including public administration, public and private enterprise, and the general public (as both individual citizens and consumers);

— responsibility will be shared through a significant broadening of the range of instruments to be applied contemporaneously to the resolution of particular issues or problems.

12.   For each of the main issues, *long-term objectives* are given as an indication of the sense of direction or thrust to be applied in the pursuit of sustainable development, certain performance targets are indicated for the period up to the year 2000 and a representative selection of actions is prescribed with a view to achieving the said targets. These objectives and targets do not constitute legal commitments but, rather, performance levels or achievements to be aimed at now in the interests of attaining a sustainable development path. Neither should all the actions indicated require legislation at Community or national level. (Note: Because of substantial disparities and short-comings in both the quantity and quality of data available, it has not been possible to have homogenous levels of precision in the objectives and targets included in the Programme.)

13.   The Programme takes account of the diversity of situations in various regions of the Community and, in particular, of the need for the economic and social development of the less wealthy regions of the Community. It aims to protect and enhance the inherent advantages of these latter regions and to afford protection to their more valuable natural assets as a resource-base for economic development and social improvement and prosperity. In the case of the more developed regions of the Community, the aim is to restore or maintain the quality of their environment and natural resource base for their continued economic activity and quality of life.

14.   The success of this approach will rely heavily on the flow and quality of information both in relation to the environment and as between the various actors, including the general public. The rôle of the European Environment Agency is seen as crucial in relation to the evaluation and dissemination of information, distinction between real and perceived risks and provision of a scientific and rational basis for decisions and actions affecting the environment and natural resources.

15.   In relation to the motivation of the general public, the main tasks will fall to levels other than the Community level. The Commission, for its part, will commit its information services to a campaign of environmental information and awareness-building.

The importance of education in the development of environmental awareness cannot be overstated and should be an integral element in school curricula from primary level onwards.

Environmental challenges and priorities

16.   The Programme addresses a number of environmental *issues*: climate change, acidification and air pollution, depletion of natural resources and bio-

diversity, depletion and pollution of water resources, deterioration of the urban environment, deterioration of coastal zones, and waste. This list is not an exhaustive one but, pursuant to the principle of subsidiarity, it comprises matters of particular seriousness which have a Community-wide dimension, either because of Internal Market, cross-boundary, shared resource or cohesion implications and because they have a crucial bearing on environmental quality and conditions in almost all regions of the Community.

17.   These issues are addressed not so much as problems, but as *symptoms* of mismanagement and abuse. The real 'problems', which cause environmental loss and damage, are the current patterns of human consumption and behaviour. With this distinction in mind and with due respect to the principle of subsidiarity, priority will be given to the following fields of action with a view to achieving tangible improvements or changes during the period covered by the Programme:

—   *Sustainable Management of Natural Resources:* soil, water, natural areas and coastal zones

—   *Integrated Pollution Control and Prevention of Waste*

—   *Reduction in the Consumption of Non-Renewable Energy*

—   *Improved Mobility Management* including more efficient and environmentally rational location decisions and transport modes

—   Coherent packages of measures to achieve improvements in *environmental quality in urban areas*

—   *Improvement of Public Health and Safety*, with special emphasis on industrial risk assessment and management, nuclear safety and radiation protection.

Selected target sectors

18.   Five target sectors have been selected for special attention under this Programme: Industry, Energy, Transport, Agriculture and Tourism. These are sectors where the Community as such has a unique role to play and where a Community approach is the most efficient level at which to tackle the problems these sectors cause or face. They are also chosen because of the particularly significant impacts that they have or could have on the environment as a whole and because, by their nature, they have crucial roles to play in the attempt to achieve sustainable development. The approach to the target sectors is designed not only for the protection of public health and the environment as such, but for the benefit and sustainability of the sectors themselves.

Industry:

19.   Whereas previous environmental measures tended to be proscriptive in character with an emphasis on the 'thou shalt not' approach, the new strategy leans more towards a 'let's work together' approach. This reflects the growing realization in industry and in the business world that not only is industry a significant part of the (environmental) problem but it must also be part of the solution. The new approach implies, in particular, a reinforcement of the dialogue with industry and the encouragement, in appropriate circumstances, of voluntary agreements and other forms of self-regulation.

Nevertheless, Community action is and will continue to be an important element in the avoidance of distortions in conditions of competition and preservation of the integrity of the Internal Market.

20.   The three pillars on which the environment/industry relationship will be based will be:

— improved resource management with a view to both rational use of resources and improvement of competitive position;

— use of information for promotion of better consumer choice and for improvement of public confidence in industrial activity and controls and in the quality of products;

— Community standards for production processes and products.

In developing measures to ensure the sustainability of the industrial sector, special consideration will be given to the position of small and medium enterprises and to the matter of international competitiveness.

In mid-1992 the Commission will publish a comprehensive Communication on international competitiveness and protection of the environment.

Energy:

21.   Energy policy is a key factor in the achievement of sustainable development. While the Community's energy sector is making steady progress in dealing with local and regional environmental problems such as acidification, global issues are daily growing in importance. The challenge of the future will be to ensure that economic growth, efficient and secure energy supplies and a clean environment are compatible objectives.

22.   The achievement of this balance requires a strategic perspective well beyond the period covered by this Programme. The key elements of the strategy up to 2000 will be improvement in energy efficiency and the develop-

ment of strategic technology programmes moving towards a less carbon-intensive energy structure including, in particular, renewable energy options.

Transport:

23.   Transport is vital to the distribution of goods and services, to trade and to regional development. Present trends in the Community's transport sector are all leading towards greater inefficiency, congestion, pollution, wastage of time and value, damage to health, danger to life and general economic loss. Transport demand and traffic are expected to increase even more rapidly with the completion of the Internal Market and the political and economic developments in Central and Eastern Europe.

24.   A strategy for sustainable mobility will require a combination of measures which includes:

—   improved land-use/economic development planning at local, regional, national and trans-national levels;

—   improved planning, management and use of transport infrastructures and facilities; incorporation of the real costs of both infrastructure and environment in investment policies and decisions and also in user costs;

—   development of public transport and improvement of its competitive position;

—   continued technical improvement of vehicles and fuels; encouraged use of less polluting fuels;

—   promotion of a more environmentally rational use of the private car, including changes in driving rules and habits.

In conjunction with this Programme, the Commission has published a more comprehensive Communication dealing with transport and the environment and the need to aim for sustainable mobility.

Agriculture:

25.   The farmer is the guardian of the soil and of the countryside. Improvements in farming efficiency, increased mechanisation levels, improved transport and marketing arrangements, increased international trade in food products and feedstuffs have all contributed to the fulfilment of the original Treaty objectives of assuring the availability of food supplies at reasonable prices, the stabilization of markets and a fair standard of living for the agricultural community. At the same time, however, changes in farming practices in many regions of the Community have led to overexploitation and degradation of the natural resources on which agriculture itself ultimately depends: soil, water and air.

26.   In addition to environmental degradation, serious problems have emerged in the case of commodity overproduction and storage, rural depopulation, the Community budget and international trade (both as regards agricultural products and wider trade agreements). It is not only environmentally desirable, therefore, but also makes sound agricultural, social and economic sense to seek to strike a more sustainable balance between agricultural activity, other forms of rural development and the natural resources of the environment.

27.   The Programme builds on the Commission's proposals for reform of the CAP and for development of the Community's forests so as to work towards a balanced and dynamic development of the rural areas of the Community which will meet the sector's productive, social and environmental functions.

Tourism:

28.   Tourism is an important element in the social and economic life of the Community. It reflects the legitimate aspirations of the individual to enjoy new places and absorb different cultures as well as to benefit from activities or relaxation away from the normal home or work setting. It is also an important economic asset to many regions and cities of the Community and has a special contribution to make to the economic and social cohesion of the peripheral regions. Tourism represents a good example of the fundamental link which exists between economic development and environment, with all the attendant benefits, tensions and potential conflicts. If well planned and managed, tourism, regional development and environment protection can go hand in hand. Respect for nature and the environment, particularly in coastal zones and mountain areas, can make tourism both profitable and long-lasting.

29.   The World Tourism Organisation predicts a significant increase in tourism activity to and within Europe during this decade. Most of this increase is likely to take place in the Mediterranean Region, and in particular types of locations such as historic towns and cities, mountain areas and coastal zones. UNEP's Blue Plan on the Mediterranean predicts a doubling, at least, of solid wastes and waste waters resulting from tourism by the year 2000, and a potential doubling in the land occupied by tourist lodgings.

30.   The European Community supports tourism through its investments in necessary infrastructures; it can also serve as a 'facilitator' in relation to other interests. But, in a practical reflection of the principle of subsidiarity and the spirit of shared responsibility, it is mainly at levels other than that of the Community that the real work of reconciling tourism activity and development and the guardianship of natural and cultural assets must be brought into a sustainable balance, i.e. by Member States, regional and local authorities, the tourism industry itself and individual tourists.

The three main lines of action indicated in the Programme deal with

— diversification of tourism activities, including better management of the phenomenon of mass tourism, and encouragement of different types of tourism;

— quality of tourist services, including information and awareness-building, and visitor management and facilities;

— tourist behaviour, including media campaigns, codes of behaviour and choice of transport.

Broadening the range of instruments

31. Previous action programmes have relied almost exclusively on legislative measures. In order to bring about substantial changes in current trends and practices and to involve all sectors of society in a full sharing of responsibility, a broader mix of instruments is needed. The mix proposed can be categorised under four headings:

i) *Legislative instruments* designed to set fundamental levels of protection for public health and the environment, particularly in cases of high risk, to implement wider international commitments and to provide Community-wide rules and standards necessary to preserve the integrity of the Internal Market.

ii) *Market-based instruments*, designed to sensitize both producers and consumers towards responsible use of natural resources, avoidance of pollution and waste by internalising of external environmental costs (through the application of economic and fiscal incentives and disincentives, civil liability, etc.) and geared towards 'getting the prices right' so that environmentally-friendly goods and services are not at a market disadvantage vis-à-vis polluting or wasteful competitors.

iii) *Horizontal, supporting instruments* including improved base-line and statistical data, scientific research and technological development, (as respects both new less-polluting technologies and technologies and techniques for solving current environmental problems) improved sectoral and spatial planning, public/consumer information and education and professional and vocational education and training.

iv) *Financial support mechanisms:* besides the budgetary lines which have direct environmental objectives, such as LIFE, the Structural Funds, notably ENVIREG, contribute significant amounts to the financing of actions for the improvement of the environment. Moreover, the new Cohesion Fund decided upon at the Maastricht Summit aims at cofinancing projects which are intended to improve the environment in Spain, Greece, Portugal and Ireland. Article 130r (2) of the new Treaty provides that environment policy must aim at a high level of protection based on the precautionary principle and preventive action, taking into account the diversity of situations in the various regions of the Community, and that environment policy must be integrated into the definition and implementation of other Community policies. In this context, it will be necessary to ensure that all Community funding operations, and in particular, these involving the Structural Funds, will be as sensitive as possible to environmental considerations and in conformity with environmental legislation. By way of qualification it must be recalled here that the new Treaty provides, in Article 130s (4), that without prejudice to certain measures of a Community nature, the Member States are responsible for financing and implementing environment policy.

The principle of subsidiarity

32.   The principle of subsidiarity will play an important part in ensuring that the objectives, targets and actions are given full effect by appropriate national, regional and local efforts and initiatives. In practice it should serve to take full account of the traditions and sensitivities of different regions of the Community and the cost-effectiveness of various actions and to improve the choice of actions and appropriate mixes of instruments at Community and/or other levels.

The objectives and targets put forward in the Programme and the ultimate goal of sustainable development can only be achieved by *concerted* action on the part of all the relevant actors working together in partnership. On the basis of the Treaty on the European Union (Article 3b), the Community will take action, in accordance with the principle of subsidiarity, only if and insofar as the objectives of the proposed action cannot be sufficiently achieved by the Member States and can therefore, by reason of the scale or effects of proposed action, be better achieved by the Community.

33.   The Programme combines the principle of subsidiarity with the wider concept of shared responsibility; this concept involves not so much a choice of action at one level to the exclusion of others but, rather, a mixing of actors and instruments at the appropriate levels, without any calling into question of the division of competences between the Community, the Member States, regional and local authorities.

Table 18 of the document and the 'actors' column of the other tables indicate respectively the manner in which the various actors are intended to combine and the different actors considered most relevant for the implementation of specific measures.

Making the Programme work

34.   Up to the present, environmental protection in the Community has mainly been based on a legislative approach ('top-down'). The new strategy advanced in this Programme implies the involvement of all economic and social partners ('bottom-up'). The complementarity and effectiveness of the two approaches together will depend, in great measure, on the level and quality of dialogue which will take place in pursuance of partnership.

35.   Inevitably, it will take some considerable time for the current patterns of consumption and behaviour to turn in the direction of sustainability. In practical terms, the effectiveness of the strategy will depend, for the foreseeable future, on the inherent quality of the measures adopted and the practical arrangements for their enforcement. This will require better preparation of measures, more effective co-ordination with and integration into other policies, more systematic follow-up and stricter compliance-checking and enforcement.

36.   For these reasons — but without prejudice to the Commission's right of initiative and its responsibility to ensure satisfactory implementation of Community rules — the following *ad hoc* dialogue groups will be convened by the Commission:

   i) a *General Consultative Forum* comprising representatives of enterprise, consumers, unions and professional organisations, non-governmental organisations and local and regional authorities;

   ii) *an Implementation Network* comprising representatives of relevant national authorities and of the Commission in the field of practical implementation with Community measures; it will be aimed primarily at exchange of information and experience and at the development of common approaches at practical level, under the supervision of the Commission.

   iii) *an Environmental Policy Review Group*, comprising representatives of the Commission and the Member States at Director-General level to develop mutual understanding and exchange of views on environment policy and measures.

37.   These three dialogue groups will serve, in a special way, to promote greater sense of responsibility among the principal actors in the partenariat,

and to ensure effective and transparent application of measures. They are not intended to duplicate the work of committees established by Community legislation for the purposes of follow-up in respect of specific measures, nor by the Commission in relation to specific fields of interest such as consumer protection, tourism development etc. nor by Member States for implementation and enforcement of policy at national level. Finally, they will not substitute the existing dialogue between industry and the Commission, which it is intended to strengthen in any event.

Review of Programme

38.   While the Programme is essentially targeted towards the year 2000, it will be reviewed and 'rolled-over' at the end of 1995 in the light of improvements in relevant data, results of current research, and forthcoming reviews of other Community policies e.g. industry, energy, transport, agriculture, and the structural funds.

Conclusion

39.   This Programme itself constitutes a turning point for the Community. Just as the challenge of the 1980s was completion of the Internal Market, the reconciliation of environment and development is one of the principal challenges facing the Community and the world at large in the 1990s. 'Towards Sustainability' is not a programme for the Commission alone, nor one geared towards environmentalists alone. It provides a framework for a new approach to the environment and to economic and social activity and development, and requires positive will at all levels of the political and corporate spectrums, and the involvement of all members of the public active as citizens and consumers in order to make it work.

40.   The Programme does not purport to 'get everything right'. It will take a long time to change patterns of behaviour and consumption and to attain a sustainable development path. The Programme, accordingly, is intended primarily to *break the current trends*. The bottom line is that the present generation must pass the environment on to the next generation in a fit state to maintain public health and social and economic welfare at a high level. As an intermediate goal, the state of the environment, the level and quality of natural resources and the potential for further development at the end of this decade should reflect a marked improvement on the situation which obtains today. The road to sustainability may be long and difficult . . . but the first steps must be taken now!

Structure of the document

41.　　The document is divided into three parts, the two main parts being related to internal and external actions. This distinction is made so as to reflect what can politically and legally be done within the Community itself in accordance with the powers and procedures incorporated in the Treaties, and what the Community and its constituent Member States can contribute or achieve in partnership with other developed and developing countries in relation to global or regional issues and problems.

42.　　Part I summarises the state of the environment in the Community and growing threats to its future health (Chapter 1) and sets out a new strategy designed to break the current trends and to set a new course for sustainable development (Chapter 2). The strategy entails active involvement of all the main actors in society (Chapter 3) using a broader range of instruments, including market-related instruments and improved information, education and training (Chapter 7) so as to achieve identifiable or quantifiable improvements in the environment or changes in consumption and behaviour (Chapter 5).

43.　　A special, concentrated, effort will be made in the case of five target sectors of Community-wide significance (Chapter 4) and in relation to the avoidance and management of risks and accidents (Chapter 6).

44.　　In an effort to be both concise and as clear as possible, the measures which together constitute the action programme are set out in a series of tables which are predominantly, though not entirely, homogenous.

These tables are structured so as to indicate:

—　the long-term objectives in the various fields;

—　the qualitative or quantitative targets to be attained by the year 2000;

—　the specific actions required to be taken;

—　the time-frame proposed for such actions;

—　the actors or sectors of activity which will be called upon to play a part.

Pursuant to the principle of subsidiarity, the lead rôle is indicated by the use of an italic type-face e.g. *MS*.

45.　　Finally, Part I attempts to indicate how responsibility can in practice be shared (Chapter 8) and the measures proposed to ensure satisfactory implementation and enforcement (Chapter 9).

46.　　Part II summarises the environmental threats and issues in the wider international sphere (Chapter 10) and what will or can be done by the Community and its constituent Member States in the context of both general international and bilateral co-operation (Chapter 11 and 12, resp.) in relation to global and regional issues and to environment and development issues in developing countries and Central and Eastern Europe. Chapter 13 deals with the United Nations Conference on Environment and Development which will take place in June 1992. It also refers to the correlation between the internal and external dimensions of the Community's policy on the environment.

47.   Part III is quite short and very general, dealing with the selection of priorities (Chapter 14), the question of costs (Chapter 15) and the intention to carry out a mid-term review of the Programme in 1995 (Chapter 16). While in a document which puts forward a policy and strategy aimed at breaking trends there is less a question of selecting priority actions than defining a *'critical path'*, nevertheless, the Programme does include a listing of horizontal measures and fields of action which require to be accorded priority. On the question of costs the document points to the difficulties of undertaking such exercise (partly because of the traditional practice of treating the environment as an infinite source of free raw materials and waste sinks, and partly because not enough has been done to determine the real costs of *'non-action'*) and puts forward a 5-point plan to devise appropriate costing mechanisms for the future.

COUNCIL REGULATION (EEC) No 792/93[1]
of 30 March 1993
establishing a cohesion financial instrument

THE COUNCIL OF THE EUROPEAN COMMUNITIES,

Having regard to the Treaty establishing the European Economic Community, and in particular Article 235 thereof,

Having regard to the proposal from the Commission[2],

Having regard to the opinion of the European Parliament[3],

Having regard to the opinion of the Economic and Social Committee[4],

Whereas Article 130a of the Treaty provides for the Community to develop and pursue its actions leading to the strengthening of its economic and social cohesion and in particular for it to aim at reducing disparities between the various regions and the backwardness of the least-favoured regions;

Whereas promoting economic and social cohesion calls for Community action to supplement the activities of the Structural Funds, the European Investment Bank and other financial instruments in the fields of the environment and of transport infrastructure of common interest;

Whereas the European Parliament adopted a resolution[5] on 10 June 1992 regarding the Commission's communication of 11 February 1992[6];

Whereas the European Council, pursuant to its meeting in Lisbon on 26 and 27 June 1992, invited, at its meeting in Edinburgh on 11 and 12 December 1992, the Commission to propose and the Council to adopt, before 1 April 1993, a regulation for an interim financial instrument pending the establishment of the Cohesion Fund and determined, for this interim financial instrument, the recipient States, the criteria and indicative allocation brackets in such a way as to ensure the provision of financial aid to Ireland, Greece, Portugal and Spain;

---

[1] OJ No L 79, 1. 4. 1993, p. 74.
[2] OJ No C 38, 12. 2. 1993, p. 18 and amended proposal transmitted on 22 March 1993.
[3] Opinion delivered on 11 March 1993 (not yet published in the Official Journal).
[4] Opinion delivered on 25 February 1993 (not yet published in the Official Journal).
[5] OJ No C 176, 13. 7. 1992, p. 74.
[6] COM(92) 2000.

Whereas, given the conclusions of the European Council and given the impossibility of implementing, on the basis of Article 235 of the EEC Treaty, the set of conditions which are linked to Article 104c of the Treaty on European Union, signed in Maastricht on 7 February 1992, the financial instrument should be of a temporary nature; whereas it should be replaced as soon as possible by the Cohesion Fund as envisaged in Article 130d of the said Treaty;

Whereas the finacial resources of the financial instrument should be those provided for the Cohesion Fund in the financial perspectives for the general budget of the European Communities for the years for which the financial instrument applies; whereas in 1994 the commitments must be proportionate to the duration of the financial instrument for that year and must comply with the requirement of continuity from the financial instrument to the Cohesion Fund;

Whereas the promotion of economic and social cohesion calls for a concentration of the funds available to the cohesion financial instrument on projects concerning the environment and transport infrastructure of common interest in Member States with a per capita GNP of less than 90 % of the Community average;

Whereas each beneficiary Member State should have a convergence programme examined by the Council, designed to avoid excessive government deficits;

Whereas Title IV of Part Two of the Treaty provides that the Council shall lay down any appropriate provisions to implement a common transport policy; whereas the Community should make a contribution, through the cohesion financial instrument, to trans-European networks in the area of transport infrastructure; whereas projects financed by the financial instrument should form part, as far as possible, of trans-European network guidelines which have been adopted by the Council or proposed by the Commission;

Whereas Article 130r of the Treaty defines the objectives of the Community in the field of the environment; whereas the Community should contribute, through the cohesion financial instrument, to actions targeted to achieve these objectives including actions taken pursuant to Article 130s of the Treaty;

Whereas an appropriate balance must be ensured between financing for transport infrastructure projects and for environmental projects;

Whereas in the light of an undertaking by the Member States concerned not to decrease their investment efforts in the field of environmental protection and transport infrastructure, additionality within the meaning of Article 9 of Council Regulation (EEC) No 4253/88 of 19 December 1988 laying down provisions for implementing Regulation (EEC) No 2052/88 as regards coordination of the activities of the different Structural Funds between themselves and with the operations of the European Investment Bank and other existing financial instruments[1] will not apply to the cohesion financial instrument;

Whereas it is necessary to coordinate action taken in the fields of the environment and trans-European transport networks through the cohesion financial instrument, the Structural Funds, the European Investment Bank and the other financial instruments in order to enhance the effectiveness of Community operations;

Whereas, with a view to helping Member States in the preparation of projects, the Commission should be in a position to ensure that they have the necessary technical support;

Whereas in the interests of the proper management of the cohesion financial instrument, it is necessary to ensure effective methods of monitoring, assessing and carrying out checks in respect of Community operations;

Whereas, to ensure value for money, thorough appraisal should precede the commitment of Community resources in order to ensure that they yield economic benefits in keeping with the resources deployed;

Whereas the operations of the cohesion financial instrument must be consistent with Community policies, including those regarding environmental protection, transport, competition and the award of public contracts;

Whereas an indicative allocation of commitment appropriations between the Member States should be provided for in order to facilitate the programming of projects;

Whereas it is necessary, given the requirements of economic and social cohesion, to provide a high rate of assistance;

Whereas provision should be made to give adequate publicity to Community assistance provided by the cohesion financial instrument;

Whereas adequate information should be given in particular through an annual report provided for in Article 10 of this Regulation and in Annex II thereto;

Whereas the Treaty does not provide, for the adoption of this Regulation, for powers other than those contained in Article 235,

HAS ADOPTED THIS REGULATION:

---

[1]   OJ No L 374, 31. 12. 1988, p. 1.

Article 1   Definition and scope

A·cohesion financial instrument (hereinafter referred to as 'the financial instrument') is hereby established, whereby the Community shall provide financial contributions to projects in the fields of the environment and trans-European transport infrastructure networks in those Member States which have a per capita GNP of less than 90 % of the Community average measured according to purchasing power parities, viz. Greece, Spain, Ireland and Portugal, each of which shall have a convergence programme examined by the Council and designed to avoid an excessive government deficit.

Article 2   Eligible projects

The financial instrument may provide assistance for:

— environmental projects contributing to the achievement of the objectives of Article 130r of the Treaty, including projects resulting from action taken pursuant to Article 130s of the Treaty,

— transport infrastructure projects of common interest financed by Member States which promote the interconnection and interoperability of national networks and access to such networks, taking account in particular of the need to link insular, landlocked or peripheral regions with the central regions of the Community, in particular the projects which are provided for in trans-European network schemes which have been adopted by the Council or proposed by the Commission in accordance with Title IV of Part Two of the Treaty,

— preparatory studies, in particular prior appraisals and analyses of costs and benefits, and technical support measures related to eligible projects.

Article 3   Financial resources

The amounts available for commitment appropriations for the financial instrument shall be ECU 1 500 million in 1993 and ECU 1 750 million for the whole of 1994 expressed in 1992 prices.

In compliance with Article 203 of the Treaty the budgetary authority shall decide in accordance with the first paragraph of this Article, as part of the budget procedure, which appropriations are to be made available for each financial year.

Commitments pursuant to this instrument in 1994 shall be proportionate to the duration of the instrument in 1994 in accordance with Article 11.

Article 4 Indicative allocation

The indicative allocation of the total resources of the financial instrument shall be based on precise and objective criteria, principally on population, GNP per capita and surface area; it shall also take account of other socio-economic factors, such as deficiencies in transport infrastructure.

The application of these criteria leads to the indicative allocation laid down in Annex I.

Article 5 Rate of assistance

1.   The rate of assistance granted by the financial instrument shall be between 80 and 85 % of public or similar expenditure as defined for the purposes of the Structural Funds. The effective rate of assistance shall be established in accordance with the nature of the operations to be undertaken.

2.   Preliminary studies, in particular prior appraisals and analyses of costs and benefits, and technical support measures necessary for the appraisal, assessment and possible adjustment of eligible projects may be financed at 100 % of total cost in exceptional cases.

The total expenses on the basis of this paragraph shall not exceed 0,5 % of the total allocation of the financial instrument.

Article 6 Coordination and compatibility with Community policies

1.   Projects financed by the financial instrument shall be in conformity with the provisions of the Treaty, with the instruments adopted pursuant thereto and with Community policies, including those concerning environmental protection, transport, competition and the award of public contracts.

2.   The Commission shall ensure coordination and coherence between projects undertaken in pursuance of this Regulation and measures undertaken with contributions from the Community budget, the European Investment Bank and the other financial instruments of the Community.

Article 7   Combination and overlapping

1.   No item of expenditure may benefit both from the financial instrument and from the European Agricultural Guidance and Guarantee Fund, the European Social Fund or the European Regional Development Fund.

2.   Combined support from the financial instrument and other Community grants shall not exceed 90 % of total expenditure.

Article 8   Approval of projects

1.   The projects to be financed under the financial instrument shall be decided upon by the Commission in agreement with the beneficiary Member State.

2.   An appropriate balance shall be ensured between projects in the fields of environment and of transport infrastructure.

3.   Applications for assistance in accordance with Article 2 shall be submitted by the beneficiary Member State. Projects, including groups of related projects, shall be of a sufficient scale to have a significant impact in the fields of environmental protection or in the improvement of trans-European transport infrastructure networks.

4.   Applications shall contain the following information: the body responsible for implementation, the nature of the investment, its location and costs, the timetable for implementation, the financing plan and the total financing the Member State is seeking from the financial instrument and any other Community source. They shall also contain any information necessary to show that the projects are in accordance with this Regulation.

5.   The following criteria shjall be employed to ensure the high quality of the projects:

—   their medium-term economic and social benefits, which shall be commensurate with the resources deployed; an assessment shall be made in the light of an analysis of costs and benefits,

—   the priorities established by the beneficiary Member States,

—   the contribution which projects can make to the implementation of Community policies on the environment and trans-European networks,

—   the compatibility of projects with Community policies and their consistency with other Community structural measures,

— the achievement of an appropriate balance between the fields of the environemnt and of transport infrastructure.

6.   Subject to the availability of commitment appropriations, the Commission shall decide on assistance from the financial instrument generally within three months of receipt of the applications. Commission decisions approving projects or groups of related projects shall determine the amount of financial assistance, a financing plan and all the provisions and conditions necessary for the realization of the projects.

7.   The decisions of the Commission shall be published in the *Official Journal of the European Communities.*

Article 9   *Financial provisions, monitoring and assessment*

1.   The Commission may, in agreement with the beneficiary Member State concerned, identify technically and financially discrete stages of a project for the purpose of granting assistance from the financial instrument.

2.   Expenditure shall not be considered eligible for assistance from the financial instrument if incurred before the date on which the corresponding application reaches the Commission. However, for applications presented to the Commission before 1 September 1993, expenditure incurred after 1 January 1993 may be regarded as eligible.

3.   For the implementation of this Regulation, the following provisions of Titles VI and VII of Regulation (EEC) No 4253/88 shall apply mutatis mutandis: Articles 19 (1), 20 (1), 21 (1) except the last sentence, 21 (5) and (7), 22, 23, 24, 25 except the last sentence of (4) and (7).

4.   The total amount of assistance from the financial instrument for each operation (project, stage of a project, study or technical support measure) shall be committed when the Commission adopts the decision approving the operation.

5.   Payments of financial assistance for a project or a stage of a project shall be made in accordance with the following provisions:

a)   the advance made following the decision may be up to 50 % of the amount of assistance related to the expenditure planned for the first year as indicated in the financial plan approved by the Commission. However, for 1993 exceptionally, the advance may be up to two-thirds of this amount, for the projects submitted before 1 September 1993;

b) interim payments may be made provided that the project is progressing satisfactorily towards completion and that two-thirds of the expenditure relating to the preceding payment and all the expenditure relating to previous payments has been incurred. Interim payments may be up to 50 % of the assistance related to the expenditure planned for the year concerned as indicated in the financial plan approved by the Commission, adjusted, where necessary, to take account of progress in implementing the project;

c) the balance of assistance for an operation shall be paid provided

- the project or stage has been completed in accordance with the objectives laid down,

- the beneficiary Member State or the designated authority submits a request for payment to the Commission within the six months following physical completion of the project, and

- the final report referred to in Article 25 (4) of Regulation (EEC) No 4253/88 has been submitted to the Commission.

The balance may not be less than 20 % of the total assistance granted.

6.   Payments shall be made to the authority or body designated by the Member States and shall, as a general rule, be made not more than two months after receipt of a valid request for payment.

7.   The beneficiary Member States concerned shall provide the Commission with a description of the management and audit systems established to ensure that projects are effectively implemented.

The Commission shall examine applications with a view in particular to checking that the administrative and financial mechanisms are adequate to ensure effective implementation.

Beneficiary Member States shall regularly inform the Commission of all cases of irregularity that have been discovered by an administrative authority or have been the subject of judicial proceedings. Beneficiary Member States and the Commission must take all the security measures necessary to ensure that information exchanged between them remains confidential.

8.   In order to ensure the effectiveness of Community assistance, the Commission and the beneficiary Member States concerned shall, in cooperation with the European Investment Bank where appropriate, carry out a systematic assessment of projects.

On receipt of a request for assistance and before approving a project, the Commission shall carry out a thorough prior appraisal in order to assess the project's consistency with the criteria laid down in Article 8 (5) and to establish its expected impact, quantified on the basis of appropriate indicators, by reference to the objectives of the financial instrument. The beneficiary Member State concerned shall provide the necessary information, including the results of feasibility studies and prior assessments, to enable this appraisal to be carried out as effectively as possible.

During the implementation of projects, and after their completion, the Commission and the beneficiary Member States concerned shall assess the manner in which they have been carried out and the potential and actual impact of their implementation in order to judge whether the original objectives can be or have been achieved.

9.   The detailed rules for monitoring and assessment shall be laid down in the decisions approving projects.

Article 10   Information and publicity

1.   The Commission shall submit a report on the operation of the financial instrument for consideration by the European Parliament, the Council and the Economic and Social Committee five months, at the latest, after the date of expiry of the instrument.

The information mentioned in this report is listed in Annex II.

2.   Member States shall ensure that adequate publicity is given to the operation of the financial instrument with a view to making the general public aware of the role played by the Community in relation to projects. They shall consult the Commission on, and inform it about, the initiatives taken for this purpose.

Article 11   *Entry into force*

This Regulation shall enter into force on 1 April 1993.

It shall remain in force until the entry into force of a regulation establishing a Cohesion Fund and until 1 April 1994 at the latest.

Should a regulation establishing a Cohesion Fund not be in force by 1 April 1994, the Council, acting by a qualified majority on a proposal from the Commission, shall take a decision regarding the extension of the financial instrument, for a limited period, in order to ensure continuity between the financial instrument and the Cohesion Fund.

This Regulation shall be binding in its entirety and directly applicable in all Member States.

Done at Brussels, 30 March 1993.

For the Council

The President

S. AUKEN

ANNEX I

Indicative allocation of the total resources of the financial instrument among beneficiary Member States

- —   Spain: 52 to 58 % of the total.
- —   Greece: 16 to 20 % of the total.
- —   Portugal: 16 to 20 % of the total.
- —   Ireland: 7 to 10 % of the total.

ANNEX II

Information referred to in Article 10 (1)

The Annual Report will provide information on the following:

1) Financial assistance committed and paid from the financial instrument, with an annual breakdown by Member States and by category of projects (environment and transport).

2) The economic and social impact of the financial instrument in Member States.

3) Summary information on the convergence programmes in Greece, Spain, Ireland and Portugal.

4) The contribution which the financial instrument has made to the efforts of beneficiary Member States to implement Community environment policy and to strengthen trans-European transport infrastructure networks; the balance between projects in the fields of environment and projects relating to transport infrastructure.

5) Assessment of the comptability of the operations of the financial instrument with Community policies including those concerning environmental protection, transport, competition and the award of public contracts.

6) Information on measures to ensure coordination and coherence between projects financed under the financial instrument and measures undertaken with contributions from the Community budget, the European Investment Bank and the other financial instruments of the Community.

7) Information on the investment efforts of the beneficiary Member States in the fields of environmental protection and transport infrastructure.

8) Information on preparatory studies and on technical support measures financed, including a specification of the types of such studies and measures.

9) Information on the results of monitoring and assessment of projects including information on any adjustment of projects to accord with the results of monitoring and assessment.

10) Information on the contribution of the European Investment Bank to the assessment of projects.

COUNCIL REGULATION (EC) No 566/94[1]
of 10 March 1994
extending Regulation (EEC) No 792/93 establishing a cohesion financial instrument

THE COUNCIL OF THE EUROPEAN UNION,

Having regard to Council Regulation (EEC) No 792/93 of 30 March 1993 establishing a cohesion financial instrument[2], and in particular Article 11 thereof,

Having regard to the proposal from the Commission,

Whereas continuity should be ensured between the cohesion financial instrument and the Cohesion Fund;

Whereas such continuity can be effective only if the beneficiary Member States are enabled to prepare projects sufficiently in advance;

Whereas, in accordance with the conclusions of the Edinburgh European Council and Article 8 (3) of Regulation (EEC) No 792/93, projects submitted must be of a sufficient scale to have a significant impact in the fields of environmental protection or in the improvement of trans-European transport infrastructure networks;

Whereas it is appropriate that the Member States concerned should be enabled to fulfil this objective,

HAS ADOPTED THIS REGULATION:

---

[1] OJ No L 72, 16. 3. 1994, p. 1.
[2] OJ No L 79, 1. 4. 1993, p. 74.

Article 1

In Article 11 of Regulation (EEC) No 792/93 '1 April 1994' shall be replaced by '31 December 1994'.

Article 2

This Regulation shall enter into force on the third day following its publication in the *Official Journal of the European Communities.*

This Regulation shall be binding in its entirety and directly applicable in all Member States.

Done at Brussels, 10 March 1994.

For the Council

The President

Y. PAPANTONIOU

COMMISSION DECISION 93/326/EEC[1]
of 13 May 1993
establishing indicative guidelines for the fixing of costs and fees in connection with the Community eco-label

THE COMMISSION OF THE EUROPEAN COMMUNITIES,

Having regard to the Treaty establishing the European Economic Community,

Having regard to Council Regulation (EEC) No 880/92 of 23 March 1992 on a Community eco-label award scheme[2], and in particular Article 11 thereof,

Whereas Article 11 of Regulation (EEC) No 880/92 provides that every application for the award of a label shall be subject to the payment of the costs of processing the application and that further the conditions of use of the label shall include the payment of a fee;

Whereas Article 11 of Regulation (EEC) No 880/92 further provides that indicative guidelines for the fixing of costs and fees should be established in accordance with the procedure laid down in Article 7 of the said Regulation;

Whereas the measures set out in this Decision are in accordance with the opinion of the Committee set up pursuant to Article 7 of Regulation (EEC) No 880/92,

HAS ADOPTED THIS DECISION:

Article 1

1.   Every application for the award of a label shall be subject to an application fee which shall cover the costs of processing the application.

2.   The guideline figure for the application fee shall be ECU 500.

Article 2

1.   A fee for the use of the label shall be paid annually by each applicant who has been awarded an eco-label in accordance with Articles 10 and 12 of Regulation (EEC) No 880/92.

---

[1]   OJ No L 129, 27. 5. 1993, p. 24.
[2]   OJ No L 99, 11. 4. 1992, p. 1.

2.   The annual fee shall relate to a period of 12 months beginning with the date of the award of the eco-label to the applicant.

3.   The annual fee shall be calculated as a percentage of the annual volume of sales within the Community of the product to which the eco-label is awarded.

4.   The guideline figure for the percentage of the annual volume of sales shall be 0,15 %.

5.   The guideline minimum figure shall be ECU 500.

Article 3

1.   Competent bodies shall have discretion to set actual fees at levels 20 % greater or smaller than the guideline figures specified above. This discretion shall be exercised so that, if a competent body chooses to set its fees at a different level from the guideline figures, the same variation in level shall apply to all the fees set by that competent body.

2.   If VAT is payable on these fees, the VAT element shall be contained within the discretionary increase which a competent body may apply.

Article 4

The fixing of the application fee and the annual fee shall be subject to the additional guidelines set out in the Annex to this Decision.

Article 5

This Decision is addressed to the Member States.

Done at Brussels, 13 May 1993.

For the Commission

Yannis PALEOKRASSAS

Member of the Commission

ANNEX

ADDITIONAL GUIDELINES

i) Figures for the annual volume of product sales should be based on ex factory prices; payment of fees to competent bodies shall not be delayed until the annual volume of product sales has been determined by end-year results, but can be made, either in part or in full, in advance of such results, subject to later validation.

ii) Neither the application fee nor the annual fee shall include any element for the cost of any testing which may be necessary for products which are the subject of applications. Applicants will be expected themselves to meet the cost of such testing.

iii) Community review of the fee structure for the eco-label award scheme may lead to a revision of the guideline figures. This should not alter the fees payable in respect of any application which resulted in the award of a label before the date of the Community decision to revise the guideline figures, until the end of the period of validity of the criteria relating to the label concerned.

GREEN PAPER on remedying environmental damage (93/C 149/08[1])

European public awareness about environmental damage is growing all the time. This applies to the damage caused by major environmental disasters, certainly, but it also applies to the less spectacular but far more extensive damage caused by non-accidental activities. Underlying this heightened sensitivity there is concern: who should bear the costs of remedying the damage? To find an answer to this question the Commission has issued a Green Paper. This paper aims to stimulate discussion about the remedying of environmental damage in the hope that this will result in the Community being given the means to deal with the issue. National legislation on this matter, which currently varies greatly between Member States, could then be harmonized.

Civil liability as a tool

'Civil liability is a legal and financial tool used to make those responsible for causing damage pay compensation for the costs of remedying that damage_, the Green Paper says. Based on environmental law, and starting from the mechanisms already existing in this respect in Member States, the principle of civil liability is proving very useful on two fronts. Firstly, it serves to identify the persons responsible and oblige them to compensate victims, thus securing respect for the principle that the polluter pays. Secondly, it plays a preventive role by discouraging people from causing further damage in future.

There are two approaches to civil liability: fault-based liability and strict liability. Fault-based liability requires proof that the liable party committed a negligent or otherwise wrongful act which caused damage. In the case of strict liability, on the other hand, there is no obligation to establish fault. The injured party must, however, prove that the damage was caused by the actions of someone other than himself.

Difficulties in applying the principle

The Commission's analysis shows that there are a number of problems and difficulties impeding the implementation of the principle of civil liability, whether with or without fault.

It is not always easy to prove the offence or the causal link between the offence and the damage suffered, or to establish what activities constitute a serious

---

[1] OJ No C 149, 29. 5. 1993, p. 12.

threat to the environment and should therefore be subject to a system of strict liability, and even if it can be shown who is responsible, damage to the environment, adequate compensation, the insurability of risks etc. still have to be defined. In short, the list of problems only shows how important the question is.

When the principles of civil liability cannot be applied, there remains the possibility of turning to different, existing systems of joint compensation and thinking about collective indemnification mechanisms, even if this might involve new limitations. The debate is still open.

The Green Paper (document COM(93) 47) is available in the official languages of the Community from the sales offices listed on the back cover (Catalogue No CB-CO-. . .-. . .-C).

Any comments regarding the Green Paper should be sent in writing to the Commission of the European Communities, Directorate-General for the Environment, Nuclear Safety and Civil Protection, before 1 October 1993.

COMMUNICATION 93/C 156/05 TO THE COUNCIL, THE PARLIAMENT AND THE ECONOMIC AND SOCIAL COMMITTEE
Public access to the institutions' documents

INTRODUCTION

During the adoption of the Treaty on European Union at Maastricht on 15 December 1991, a declaration was made on improved public access to information. The text of the declaration is the following:

> ' the Conference considers that transparency of the decision-making process strengthens the democratic nature of the institutions and the public's confidence in the administration. The Conference accordingly recommends that the Commission submit to the Council no later than 1993 a report on measures designed to improve public access to the information available to the institutions. '

The European Council at Birmingham subsequently declared that the Community must demonstrate to its citizens the benefits of the Community and the Maastricht Treaty and that the Council, Commission and Parliament must do more to make this clear. Moreover, in Birmingham the Commission was asked to complete by early 1993 its work on improving public access to the information available to the Community institutions.

The Edinburgh European Council continued the work for a more open and transparent Community. Specific measures were adopted to start the process of opening up the work of the Council. Before Edinburgh the Commission had already taken a package of measures to increase transparency.

This package included producing the annual work programme in October, to allow for wider debate including in national parliaments; wider consultation before making proposals, including the use of Green Papers; making Commission documents more rapidly available to the public in all Community languages; and attaching higher priority to the consolidation and codification of legal texts. The Commission has taken these initiatives whilst being aware that it has already a commendable history of an open door policy, especially in comparison with existing practices in national administrations. Traditionally it has been open to input from the public. This stems from the belief that such a process is fundamental for the development of sound and workable policies.

The Edinburgh European Council welcomed these measures taken by the Commission. At the same occasion the European Council reconfirmed its invitation made at Birmingham for the Commission to complete by early next year its work resulting from the declaration in the Maastricht Treaty on improving access to information.

RESPONSE

The Commission views this declaration as an important element of the Community's policy on transparency of the institutions. Improved access to information will be a means of bringing the public closer to the Community institutions and of stimulating a more informed and involved debate on Community policy matters. It will also be a means of increasing the public's confidence in the Community.

In order to implement the Maastricht declaration the Commission has undertaken a comparative survey on existing access to information policies in the Member States and in some third countries. The results of this survey are summarized in the Annex as requested in Maastricht.

The fact finding survey has shown the different experiences of improved access to information. Access to information consists of two main elements.

Firstly it encompasses a series of measures taken by the public authorities themselves aimed at informing the general public of their actions. In this respect the Commission has noted that from the time the Community was established both Community institutions and Member States have taken numerous initiatives in this field to inform the public and to make them more aware of Community policies.

Secondly, access to information also consists of making information available upon request from a member of the public. Some countries have developed a relatively long tradition in this respect, which has evolved over the years. This policy is based on the principle that access is granted while at the same time protection is given to public and private interests, and the proper functioning of the public authority concerned is preserved.

The public is granted access to specific types of information in some countries, while in other cases these were combined with general access rules. Directive 90/313/EEC on access to environmental information is an example of a Community initiative on access to a specific area of information.

FURTHER STEPS

Taking account of the comparative survey on the situation in different Member States and third countries there is a strong case for developing further the access to documents at Community level.

The Commission therefore is prepared to take further steps in order to establish a framework for granting general access to documents. This will entail some adjustments of the Commission's working practices but the Commission considers that general access is a particularly important instrument to bring the Community closer to its citizens.

The Commission feels that the principle of access to information held should be shared by the other institutions and Member States. It invites the other institutions to cooperate in the development of such an approach which should contain at least the fundamental principles and a minimum set of requirements. As a first step, this could take the form of an inter-institutional agreement. Special attention should be given to the specific role of each institution within the existing inter-institutional framework.

In order to contribute to this common approach, the Commission, for its part, suggests that work be based on the following principles which it intends to elaborate upon further:

— access to information is granted to documents, the precise definition of which will be established,

— access to such documents will be provided subsequent to a sufficiently precise request from the public,

— there shall be no obligation on the person making the request to justify the reasons for wanting the document,

— a reply to a request for information should be given as soon as possible.

A request for a document may be refused in order to safeguard:

— personal privacy,

— industrial and financial confidentiality,

— public security including international relations and monetary stability,

— information passed to the institutions in confidence.

Should a request meet with a refusal, then the institution must reply in writing giving the reasons for the decision.

The Commission will use the time remaining before the European Council to be held at Copenhagen by the end of June to prepare a further outline of the general access to documents policy. It intends to submit this to the other institutions in the context of a second communication on transparency which will focus on a general framework and specific actions to improve the Community's transparency.

ANNEX

PUBLIC ACCESS TO INFORMATION
(Comparative survey)

1. HISTORICAL OVERVIEW

Public administrations in many countries have in the past often tended to carry out their work within a framework of secrecy laws designed to protect major public interests (e.g. defence, foreign affairs, etc.). Security regulations were thus established to ensure that information not destined for public release remained protected.

Furthermore, legislation protecting the citizens themselves with regard to such issues as health and fiscal matters traditionally has been quite important.

A dual track rationale for restricting information on public administration can therefore be seen: to protect both public and private interests.

The traditional way in which a government administration informs the public of its decisions is through some form of official publication (journal, gazette, etc.). The public is also kept informed through the accountability of ministers to parliament, through the oversight of such external bodies as the court of auditors and law courts, through public access to plenary meetings of parliament and its various select committees and, finally, through a statutory right of petition.

Turning point

During the course of the 1960s there was a growing belief that such a relationship between government and those it governs should be supplemented with a more open approach. This belief arose from a desire for a stronger form of democracy, i.e., a more democratic form of government. It was felt that the public's business, in particular the way its affairs are administrated, should be conducted more publicly. Another driving force was the fact that whilst administrations were being entrusted with more and more tasks parliamentary control appeared to be less effective.

It was also assumed that a more open approach stimulates an informed debate on public policy issues and also opens up the possibility of improving control over the workings of the administration.

Policies adopted

A number of Member States and third countries therefore gradually adopted a series of measures designed to open up and improve public administration.

These national measures included mechanisms to increase the public participation in the administrative decision-making process. The measures vary from an obligation to pre-consult the public (through, for example, the issuing of Green and White Papers), the right to call for a public hearing and the granting of a right to the public to propose legislation which the relevant public authority would then be obliged to adopt or to consider.

The measures also included the reinforcement of provisions dealing with improved explanation and justification of decisions to the public; the improved publication of final decisions and increased opportunities for appeal against administrative decisions. In certain cases, new ways of appeal were created, such as the establishment of an ombudsman.

Finally, a number of countries also adopted the principle whereby information held by public authorities is generally open to the public unless such access has been explicitly exempted for a limited number of specified reasons.

2. ACCESS TO INFORMATION - A COMPARATIVE SURVEY

2.1.   General

Three trends can be identified which relate to the strengthening of access to information held by public authorities:

—   access to consult administrative files was given to those members of the public who are a party in a lawsuit. The consultation of such files stems from the general right of defence. In several instances this form of access is granted regardless of whether or not the member of the public is involved in a judicial (appeal) procedure. This development led to the establishment of a number of specific access rules for each subject of information,

—   access for the individual concerned to consult files containing personal data. These could be files held by the public sector concerning such things as appointments and nominations. It could also comprise access to files held by the private sector (insurance companies, for example). This has resulted in a number of specific access rules for each subject of information,

—   general access to information held by public authorities (regardless of whether or not the individual/company concerned has a specific interest or is involved in a lawsuit). This has led to a number of general access to information laws.

The fact-finding carried out indicates that, following the developments described above, however, the situation in individual countries varies. Only access to a specific kind of information was granted to the public in some countries while general access rules came into force in other countries. In a third group of countries both types of rules were established.

Active and passive information supply

The survey has shown that there are essentially two ways in which more access to information can be achieved. Firstly, there is the general (legal) obligation upon government departments actively to make all appropriate information (e.g. circulars, policy statements, departmental organigrams, etc.) available to the public at their own initiative.

Secondly, there is the more passive (legal) requirement for government departments to make information available upon request by a member of the public. This includes access to information which forms the basis of governmental decisions such as reports, studies, minutes, notes, circulars, instructions, opinions, forecasts, invoices, registers, indexes and other sorts of information which are held in written, computerized or audiovisual form.

Focus

The comparative survey focused on rules dealing with access to information available upon request (passive information supply), as laid down in general access to information legislation. It does not deal with specific access laws to a particular kind of information nor with active information supply by public authorities. The first of these issues has been extensively examined in the framework of another study, at the request of the Commission (Publaw 1, 1991). In the light of this study, the Commission has made certain proposals in this area (see below).

2.2. Member States and third countries

Inside the Community, Denmark, France, Greece and the Netherlands have statutes establishing general public rights of access to government information. In Belgium, draft proposals on establishing the right of access to information are currently under discussion at federal and regional level. As is also the case in many other countries, Portugal, Spain and the Netherlands have constitutional provisions regarding a general right of access to information without, however, Portugal and Spain having yet implemented specific legislation.

Outside the Community, statutes granting access to information in the United States, Canada, Norway and Sweden have been studied. In the case of the latter country, a right of access to information has been established for over two hundred years.

All of these statutes (see Annex II) have one thing in common: they provide the public with a right of access to information upon request (albeit with certain exemptions from compulsory disclosure in order to protect public and private interests).

Main features

•   Aim of the legislation

The introduction of specific legislation dealing with the public's right of access to information is considered to be a vital element in the proper functioning of a free society as it further extends democracy within the administrative process. The right of access to information is consequently viewed as a fundamental civil right. It deals with the relations between an administration and the citizens it serves (third generation of human rights). In this regard the Council of Europe adopted a recommendation on a right of access to information held by public authorities. It invited the Member States to introduce a systematic right of access to such information.

A number of other benefits are cited in support of the introduction of access to information legislation. These include providing a system of checks and balances with which to oversee and control the workings of public bodies: improving management and ensuring a better allocation of resources, encouraging citizens to participate willingly in the workings of government and stimulating an informed debate on, as well as interest in, public policy.

•   The subject of the information requested

The statutes examined in the survey grant, in principle, public access to any kind of information held by a public authority which is contained in existing documents. The term 'document' is defined broadly to include not only traditional formats such as written papers and photographs but also more modern information carriers (e.g. microfilms, computer discs, magnetic, video and audio tapes). It is also taken as a basic principle that a request for information will only be granted provided it does not necessitate the creation of information that does not exist (e.g. compiling and summarizing data from a number of separate sources).

In the case of automatic data processing, however, this principle is sometimes difficult to maintain. To take the case of Sweden as an example, the rule has been established that a certain selection or merging of data should be regarded as an existing document if the selection or merging can be produced by routine measures.

•   Which authorities are obliged to grant access?

The public authorities bound by the access to information legislation differ from one country to another depending on the form of government. Broadly speaking, in federal systems, federal authorities (including the independent regulatory agencies) are the object of access legislation. Moreover, often State (as opposed to federal) legislation exists which provides access to information held by State authorities. In Belgium, for example, initiatives are taken at both federal and regional levels to provide access to information.

In other governmental systems it is often the case that all public authorities (including the agencies) are governed by legislation concerning access to information.

Some statutes also include specific provisions with regard to the right of access to information and opinions originating from independent advisory bodies i.e. bodies to advise one or more public authorities on a particular subject.

•   Who may make a request for information?

Most of the general access laws studied contain provisions whereby any person, regardless of his or her nationality, has the right to exercise access to information. In virtually all cases the individual making the request for information is under no obligation to give a reason for his or her request.

•   How is information made available to the public?

There are essentially four ways in which an individual can obtain the information: either by requesting a full copy, a summary, an extract or an opportunity to examine the document in person. In deciding which of these alternatives it should choose, the public authority concerned must bear in mind the preferences expressed by the individual making the request.

•   Exemptions from the right of access to information

The study has shown that grounds for exemption from access to information legislation vary considerably from country to country. In certain cases exemption is compulsory, it is sometimes optional and in other instances it can be either one or the other.

Regulations in all the countries examined contain exemptions. These can be divided into two main categories:

— exemptions with regard to the protection of general public interest. Information shall not be disclosed if it damages international relations, the security of the State, national security and defence matters, economic and financial interests, the investigation of criminal offences and the prosecution of offenders, inspection activities,

— exemptions with regard to the protection of personal privacy. In this respect, data specifically related to a person is not disclosed to third persons if this would cause disproportionate harm to the privacy of the person concerned.

In some countries internal documents containing personal opinions on policy are also exempt from the legislation.

• Time limits within which the public can expect to receive a reply

These range from 10 days to two months. In some cases the authorities simply commit themselves 'to reply as soon as possible'. Most acts provide an opportunity for the time limit to be extended in exceptional circumstances and for a varying number of working days.

• Charges for making information available to the public

In the great majority of cases, copies of requested documents are provided at cost price. However, personnel costs are not included in the calculation of this figure.

• Appeal procedures in the event of a request for information being refused

In all the cases studied there exists the possibility of an appeal to an independent body, such as an administrative court, a council of State, an ombudsman or an information commissioner.

2.3. Quantitative analysis

It has proved difficult to find material with which to quantify the use to which these regulations have been put. There do not appear to be any central registers for the filing of requests received. However, in some of the literature consulted, it is indicated that access to government information is used more by individuals or companies who have economic rather than purely civil interests.

Should a request for information be refused or not answered within a given time period under the French system, the individual making the request can turn to the Commission d'accès aux documents administratifs (CADA) for an 'avis'. There has been a steady increase in the number of 'avis' issued: from 470 in 1979/80 to 2 098 in 1989. The 10 000th 'avis' was given out in 1989.

In Canada, 48 493 people exercised their right to request government records during the period 1983 to 1991. In that same period, 31 % of all requested information was disclosed, 37 % was disclosed in part and 8 % was dealt with in an informal way. In total, 4 % was not disclosed while 20 % of the requests could not be processed. The most frequently used exemptions were third party information and personal information. The total cost of operations was 39,5 million dollars, being 817 dollars per request. The total fees collected were 586 961 being slightly more than 12 dollars per request. During the period 1990 to 1991 54 % of all requests made under the Access to Information Act came from the business sector and 28 % from individuals. In Australia, some 25 000 freedom of information requests were made in 1990/91.

2.4. Community institutions

Present situation

The EEC Treaty contains a number of rules relating to administrative transparency which are related to this subject. These include rules governing the non-disclosure of information of a kind covered by the duty of professional secrecy (Article 214 EEC); the non-disclosure by Member States of information which is considered to be contrary to its essential security interests (Article 223 EEC); the obligation to publish legal acts of the Community (Article 191 EEC); the obligation to state the reasons upon which such legal acts are based (Article 190 EEC); the establishment of rules under which the Commission is obliged to give interested parties the opportunity to express their views on, for example, cases falling under Community regulations on competition rules applying to undertakings (Articles 85/90 EEC) and the obligatory annual publication of a General Report on the activities of the European Communities (Article 18 of the Merger Treaty).

Many of the relevant provisions of the EEC Treaty have been implemented through detailed legislation in, for example, the Staff Regulations for officials of the European Communities; Council Regulation No 3 (Euratom) implementing Article 24 of the EEC Treaty establishing the European Atomic Energy Community[1]; Council Regulation of 1 February 1983 concerning the opening to the public of the historical archives of the Community and Euratom which foresees access to the archives after a period of 30 years[2]; Commission's decision of 7 July 1986 on classified[3] documents and the security measures

---

[1]   OJ No 17, 6. 10. 1958, p. 406/58.
[2]   OJ No L 43, 15. 2. 1983, p. 1.
[3]   SEC(86) 1132 final.

applicable to such documents which, for example, implies that sensitive commercial information made available in the context of competition policy will obtain the appropriate security classification, and also contains rules on classification and declassification of documents and handling of information received from Member States; and the Council Regulation of 11 June 1990 on data subject to statistical confidentiality addressed to the Statistical Office of the European Communities[1]. This applies to the transmission to the Statistical Office of data which falls within the national statistical institutes' field of competence and is covered by statistical confidentiality. Moreover, a number of internal regulations have been established dealing with the internal functioning of each institution.

Over the years, relevant case-law has been established on this issue by the Court of Justice (see, for example, the February 1988 case of Zwartveld versus the Commission, as reported on 13 July 1990).

At Community level, no general legislation exists with specific regard to access of information although the Commission has established certain explicit rules which do allow for it in the field of competition policy (see 12th yearly report on competition, 1982, pp. 42 to 43). A company involved on a proceeding is allowed to have access to the file on a particular case. However, any such access is limited by the Commission's obligation to refrain from discussing business secrets to third companies and the need to preserve the confidential nature of the Commission's internal and/or working documents.

Furthermore the content of Article 47 of the Treaty establishing the European Coal and Steel Community should be noted as it indicates that the Commission must not disclose information of the kind covered by the obligation of professional secrecy.

In 1990 the Council of Ministers adopted Directive 90/313/EEC to allow the possibility of access for any legal or natural person throughout the Community to information held by public authorities relating to the environment[2]. In certain specified cases this information may be refused. This Directive came into force on 1 January 1993.

The rules apply to environmental information held by the competent authorities of the Member States. It does not apply to environmental information held by the European institutions. However, the Commission indicated, in the explanatory memorandum accompanying the proposed Directive, that it would take initiatives with the object of applying the principle of access to information (with regard to the environment) to the Community bodies[3].

---

[1] OJ No L 151, 15. 6. 1990, p. 1.
[2] OJ No L 158, 23. 6. 1990, p. 56.

The Commission has recently proposed specific rules for personal data protection and the free circulation of data[1]. This proposal is aimed at facilitating the free movement of data in the Community while ensuring a high level of protection for the individual with regard to the processing of personal data. It includes provisions for an individual's right of access to his or her own personal data. It also lists exhaustively the exceptions with regard to personal data contained in public sector files in order to safeguard such interests as national security, defence, criminal proceedings, etc. The draft Directive was accompanied by a Commission declaration on the application of the data protection principles to personal data held by the Commission and other Community institutions. Work is under way to implement these principles.

OVERVIEW OF GENERAL ACCESS LAWS

Introduction

By 'general access laws' this survey refers to such rules as provide a general access to administrative documents. This means access which is neither restricted to a particular area nor demanding a special involvement of the person seeking the information. There are other types of rules on access which are restricted to certain persons or may demand that a person state a legal or at least a legitimate interest. These rules deal for example with company registers, population registers, and credit risk information. Such access rules exist in most of the Member States.

The situation on general access both in the Community and in certain other countries is as follows:

Belgium

Several draft proposals granting general access to information are under discussion at different levels of government.

Denmark

Act No 572 of 19 December 1985 'on access to public administration files'.

France

Loi No 78-753 du 17 juillet 1978: Titre premier: 'de la liberté d'accès aux documents administratifs' and Loi No 79-587 du 11 juillet 1979 'relative à la moti-

---

[3]   COM(88) 484 final.
[1]   COM(92) 422 final.

vation des actes administratifs et à l'amélioration des relations entre l'administration et le public'.

Germany

There is no general access to information law in Germany. The regulation closest to such a law is the Administrative Procedure Act. However, access to information exists in specific areas, mainly to public registers.

Greece

Law No 1599/1986, 'on the relationship between State and citizen, the establishment of a new type of identification card and other provisions', Article 16.

Ireland

There exists no general access legislation, however, in specific areas access to information exists.

Italy

There is no general access to information law in Italy. The regulation closest to such a law is the Access to Administrative Documents Law of 7 August 1990 (No 241). Access is possible for those who have a legal interest.

Luxembourg

There is no general access to information law. Access to administrative documents is regulated in the context of non-contentious administrative procedure.

The Netherlands

Act of 31 October 1991, Stbl. 703 'on public access to government information'.

Portugal

Constitutional provision regarding a general right of access to information. Moreover, in specific areas access to information exists.

Spain

Constitutional provision regarding a general right of access to information. Moreover, in specific areas access to information exists.

United Kingdom

No legislation exists on a general right of access to information.

Canada

'Access to Information Act' of 1983.

Norway

Act No 69 of 19 June 1970 concerning public access to documents in the (public administration as subsequently amended by Act No 47 of 11 June 1982 and Act No 86 of 17 December 1982.

Sweden

1976 Freedom of the Press Act, Chapter 2, 'on the public nature of official documents'.

United States of America

Freedom of Information Act of 1982 (5 USC Section 552), as part of the Public Information, Agency Rules, Opinions, Orders, Records and Proceedings (5 USC Section 551 to 559).

COMMISSION DECISION 93/430/EEC[1]
of 28 June 1993
establishing the ecological criteria for the award of the Community eco-label to washing machines

THE COMMISSION OF THE EUROPEAN COMMUNITIES,

Having regard to the Treaty establishing the European Economic Community,

Having regard to Council Regulation (EEC) No 880/92 of 23 March 1992 on a Community eco-label award scheme[2], and in particular Article 5 thereof,

Whereas the first subparagraph of Article 5 (1) of Regulation (EEC) No 880/92 provides that the conditions for the award of the Community eco-label shall be defined by product group;

Whereas Article 10 (2) of Regulation (EEC) No 880/92 states that the environmental performance of a product shall be assessed by reference to the specific criteria for product groups;

Whereas the second subparagraph of Article 5 (1) of Regulation (EEC) No 880/92 provides further that product groups, the specific ecological criteria for each group and their respective periods of validity are to be established in accordance with the procedure laid down in Article 7 of that Regulation, following the consultation procedure provided for in Article 6 thereof;

Whereas in accordance with Article 6 of Regulation (EEC) No 880/92 the Commission has consulted the principal interest groups within a consultation forum;

Whereas the measures provided for in this Decision are in accordance with the opinion of the Committee set up pursuant to Article 7 of Regulation (EEC) No 880/92,

HAS ADOPTED THIS DECISION:

---

[1]   OJ L 198, 7; 8; 1993, p. 35.
[2]   OJ No L 99, 11. 4. 1992, p. 1.

Article 1

The product group to which this Decision relates is defined as:

> front and top loading washing machines sold to the general public, excluding twin tubs and washer dryers,

> (hereinafter referred to as 'the product group').

Article 2

The environmental performance of the product group shall be assessed by reference to the specific ecological criteria set out in the Annex.

Article 3

The definition of the product group and the specific ecological criteria for the product group shall be valid until 30 June 1996.

Article 4

This Decision is addressed to the Member States.

Done at Brussels, 28 June 1993.

For the Commission

Yannis PALEOKRASSAS

Member of the Commission

ANNEX

ECO-LABEL CRITERIA FOR WASHING MACHINES

A.   Key criteria

These criteria are based on the major environmental impacts as highlighted in the cradle-to-grave assessment. The threshold levels must all be achieved in order to qualify for an eco-label.

i)   *Energy consumption*

The machine must use less than or equal to 0,23 kWh of electrical energy per kg of washload in an IEC 456 test for a cotton wash without prewash at 60 °C using cold fill only.

The machine must use less than or equal to 0,11 kWh of electrical energy per kg of washload in an IEC 456 test for a cotton wash without prewash at 40 °C using cold fill only.

ii)   *Water consumption*

The machine must use less than or equal to 17 litres of water per kg of washold in an IEC 456 test for a cotton wash without prewash at either 60 or 40 °C.

iii)   *Detergent consumption*

The machine must lose less than or equal to 5 % of detergent in an IEC 456 test with the detergent added via the detergent drawer.

B.   Best practice criteria

Best practice criteria relate to features of a washing machine which make a smaller contribution to the overall environmental impact of the product. The qualifying levels for these criteria reflect best environmental practice. All of these criteria must be achieved in order to qualify for an eco-label.

i)   *User instructions*

1)   The machine must have clear markings on it identifying the settings appropriate according to fabric type and laundry code.

2)   The machine must have clear markings on it identifying energy and water saving programmes and options.

3)   Clear instructions must be made available to the consumer providing:

- advice to use a full load rather than part loads wherever possible,

- advice about the best wash temperature to use according to the fabric type,

- advice on varying the detergent dose according to water hardness, load size and the degree of soil,

- advice on the machine installation which makes the most appropriate use of the hot and cold fill, if available on the machine, including advice based on the fuel used for home water heating,

- advice on sorting fabrics appropriately,

- advice on situations where a prewash, if available, is likely to be required,

- information about the energy consumption and the water consumption of the machine for different temperature settings and for different load settings and according to whether hot and cold fill is an option,

- advice about the machine being made of materials which are recyclable and that it should be disposed of accordingly.

ii)   *Encouragement to recycling*

Where they occur in components in quantities greater than 50 g the following polymeric materials must have a permanent marking identifying the material:

- polypropylene,

- polystyrene,

- PVC,

- HDPE,

- LDPE,

- ABS,

- polyamide,

- other.

The marking must use the symbols or abbreviated terms given in ISO 1043.

C.   Performance criteria

i)   *Wash performance*

The machine must achieve at least a minimum of 20 % stain removal based on the carbon black soiled sample EMPA test cloth in an IEC 456 test at 60 °C.

The machine must achieve at least a minimum of 6 % stain removal based on the carbon black soiled sample EMPA test cloth in an IEC 456 test at 40 °C.

ii)   *Rinse efficiency*

The machine must achieve at least a minimum rinsing efficiency of 60 dilutions as defined in IEC 456.

COMMISSION DECISION 93/431/EEC[1]
of 28 June 1993
establishing the ecological criteria for the award of the Community eco-label to dishwashers

THE COMMISSION OF THE EUROPEAN COMMUNITIES,

Having regard to the Treaty establishing the European Economic Community,

Having regard to Council Regulation (EEC) No 880/92 of 23 March 1992 on a Community eco-label award scheme[2], and in particular Article 5 thereof,

Whereas the first subparagraph of Article 5 (1) of Regulation (EEC) No 880/92 provides that the conditions for the award of the Community eco-label shall be defined by product group;

Whereas Article 10 (2) of Regulation (EEC) No 880/92 states that the environmental performance of a product shall be assessed by reference to the specific criteria for product groups;

Whereas the second subparagraph of Article 5 (1) of Regulation (EEC) No 880/92 provides further that product groups, the specific ecological criteria for each group and their respective periods of validity are to be established in accordance with the procedure laid down in Article 7 of that Regulation, following the consultation procedure provided for in Article 6 thereof;

Whereas in accordance with Article 6 of Regulation (EEC) No 880/92 the Commission has consulted the principal interest groups within a consultation forum;

Whereas the measures provided for in this Decision are in accordance with the opinion of the Committee set up pursuant to Article 7 of Regulation (EEC) No 880/92,

HAS ADOPTED THIS DECISION:

---

[1] OJ No 198, 7. 8. 1993, p. 38.
[2] OJ No L 99, 11. 4. 1992, p. 1.

Article 1

The product group to which this Decision relates is defined as:

dishwashers sold to the general public,

(hereinafter referred to as 'the product group_).

Article 2

The environmental performance of the product group shall be assessed by reference to the specific ecological criteria set out in the Annex.

Article 3

The definition of the product group and the specific ecological criteria for the product group shall be valid until 30 June 1996.

Article 4

This Decision is addressed to the Member States.

Done at Brussels, 28 June 1993.

For the Commission

Yannis PALEOKRASSAS

Member of the Commission

ANNEX

ECO-LABEL CRITERIA FOR DISHWASHERS

A.   Key Criteria

These criteria are based on the major environmental impacts as highlighted in the cradle-to-grave assessment. The threshold levels must all be achieved in order to qualify for an eco-label.

i)   *Energy Consumption*

Standard size models (10 or more place settings)

The machine must use less than or equal to 0,125 kWh of electrical energy per place setting in an IEC 436 test.

Slimline and compact models (less than 10 place settings)

The machine must use less than or equal to 0,15 kWh of electrical energy per place setting in an IEC 436 test.

ii)   *Water Consumption*

Standard size models (10 or more place settings)

The machine must use less than or equal to 1,85 litres of water per place setting in an IEC 436 test.

Slimline and compact models (less than 10 place settings)

The machine must use less than or equal to 2,25 litres of water per place setting in an IEC 436 test.

B.   Best practice criteria

Best practice criteria relate to features of a dishwasher which make a smaller contribution to the overall environmental impact of the product. The qualifying levels for these criteria reflect best environmental practice. All of these criteria must be achieved in order to qualify for an eco-label.

i)   *User instructions*

1)   The machine must have clear markings on it identifying the settings appropriate according to the type of load (e.g. glass, china, pots and pans, crockery) and degree of soil.

2) Where dry heat boost is provided, it must be an option; it should not occur automatically.

3) On the machine there must be clear instructions to use a full load wherever possible.

4) Clear instructions must be made available to the consumer providing:

- advice on varying the detergent dosing according to the degree of soil,

- advice on varying the salt dosing according to water hardness,

- advice on the machine installation which makes the most appropriate use of the hot and cold fill, if available on the machine, including advice based on the fuel used for home water heating,

- advice to avoid rinsing items before placing them in the dishwater,

- advice on the best use of the rinse and hold option, if available,

- advice on the best use of the dry heat boost option, if available,

- information about the energy consumption of the machine for different programmes and with and without dry heat boost,

- information about the water consumption of the machine for different programmes and options,

- advice about te machine being made of materials which are recyclable and that it houd be disposed of accordingly.

ii) *Encouragement to recycling*

Where they occur in components in quantities greater than 50 g the following polymeric materials must have a permanent marking identifying the material:

- polypropylene,

- polystyrene,

- PVC,

- HDPE,

- LDPE,

- ABS,

- polyamide,

- other.

The marking must use the symbols or abbreviated terms given in ISO 1043.

C.   Performance criteria

i)   *Wash performance*

The machine must achieve at least a minimum wash efficiency of 85 % in an IEC 436 test.

ii)   *Drying efficiency*

The machine must achieve at least a minimum drying efficiency of 70 % in an IEC 436 test.

COUNCIL REGULATION (EEC) No 1836/93[1] of 29 June 1993 allowing voluntary participation by companies in the industrial sector in a Community eco-management and audit scheme

THE COUNCIL OF THE EUROPEAN COMMUNITIES,

Having regard to the Treaty establishing the European Economic Community, and in particular Article 130s thereof,

Having regard to the proposal from the Commission[2],

Having regard to the opinion of the European Parliament[3],

Having regard to the opinion of the Economic and Social Committee[4],

Whereas the objectives and principles of the Community's environment policy, as set out in the Treaty and detailed in the resolution of the Council of the European Communities and the representatives of the Governments of the Member States, meeting within the Council of 1 February 1993 on a Community programme of policy and action in relation to the environment and sustainable development[5], as well as in the preceding resolutions of 1973[6], 1977[7], 1983[8] and 1987[9] on a policy and action programme of the Community regarding the protection of the environment are, in particular, to prevent, reduce and as far as possible eliminate pollution, particularly at source on the basis of the polluter pays principle, to ensure sound management of resources and to use clean or cleaner technology;

Whereas Article 2 of the Treaty, as it will read according to the Treaty on the European Union signed at Maastricht on 7 February 1992, stipulates that the Community shall have among its tasks to promote throughout the Community

---

[1] OJ No L 168, 10. 7. 1993, p. 1.
[2] OJ No C 120, 30. 4. 1993, p. 3.
[3] OJ No C 42, 15. 2. 1993, p. 44.
[4] OJ No C 332, 16. 12. 1992, p. 44.
[5] OJ No C 138, 17. 5. 1993, p. 1..
    See also Community Legislation concerning the environment, volume 1, General Policy, first edition.
[6] OJ No C 112, 20. 12. 1973, p. 1.
[7] OJ No C 139, 13. 6. 1977, p. 1.
[8] OJ No C 46, 17. 2. 1983, p. 1.
[9] OJ No C 70, 18. 3. 1987, p. 1.

sustainable growth and the Council resolution of 1 February 1993 stresses the importance of such sustainable growth;

Whereas the programme 'Towards Sustainability', presented by the Commission and approved as to its general approach by the Council resolution of 1 February 1993, underlines the role and responsibilities of companies, both to reinforce the economy and to protect the environment throughout the Community;

Whereas industry has its own responsibility to manage the environmental impact of its activities and should therefore adopt a pro-active approach in this field;

Whereas this responsibility calls for companies to establish and implement environmental policies, objectives and programmes and effective environmental management systems; whereas companies should adopt an environmental policy which, in addition to providing for compliance with all relevant regulatory requirements regarding the environment, must include commitments aimed at the reasonable continuous improvement of environmental performance;

Whereas the application of environmental management systems by companies shall take acccount of the need to ensure awareness and training of workers in the establishment and implementation of such systems;

Whereas environmental management systems should include environmental auditing procedures to help management assess compliance with the system and the effectiveness of the system in fulfilling the company's environmental policy;

Whereas the provision of information to the public, by companies, on the environmental aspects of their activities is an essential element of good environmental management and a response to the growing interest of the public in information on this subject;

Whereas companies should therefore be encouraged to produce and disseminate periodic environmental statements containing information for the public on the factual environmental situation in their industrial sites and on their environmental policies, programmes, objectives and management system;

Whereas the transparency and credibility of companies' activities in this field are enhanced when the companies' environmental policies, programmes, management systems, audit procedures and environmental statements are examined to verify that they meet the relevant requirements of this Regulation and when the environmental statements are validated by accredited environmental verifiers;

Whereas it is necessary to provide for an independent and neutral accreditation and supervision of environmental verifiers in order to ensure the credibility of the scheme;

Whereas companies should be encouraged to participate in such a scheme on a voluntary basis; whereas, in order to ensure an equal implementation of the scheme throughout the Community, the rules, procedures and essential requirements have to be the same in each Member State;

Whereas a Community eco-management and audit scheme should at the first stage focus on the industrial sector where environmental management systems and environmental auditing are already practised; whereas it is desirable to apply on an experimental basis similar provisions to sectors outside industry such as the distributive trades and the public service;

Whereas, in order to avoid unjustified burdens on companies and to ensure consistency between the Community scheme and national, European and international standards for environmental management systems and audits, those standards recognized by the Commision according to an appropriate procedure shall be considered as meeting the corresponding requirements of this Regulation and companies should not be required to duplicate the relevant procedures;

Whereas it is important that small and medium-sized companies participate in the Community eco-management and audit scheme and that their participation should be promoted by establishing or promoting technical assistance measures and structures aimed at providing such firms with the expertise and support needed;

Whereas the Commission should, according to a Community procedure, adapt the Annexes to this Regulation, recognize national, European and international standards for environmental management systems, establish guidelines for setting the environmental audit frequency and promote collaboration between Member States regarding the accreditation and supervision of environmental verifier;

Whereas this Regulation should be revised in the light of experience gained after a certain period of operation,

HAS ADOPTED THIS REGULATION:

Article 1 *The eco-management and audit scheme and its objectives*

1.   A Community scheme allowing voluntary participation by companies performing industrial activities, hereinafter referred to as the 'Community eco-management and audit scheme' or 'the scheme', is hereby established for the evaluation and improvement of the environmental performance of industrial activities and the provision of the relevant information to the public.

2.   The objective of the scheme shall be to promote continuous improvements in the environmental performance of industrial activities by:

   a)   the establishment and implementation of environmental policies, programmes and management systems by companies, in relation to their sites;

   b)   the systematic, objective and periodic evaluation of the performance of such elements;

   c)   the provision of information of environmental performance to the public.

3.   The scheme shall be without prejudice to existing Community or national laws or technical standards regarding environmental controls and without prejudice to the duties of companies under those laws and standards.

Article 2 *Definitions*

For the purposes of this Regulation:

   a)   environmental policy shall mean the company's overall aims and principles of action with respect to the environment including compliance with all relevant regulatory requirements regarding the environment;

   b)   environmental review shall mean an initial comprehensive analysis of the environmental issues, impact and performance related to activities at a site;

   c)   environmental programme shall mean a description of the company's specific objectives and activities to ensure greater protection of the environment at a given site, including a description of the measures taken or envisaged to achieve such objectives and where appropriate the deadlines set for implementation of such measures;

   d)   environmental objectives shall mean the detailed goals, in terms of environmental performance, which a company sets itself;

e) environmental management system shall mean that part of the overall management system which includes the organizational structure, responsibilities practices, procedures, processes and resources for determining and implementing the environmental policy;

f) environmental audit shall mean a management tool comprising a systematic, documented, periodic and objective evaluation of the performance of the organization, management system and processes designed to protect the environment with the aim of:

   i) facilitating management control of practices which may have impact on the environment;

   ii) assessing compliance with company environmental policies;

g) audit cycle shall mean the period of time in which all the activities in a given site are audited, according to the requirements of Article 4 and Annex II, on all the relevant environmental aspects mentioned in Annex I.C;

h) environmental statement shall mean a statement prepared by the company in line with the requirements of this Regulation and, in particular, of Article 5;

i) industrial activity shall mean any activity listed under sections C and D of the classification of economic activities in the European Community (NACE rev. 1) as established by Council Regulation (EEC) No 3037/90[1], with the addition of electricity, gas, steam, and hot water production and the recycling, treatment, destruction or disposal of solid or liquid waste;

j) company shall mean the organization which has overall management control over activities at a given site;

k) site shall mean all land on which the industrial activities under the control of a company at a given location are carried out, including any connected or associated storage of raw materials, by-products, intermediate products, end products and waste material, and any equipment and infrastructure involved in the activities, whether or not fixed:

l) auditor shall mean a individual or a team, belonging to company personnel or external to the company, acting on behalf of company top management, possessing, individually or collectively, the competencies referred to in Annex II paragraph C and being sufficiently independent of the activities they audit to make an objective judgement;

m) accredited environmental verifier shall mean any person or organization independent of the company being verified, who has obtained accredi-

---

[1] OJ No L 293, 24. 10. 1990, p. 1.

tation, in line with the conditions and procedures referred to in Article 6;

n) accreditation system shall mean a system for the accreditation and supervision of environmental verifiers operated by an impartial institution or organization designated or created by the Member State, with sufficient resources and competency and having appropriate procedures for performing the functions defined by this Regulation for such a system;

o) competent bodies shall mean the bodies designated by Member States, in line with Article 18, to perform the tasks mentioned in this Regulation.

Article 3   Participation in the scheme

The scheme is open to companies operating a site or sites where an industrial activity is performed. In order for a site to be registered in the scheme the company must:

a) adopt a company environmental policy, in accordance with the relevant requirements in Annex I, which, in addition to providing for compliance with all relevant regulatory requirements regarding the environment, must include commitments aimed at the reasonable continuous improvement of environmental performance, with a view to reducing environmental impacts to levels not exceeding those corresponding to economically viable application of best available technology;

b) conduct an environmental review of the site on the aspects referred to in Annex I, part C;

c) introduce, in the light of the results of that review, an environmental programme for the site and an environmental management system applicable to all activities at the site. The environmental programme will be aimed at achieving the commitments contained in the company environmental policy towards continuous improvement of environmental performance. The environmental management system must comply with the requirements of Annex I;

d) carry out, or cause to be carried out, in accordance with Article 4, environmental audits at the sites concerned;

e) set objectives at the highest appropriate management level, aimed at the continuous improvement of environmental performance in the light of the findings of the audit, and appropriately revise the environmental programme to enable the set objectives to be achieved at the site;

f) prepare, in accordance with Article 5, an environmental statement specific to each site audited. The first statement must also include the information referred to in Annex V;

g) have the environmental policy, programme, management system, review or audit procedure and environmental statement or statements examined to verify that they meet the relevant requirements of this Regulation and the environmental statements validated in accordance with Article 4 and Annex III;

h) forward the validated environmental statement to the competent body of the Member State where the site is located and disseminate it as appropriate to the public in that State after registration of the site in question in accordance with Article 8.

Article 4   *Auditing and validation*

1.   The internal environmental audit of a site may be conducted by either auditors belonging to the company or external persons or organizations acting on its behalf. In both cases the audit shall be performed in line with the criteria set out in part C of Annex I and in Annex II.

2.   The audit frequency shall be determined in accordance with the criteria set out in Annex II H on the basis of guidelines established by the Commission in accordance with the procedure laid down in Article 19.

3.   The environmental policies, programmes, management systems, reviews or audit procedures and the environmental statements shall be examined to verify that they meet the requirements of this Regulation, and the environmental statements shall be validated, by the independent accredited environmental verifier, on the basis of Annex III.

4.   The accredited environmental verifier must be independent of the site's auditor.

5.   For the purposes of paragraph 3 and without prejudice to the competence of the enforcement authorities in the Member States with regard to regulatory requirements, the accredited environmental verifier shall check:

a) whether the environmental policy has been established and if it meets the requirements of Article 3 and the relevant requirements in Annex I;

b) whether an environmental management system and programme are in place and operational at the site and whether they comply with the relevant requirements in Annex I;

c) whether the environmental review and audit are carried out in accordance with the relevant requirements in Annex I and II;

d) whether the data and information in the environmental statement are reliable and whether the statement adequately covers all the significant environmental issues of relevance to the site.

6) The environmental statement shall be validated by the accredited environmental verifier only if the conditions referred to in paragraphs 3 to 5 are met.

7) External auditors and accredited environmental verifiers shall not divulge, without authorization from the company management, any information or data obtained in the course of their auditing or verification activities.

Article 5   Environmental statement

1. An environmental statement shall be prepared following in initial environmental review and the completion of each subsequent audit or audit cycle for every site participating in the scheme.

2. The environmental statement shall be designed for the public and written in a concise, comprehensible form. Technical material may be appended.

3. The environmental statement shall include, in particular, the following:

a) a description of the company's activities at the site considered;

b) an assessment of all the significant environmental issues of relevance to the activities concerned;

c) a summary of the figures on pollutant emissions, waste generation, consumption of raw material, energy and water, noise and other significant environmental aspects, as appropriate;

d) other factors regarding environmental performance;

e) a presentation of the company's environmental policy, programme and management system implemented at the site considered;

f) the deadline set for submission of the next statement;

g) the name of the accredited environmental verifier.

4.   The environmental statement shall draw attention to significant changes since the previous statement.

5.   A simplified environmental statement shall be prepared annually in intervening years, based as a minimum on the requirements set out in paragraph 3 (c) and drawing attention where appropriate to significant changes since the previous statement. Such simplified statements will require validation only at the end of the audit or audit cycle.

6.   The annual preparation of environmental statements will, however, not be required for sites:

—   where the accredited environmental verifier considers, in particular in the case of small and medium-sized enterprises, that the nature and scale of the operations at the site are such that no further environmental statement is required until completion of the next audit, and

—   where there have been few significant changes since the last environmental statement.

Article 6   Accreditation and supervision of environmental verifiers

1.   Member States shall each establish a system for the accreditation of independent environmental verifiers and for the supervision of their activities. To this end, Member States may either use existing accreditation institutions or the competent bodies referred to in Article 18, or designate or set up any other body with an appropriate status.

Member States shall ensure that the composition of these systems is such as to guarantee their independence and neutrality in the execution of their tasks.

2.   Member States shall ensure that these systems are fully operational within 21 months following the date of entry into force of this Regulation.

3.   Member States shall ensure appropriate consultation of parties involved, in setting up and directing the accreditation systems.

4.   The accreditation of environmental verifiers and supervision of their activities shall be in accordance with the requirements of Annex III.

5.   Member States shall inform the Commission of the measures taken pursuant to this Article.

6.   The Commission shall, in accordance with the procedure laid down in Article 19, promote collaboration between Member States in order in particular to:

—   avoid inconsistency between the criteria, conditions and procedures they apply for the accreditation of environmental verifiers,

—   facilitate the supervision of the activities of environmental verifiers in Member States other than those where they have obtained their accreditation.

7.   Environmental verifiers accredited in one Member State may perform verification activities in any other Member State, subject to prior notification to, and subject to supervision of, the accreditation system of the Member State where the verification takes place.

Article 7   List of accredited environmental verifiers

The accreditation systems shall establish, revise and update a list of acredited environmental verifiers in each Member State and shall communicate this list every six months to the Commission.

The Commission shall publish an overall Community list in the *Official Journal of the European Communities.*

Article 8   Registration of sites

1.   The competent body shall register a site and give it a registration number once it has received a validated environmental statement and any registration fee that may be payable under Article 11 and it is satisfied that the site meets all the conditions of this Regulation. It shall inform the site management that the site appears on the register.

2.   The competent body shall update the list of sites referred to in paragraph 1 annually.

3.   If a company fails to submit a validated environmental statement and registration fee to the competent body within three months of being required to do so or if at any time the competent body concludes that the site is no longer complying with all the conditions of this Regulation, the site shall be deleted from the register and the site management shall be so informed.

4.   If a competent body is informed by the competent enforcement authority of a breach at the site of relevant regulatory requirements regarding

the environment, it shall refuse registration of that site or suspend it from the register as the case may be and inform the site management thereof.

Refusal or suspension shall be lifted if the competent body has received satisfactory assurances from the competent enforcement authority that the breach has been rectified and that satisfactory arrangements are in place to ensure that it does not recur.

Article 9   Publication of the list of registered sites

The competent bodies directly, or via the national authorities as decided by the Member State concerned, shall communicate to the Commission before the end of each year the lists referred to in Article 8 and updates thereof.

Each year the Commission shall publish in the *Official Journal of the European Communities* a list of all the registered sites in the Community.

Article 10   Statement of participation

1.   Companies may use for their registered site(s), one of the statements of participation listed in Annex IV, which are designed to bring out clearly the nature of the scheme.

The graphic may not be used without one of the accompanying statements of participation.

2.   The names of the site(s) must be given where appropriate with the statement of participation.

3.   The statement of participation may not be used to advertise products, or on the products themselves or on their packaging.

Article 11   Costs and fees

A system of fees in accordance with modalities established by Member States may be set up for the administrative costs incurred in connection with the registration procedures for sites and the accreditation of environmental verifiers and the promotional costs of the scheme.

Article 12   *Relationship with national, European and i*
                    international standards

1.   Companies implementing national, European or international standards
for environmental management systems and audits and certified, according to
appropriate certification procedures, as complying with those standards shall
be considered as meeting the corresponding requirements of this Regulation,
provided that:

   a) the standards and procedures are recognized by the Commission acting
       in accordance with the procedure laid down in Article 19;
   b) the certification is undertaken by a body whose accreditation is recog-
       nized in the Member State where the site is located.

The references of the recognized standards and criteria shall be published in
the *Official Journal of the European Communities.*

2.   To enable such sites to be registered under the scheme, the companies
concerned must in all cases meet the requirements regarding the environmental
statement in Articles 3 and 5 including validation and the requirements in
Article 8.

Article 13   *Promotion of companies' participation,*
                    in particular of small and medium-sized
                    enterprises

1.   Member States may promote companies' participation in the eco-management and audit scheme, in particular the participation of small and medium-
sized enterprises, by establishing or promoting technical assistance measures
and structures, aimed at providing such firms with the expertise and support
needed in order to comply with the rules, conditions and procedures defined by
this Regulation and, in particular, to set up environmental policies, programmes and management systems, conduct audits and prepare and validate
statements.

2.   The Commission shall present appropriate proposals to the Council
aiming at greater participation in the scheme by small and medium-sized enterprises, in particular by providing information, training and structural and technical support, and concerning auditing and verification procedures.

Article 14   Inclusion of other sectors

The Member States may, on an experimental basis, apply provisions analogous to the eco-management and audit scheme to sectors outside industry, e.g. the distributive trades and public service.

Article 15   Information

Each Member State shall ensure by appropriate means that:

— companies are informed of the content of this Regulation,

— the public is informed of the objectives and principal arrangements of the system.

Article 16   Infringements

Member States shall take appropriate legal or administrative measures in case of non-compliance with the provisions of this Regulation.

Article 17   Annexes

The Annexes to this Regulation shall be adapted by the Commission, acting in accordance with the procedure of Article 19 in the light of experience gained in the operation of the scheme.

Article 18   Competent bodies

1.   Within 12 months of the entry into force of this Regulation, each Member State shall designate the competent body responsible for carrying out the tasks provided for in this Regulation, particularly in Articles 8 and 9, and shall inform the Commission thereof.

2.   Member States shall ensure that the composition of the competent bodies is such as to guarantee their independence and neutrality, and that the competent bodies apply the provisions of this Regulation in a consistent manner. The competent bodies shall, in particular, have procedures for considering observations from interested parties concerning registered sites, or deletion or suspension of sites from registration.

Article 19   *Committee*

1.   The Commission shall be assisted by a committee composed of the representatives of the Member States and chaired by the representative of the Commission.

2.   The representative of the Commission shall submit to the committee a draft of the measures to be taken. The committee shall deliver its opinion on the draft within a time limit which the chairman may lay down according to the urgency of the matter. The opinion shall be delivered by the majority laid down in Article 148 (2) of the Treaty in the case of decisions which the Council is required to adopt on a proposal from the Commission. The votes of the representatives of the Member States within the committee shall be weighted in the manner set out in that Article. The chairman shall not vote.

3.

   a)   The Commission shall adopt the measures envisaged if they are in accordance with the opinion of the committee.

   b)   If the measures envisaged are not in accordance with the opinion of the committee, or if no opinion is delivered, the Commission shall, without delay, submit to the Council a proposal relating to the measures to be taken. The Council shall act by a qualified majority.

If the Council has not acted within three months of the date of referral to it, the proposed measures shall be adopted by the Commission.

Article 20   *Revision*

Not more than five years after the entry into force of this Regulation, the Commission shall review the scheme in the light of the experience gained during its operation and shall, if necessary, propose to the Council the appropriate amendments, particularly concerning the scope of the scheme and the possible introduction of a logo.

Article 21   *Entry into force*

This Regulation shall enter into force on the third day following its publication in the *Official Journal of the European Communities*.

It shall apply 21 months after publication.

This Regulation shall be binding in its entirety and directly applicable in all Member States.

Done at Luxembourg, 29 June 1993.

For the Council

The President

S. AUKEN

ANNEX I

REQUIREMENTS CONCERNING ENVIRONMENTAL POLICIES, PROGRAMMES AND MANAGEMENT SYSTEMS

A. Environmental policies, objectives and programmes

1) The company environmental policy, and the programme for the site, shall be established in writing. Associated documents will explain how the environmental programme and the management system at the site relate to the policy and systems of the company as a whole.

2) The company environmental policy shall be adopted and periodically reviewed, in particular in the light of environmental audits, and revised as appropriate, at the highest management level. It shall be communicated to the company's personnel and be publicly available.

3) The company's environmental policy shall be based on the principles of action in section D.

   The policy will aim, in addition to providing for compliance with all relevant regulatory requirements regarding the environment, at the continual improvement of environmental performance.

   The environmental policy and the programme for the site shall address, in particular, the issues in section C.

4) *Environmental objectives*

   The company shall specify its environmental objectives at all relevant levels within the company.

   The objectives shall be consistent with the environmental policy and shall quantify wherever practicable the commitment to continual improvement in environmental performance over defined time-scales.

5) *Environmental programme for the site*

   The company shall establish and maintain a programme for achieving the objectives at the site. It shall include:

   a) designation of responsibility for objectives at each function and level of the company;

   b) the means by which they are to be achieved.

   Separate programmes shall be established in respect of the environmental management of projects relating to new developments, or to new or modified products, services or processes, to define:

1) the environmental objectives to be attained;

2) the mechanisms for their achievement;

3) the procedures for dealing with changes and modifications as projects proceed;

4) the corrective mechanisms which shall be employed should the need arise, how they shall be activated and how their adequacy shall be measured in any particular situation in which they are applied.

B. Environmental management systems

The environmental management system shall be designed, implemented and maintained in such a way as to ensure the fulfilment of the requirements defined below.

1) *Environmental policy, objectives and programmes*

   The establishment and periodical review, and revision as appropriate, of the company's environmental policy, objectives and programmes for the site, at the highest appropriate management level.

2) *Organization and personnel*

   Responsibility and authority

   Definition and documentation of responsibility, authority and interrelations of key personnel who manage, perform and monitor work affecting the environment.

   Management representative

   Appointment of a management representative having authority and responsibility for ensuring that the management system is implemented and maintained.

   Personnel, communication and training

   Ensuring among personnel, at all levels, awareness of:

a) the importance of compliance with the environmental policy and objectives, and with the requirements applicable under the management system established;

b) the potential environmental effects of their work activities and the environmental benefits of improved performance;

c) their roles and responsibilities in achieving compliance with the environmental policy and objectives, and with the requirements of the management system;

d)   the potential consequences of departure from the agreed operating procedures.

Identifying training needs, and providing appropriate training for all personnel whose work may have a significant effect upon the environment.

The company shall establish and maintain procedures for receiving, documenting and responding to communications (internal and external) from relevant interested parties concerning its environmental effects and management.

3)   *Environmental effects*

Environmental effects evaluation and registration

Examining and assessing the environmental effects of company's activities at the site, and compiling a register of those identified as significant. This shall include, where appropriate, consideration of:

a)   controlled and uncontrolled emissions to atmosphere;

b)   controlled and uncontrolled discharges to water or sewers;

c)   solid and other wastes, particularly hazardous wastes;

d)   contamination of land;

e)   use of land, water, fuels and energy, and other natural resources;

f)   discharge of thermal energy, noise, odour, dust, vibration and visual impact;

g)   effects on specific parts of the environment and ecosystems.

This shall include effects arising, or likely to arise, as consequences of:

1)   normal operating conditions;

2)   abnormal operating conditions;

3)   incidents, accidents and potential emergency situations;

4)   past activities, current activities and planned activities.

Register of legislative, regulatory and other policy requirements

The company shall establish and maintain procedures to record all legislative, regulatory and other policy requirements pertaining to the environmental aspects of its activities, products and services.

4)   *Operational control*

Establishment of operating procedures

Identification of functions, activities and processes which affect, or have the potential to affect, the environment, and are relevant to the company's policy and objectives.

Planning and control of such functions, activities and processes, and with particular attention to:

a) documented work instructions defining the manner of conducting the activity, whether by the company's own employees or by others acting on its behalf. Such instructions shall be prepared for situations in which the absence of such instructions could result in infringement of the environmental policy;

b) procedures dealing with procurement and contracted activities, to ensure that suppliers and those acting on the company's behalf comply with the company's environmental policy as it relates to them;

c) monitoring and control of relevant process characteristics (e.g. effluent streams and waste disposal);

d) approval of planned processes and equipment;

e) criteria for performance, which shall be stipulated in written standards.

Monitoring

Monitoring by the company of meeting the requirements established by the company's environmental policy, programme and management system for the site; and for establishing and maintaining records of the results.

For each relevant activity or area, this implies:

a) identifying and documenting the monitoring information to be obtained;

b) specifying and documenting the monitoring procedures to be used;

c) establishing and documenting acceptance criteria and the action to be taken when results are unsatisfactory;

d) assessing and documenting the validity of previous monitoring information when monitoring systems are found to be malfunctioning.

Non-compliance and corrective action

Investigation and corrective action, in case of non-compliance with company's environmental policy, objectives or standards, in order to:

a) determine the cause;

b) draw up a plan of action;

c) initiate preventive actions, to a level corresponding to the risks encountered;

d) apply controls to ensure that any preventive actions taken are effective;

e) record any changes in procedures resulting from corrective action.

5) *Environmental management documentation records*

Establishing documentation with a view to:

a) present in a comprehensive way the environmental policy, objectives, and programme;

b) document the key roles and responsibilities;

c) describe the interactions of system elements.

Establishing records in order to demonstrate compliance with the requirements of the environmental management system, and to record the extent to which planned environmental objectives have been met.

6) *Environmental audits*

Management, implementation and review of a systematic and periodical programme concerning:

a) whether or not environmental management activities conform to the environmental programme, and are implemented effectively;

b) the effectiveness of the environmental management system in fulfilling the company's environmental policy.

C. Issues to be covered

The following issues shall be addressed, within the framework of the environmental policy and programmes and of environmental audits.

1) Assessment, control, and reduction of the impact of the activity concerned on the various sectors of the environment.

2) Energy management, savings and choice.

3) Raw materials management, savings, choice and transportation; water management and savings.

4) Waste avoidance, recyling, reuse, transportation and disposal.

5) Evaluation, control and reduction of noise within and outside the site.

6) Selection of new production processes and changes to production processes.

7) Product planning (design, packaging, transportation, use and disposal).

8) Environmental performance and practices of contractors, subcontractors and suppliers.

9) Prevention and limitation of environmental accidents.

10) Contingency procedures in cases of environmental accidents.

11) Staff information and training on environmental issues.

12) External information on environmental issues.

D. Good management practices

The company's environmental policy shall be based on the principles of action set out below; the activities of the company shall be checked regularly to see if they are consistent with these principles and that of continual improvement in environmental performance.

1) A sense of responsibility for the environment amongst employees at all levels, shall be fostered.

2) The environmental impact of all new activities, products and processes shall be assessed in advance.

3) The impact of current activities on the local environment shall be assessed and monitored, and any significant impact of these activities on the environment in general, shall be examined.

4) Measures necessary to prevent or eliminate pollution, and where this is not feasible, to reduce pollutant emissions and waste generation to the minimum and to conserve resources shall be taken, taking account of possible clean technologies.

5) Measures necessary to prevent accidental emissions of materials or energy shall be taken.

6) Monitoring procedures shall be established and applied, to check compliance with the environmental policy and, where these procedures require measurement and testing, to establish and update records of the results.

7)   Procedures and action to be pursued in the event of detection of non-compliance with its environmental policy, objectives or targets, shall be established and updated.

8)   Cooperation with the public authorities shall be ensured to establish and update contingency procedures to minimize the impact of any accidental discharges to the environment that nevertheless occur.

9)   Information necessary to understand the environmental impact of the company's activities shall be provided to the public, and an open dialogue with the public should be pursued.

10)   Appropriate advice shall be provided to customers on the relevant environmental aspects of the handling, use and disposal of the products made by the company.

11)   Provisions shall be taken to ensure that contractors working at the site on the company's behalf apply environmental standards equivalent to the company's own.

ANNEX II

REQUIREMENTS CONCERNING ENVIRONMENTAL AUDITING

The audit will be planned and executed in the light of the relevant guidelines in the ISO 10011 international standard (1990, Part 1, in particular paragraphs 4.2, 5.1, 5.2, 5.3, 5.4.1, 5.4.2) and other relevant international standards, and within the framework of the specific principles and requirements of this Regulation[1].

In particular:

A. Objectives

The site's environmental auditing programmes will define in writing the objectives of each audit or audit cycle including the audit frequency for each activity.

The objectives must include, in particular, assessing the management systems in place, and determining conformity with company policies and the site programme, which must include compliance with relevant environmental regulatory requirements.

B. Scope

The overall scope of the individual audits, or of each stage of an audit cycle where appropriate, must be clearly defined and must explicitly specify the:

1)   subject areas covered;

2)   activities to be audited;

3)   environmental standards to be considered;

4)   period covered by the audit.

---

[1]   For the specific purpose of this Regulation, the terms of the abovementioned standard will be interpreted as follows:
— 'quality system' shall read 'environmental management system' ,
— 'quality standard' shall read 'environmental standard' ,
— 'quality manual' shall read 'environmental management manual' ,
— 'quality audit' shall read 'environmental audit' ,
— 'client' shall read 'the company's top management' ,
— 'auditee' shall read 'the site' .

Environmental audit includes assessment of the factual data neessary to evaluate performance.

C. Organization and resources

Environmental audits must be performed by persons or groups of persons with appropriate knowledge of the sectors and fields audited, including knowledge and experience on the relevant environmental management, technical, environmental and regulatory issues, and sufficient training and proficiency in the specific skills of auditing to achieve the stated objectives. The resources and time allocated to the audit must be commensurate with the scope and objectives of the audit.

The top company management shall support the auditing.

The auditors shall be sufficiently independent of the activities they audit to make an objective and impartial judgment.

D. Planning and preparation for a site audit

Each audit will be planned and prepared with the objectives, in particular, of:

— ensuring the appropriate resources are allocated,

— ensuring that each individual involved in the audit process (including auditors, site management, and staff) understands his or her role and responsibilities.

Preparation will include familiarization with activities on the site and with the environmental management system established there and review of the findings and conclusions of previous audits.

E. Audit activities

1) On-site audit activities will include discussions with site personnel, inspection of operating conditions and equipment and reviewing of records, written procedures and other relevant documentation, with the objective of evaluating environmental performance at the site by determining whether the site meets the applicable standards and whether the system in place to manage environmental responsibilities is effective and appropriate.

2) The following steps, in particular, will be included in the audit process:

   a) understanding of the management systems;

b) assessing strengths and weaknesses of the management systems;

c) gathering relevant evidence;

d) evaluating audit findings;

e) preparing audit conclusions;

f) reporting audit findings and conclusions.

F. Reporting audit findings and conclusions

1) A written audit report of the appropriate form and content will be prepared by the auditors to ensure full, formal submission of the findings and conclusions of the audit, at the end of each audit and audit cycle.

The findings and conclusions of the audit must be formally communicated to the top company management.

2) The fundamental objectives of a written audit report are:

a) to document the scope of the audit;

b) to provide management with information on the state of compliance with the company's environmental policy and the environmental progress at the site;

c) to provide management with information on the effectiveness and reliability of the arrangements for monitoring environmental impacts at the site;

d) to demonstrate the need for corrective action, where appropriate.

G. Audit follow-up

The audit process will culminate in the preparation and implementation of a plan of appropriate corrective action.

Appropriate mechanisms must be in place and in operation to ensure that the audit results are followed up.

H. Audit frequency

The audit will be executed, or the audit cycle will be completed, as appropriate, at intervals no longer than three years. The frequency for each activity at a site will be established by the top company management, taking account of the potential overall environmental impact of the activities at the site, and of the site's environmental programme depending, in particular, on the following elements:

a) nature, scale and complexity of the activities;

b) nature and scale of emissions, waste, raw material and energy consumption and, in general, of interaction with the environment;

c) importance and urgency of the problems detected, following the initial environmental review or the previous audit;

d) history of environmental problems.

ANNEX III

REQUIREMENTS CONCERNING THE ACCREDITATION OF ENVIRONMENTAL VERIFIERS AND THE FUNCTION OF THE VERIFIER

A. Requirements for the accreditation of environmental verifiers

1.   Accreditation criteria for environmental verifiers shall include the following:

Personnel

The environmental verifier shall be competent in relation to the functions within the accredited scope and must demonstrate and maintain records on the qualifications, training and experience of its personnel with respect to, at least, the following:

—   environmental auditing methodologies,

—   management information and process,

—   environmental issues,

—   relevant legislation and standards including specific guidances developed for the purposes of this Regulation, and

—   relevant technical knowledge of the activity subject to verification.

Independence and objectivity

A verifier shall be independent and impartial.

The environmental verifier must demonstrate that its organization and its staff are free of any commercial, financial or other pressures which might influence their judgment or endanger trust in their independence of judgment and integrity in relation to their activities, and that they comply with any rules applicable in this respect.

Verifiers complying with EN 45012, Articles 4 and 5, comply with these requirements.

Procedures

The environmental verifier shall have documented methodologies and procedures, including quality control mechanisms and confidentiality provisions, for the verification requirements of this Regulation.

Organization

In the case of organizations, the environmental verifier shall have and make available on request an organization chart detailing structures and responsibilities within the organization and a statement of legal status, ownership and funding sources.

2.   Accreditation of individuals

Accreditation may be granted to individuals, limited in scope to those activities of a nature and scale for which the individual concerned possesses all the competences and experience necessary for fulfilling the task referred to in section B.

In relation to sites where such activities are performed the applicant shall demonstrate, in particular, sufficient competence and expertise on technical, and environmental and regulatory issues relevant to the scope of the accreditation, and on the verification methods and procedures. The applicant shall meet the criteria given in paragraph 1, concerning independence, objectivity and procedures.

3.   Applications for accreditation

The applicant environmental verifier shall complete and sign an official application form in which the applicant declares knowledge of functioning of the accreditation system; agrees to fulfil the accreditation procedure and pay the necessary fees; agrees to comply with the accreditation criteria; and, divulges previous applications or accreditations.

Applicant environmental verifiers shall receive documented descriptions of accreditation procedures and the rights and duties, including fees, of accredited environmental verifiers. Additional relevant information shall be provided to the applicant on request.

4.   The accreditation process

The accreditation process shall include:

   a)   gathering relevant information needed for the evaluation of the applicant environmental verifier, which shall include general information such as name, address, legal status, human resources, relationship in a larger corporate entity etc., information to assess compliance with criteria specified under section 1 and to establish any limitation to the scope of the accreditation;

b) assessment of the applicant be either the accreditaiton body staff or their appointed representatives forming a view on whether the applicant meets the accreditation criteria by reviewing submitted information and relevant work, and making additional enquiries, if necessary, which may include interviewing personnel. The applicant shall be informed of the review and be able to comment on its contents;

c) a review by the accreditation body of all the evaluation material necessary to determine an accreditation;

d) the decision to grant or withhold accreditation with terms and conditions or any limitations in the scope of accreditation shall be taken on the basis of the review in section (b) by the accreditation body and documented. Accreditation bodies shall have written procedures for assessing the extension of accreditation scope of accredited environmental verifiers.

5. Supervision of accredited environmental verifiers

Provision shall be made, at regular intervals not exceeding 36 months, to ensure that the accredited environmental verifier continues to comply with the accreditation requirements and to monitor the quality of the verifications undertaken.

The accredited environmental verifier must immediately inform the accreditation body of any changes which have bearing on the accreditation or its scope.

Any decision taken by the accreditation body to terminate or suspend accreditation or curtail the scope of accreditation shall be taken only after the accredited environmental verifier has had the possibility of a hearing.

When performing verification activities in a Member State, a verifier accredited in another Member State shall notify its activities to the accreditation organization of the Member State where the verification takes place.

6. Extension of accredited scope

The accreditation body shall have written procedures for assessing accredited environmental verifiers applying for an extension of accredited scope.

B. The function of verifiers

1.   Examination of environmental policies, programmes, management systems, review and audit procedures and environmental statements, and the validation of the last, will be carried out by accredited environmental verifiers.

The function of the verifier is to check, without prejudice to the powers of Member States in respect of supervision of regulatory requirements:

—   compliance with all the requirements of this Regulation, particularly concerning the environmental policy, and programme, the environmental review, the functioning of the environmental management system, the environmental audit process and the environmental statements,

—   the reliability of the data and information in the environmental statement and whether the statement adequately covers all the significant environmental issues of relevance to the site.

The verifier will, in particular, investigate in a sound professional manner, the technical validity of the environmental review or audit or other procedures carried out by the company, without unnecessarily duplicating those procedures.

2.   The verifier will operate on the basis of a written agreement with the company which defines the scope of the work, enables the verifier to operate in an independent professional manner and commits the company to providing the necessary cooperation.

The verification will involve examination of documentation, a visit to the site including, in particular, interviews with personnel, preparation of a report to the company management and solution of the issues raised by the report.

The documentation to be examined in advance of the site visit will include basis information about the site and activities there, the environmental policy and programme, the description of the environmental management system in operation at the site, details of the previous environmental review or audit carried out, the report on that review or audit and on any corrective action taken afterwards, and the draft environmental statement.

3. The verifier's report to the company management will specify:

    a) in general, cases of non-compliance with the provisions of this Regulation, and in particular;

    b) technical defects in the environmental review, or audit method, or environmental management system, or any other relevant process;

    c) points of disagreement with the draft environmental statement, together with details of the amendments or additions that should be made to the environmental statement.

4. The following cases can arise:

    a) If

    — the environmental policy is established in conformity with the relevant requirements of this Regulation,

    — the environmental review or audit appears to have been technically satisfactory,

    — the environmental programme addresses all the significant issues raised,

    — the environmental management system meets the requirements of Annex I and,

    — the statement proves accurate, sufficiently detailed and in compliance with the requirements of the scheme,

    the verifier will validate the statement.

    b) If

    — the environmental policy is established in conformity with relevant requirements of this Regulation,

    — the environmental review or audit appears to have been technically satisfactory,

    — the environmental programme addresses all the significant issues raised,

    — the environmental management system meets the requirements of Annex I, but

    — the statement needs to be revised and/or completed, or the statement for an intervening year in which there has been no validation has been found to be incorrect or misleading, or there has been no statement for an intervening year in which there should have been one, the verifier will discuss the changes needed with the company management and will not validate the statement until the company has made the appropriate additions and/or amendments to the statement, including reference if necessary to amendments required to earlier unvalidated statements, or to additional information which should have been published in intermediate years.

c) If

— the environmental policy had not been established in conformity with the relevant requirements of this Regulation, or

— the environmental review or audit is not technically satisfactory, or,

— the environmental programme does not address all the significant issues raised, or,

— the environmental management system does not meet the requirements of Annex I,

the verifier will make the appropriate recommendations to the company's management on the improvements needed and will not validate the statement until the shortcomings in the policy and/or programmes and/or processes have been corrected, the processes repeated as far as is necessary, and the statement revised accordingly.

ANNEX IV
STATEMENTS OF PARTICIPATION

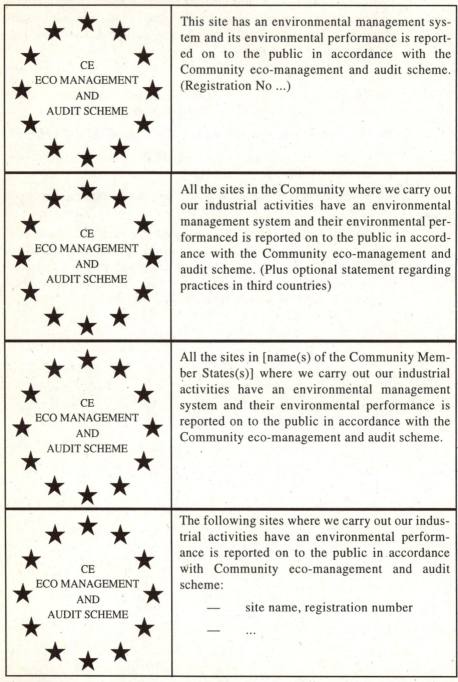

CE ECO MANAGEMENT AND AUDIT SCHEME	This site has an environmental management system and its environmental performance is reported on to the public in accordance with the Community eco-management and audit scheme. (Registration No ...)
CE ECO MANAGEMENT AND AUDIT SCHEME	All the sites in the Community where we carry out our industrial activities have an environmental management system and their environmental performanced is reported on to the public in accordance with the Community eco-management and audit scheme. (Plus optional statement regarding practices in third countries)
CE ECO MANAGEMENT AND AUDIT SCHEME	All the sites in [name(s) of the Community Member States(s)] where we carry out our industrial activities have an environmental management system and their environmental performance is reported on to the public in accordance with the Community eco-management and audit scheme.
CE ECO MANAGEMENT AND AUDIT SCHEME	The following sites where we carry out our industrial activities have an environmental performance is reported on to the public in accordance with Community eco-management and audit scheme: — site name, registration number — ...

ANNEX V

INFORMATION TO BE PROVIDED TO THE COMPETENT BODIES AT THE TIME OF APPLICATION FOR REGISTRATION OR SUBMISSION OF A SUBSEQUENT VALIDATED ENVIRONMENTAL STATEMENT

1) Name of company.

2) Name and location of the site.

3) Brief description of the activities at the site (refer to annexed documents if necessary).

4) Name and address of the accredited environmental verifier who validated the statement annexed.

5) Deadline for submission of the next validated environmental statement.

The following details must be included in the application.

a) A brief description of the environmental management system.

b) A description of the auditing programme established for the site.

c) The validated environmental statement.

COUNCIL DECISION 93/500/EEC[1]
of 13 September 1993
concerning the promotion of renewable energy sources in the Community (Altener programme)

THE COUNCIL OF THE EUROPEAN COMMUNITIES,

Having regard to the Treaty establishing the European Economic Community, and in particular Articles 130s and 235 thereof,

Having regard to the proposal from the Commission[2],

Having regard to the opinion of the European Parliament[3],

Having regard to the opinion of the Economic and Social Committee[4],

Whereas, at their meeting on 29 October 1990, the Council (Environment and Energy Ministers) agreed that the Community and Member States, assuming that other leading countries would enter into similar commitments, and acknowledging the targets identified by a number of Member States for stabilizing or reducing emissions by different dates, were willing to take action aimed at reaching stabilization of the total CO_2 emissions by 2000 at the 1990 level in the Community as a whole and that Member States which start from relatively low levels of energy consumption and therefore low emissions measured on a per capita or other appropriate basis are entitled to have CO_2 targets and/or strategies corresponding to their economic and social development, while continuing to improve the energy efficiency of their economic activities;

Whereas, in its communication to the Council concerning a Community strategy to limit carbon dioxide emissions and to improve energy efficiency, the Commission indicated the action the Community should take to limit CO_2 emissions;

Whereas, at its meeting on 13 December 1991, the Council invited the Commission to put forward formal proposals for the adoption of measures as part of a Community strategy;

---

[1] OJ No L 235, 18. 9. 1993, p. 41.
[2] OJ No C 179, 16. 7. 1992, p. 4.
[3] OJ No C 176, 28. 6. 1993.
[4] OJ No C 19, 25. 1. 1993, p. 7.

Whereas a significant increase in the use of renewable energy sources will contribute towards achieving the objective of stabilizing CO_2 emissions;

Whereas, pursuant to Article 130r of the Treaty, action by the Community relating to the environment should improve the quality of the environment and ensure a prudent and rational utilization of natural resources, objectives which are furthered by the use of renewable energy sources;

Whereas the development of renewable energy sources can make a significant contribution to the reduction of polluting emissions arising from the consumption of fossil fuels;

Whereas the development of renewable energy sources will contribute to the reduction of greenhouse gases and the danger of global warming; whereas wide-ranging international cooperation is therefore desirable in order to obtain significant results;

Whereas, since the Treaty does not provide for other powers to cover the energy aspects of the programme referred to in Article 2, Article 235 should also be invoked;

Whereas the Council resolution of 16 September 1986 concerning new Community energy policy objectives for 1995 and convergence of the policies of the Member States[1] states that the contribution of new and renewable energy sources to the replacement of traditional fuels should increase substantially, so that those energy sources can play a significant part in the overall energy balance sheet;

Whereas some renewable energy sources today occupy only a few market slots; whereas, if they are not yet competitive, this is to be explained in part by the fact that the present pricing system does not always take into account fully the ecological cost of the principal traditional sources of energy; whereas, in order to strengthen the future contribution of renewable energy sources to energy supplies, the Member States will have to avoid such distortions;

Whereas, by its recommendation of 9 June 1988 on developing the exploitation of renewable energy sources in the Community[2], the Council confirmed in detail its desire to pursue a policy of developing renewable energy sources;

Whereas, when reviewing the progress made towards achieving the energy objectives for 1995 provided for in its resolution of 16 September 1986, the

---

[1]   OJ No C 241, 25. 9. 1986, p. 1.
[2]   OJ No L 160, 28. 6. 1988, p. 46.

Council stated in its conclusions of 8 November 1988 that it attributed particular importance to renewable energy sources for future energy supplies;

Whereas the development of renewable energy sources and in particular the exploitation of biomass offer secondary economic advantages in terms of employment and keeping local populations in situ;

Whereas the promotion and wider use of renewable energy sources throughout the Community are likely to strengthen its economic and social cohesion, as called for by Article 130a of the Treaty;

Whereas, to this end, it is appropriate to take account of the Community's indicative objectives and make provision for resources to further the attainment of those objectives, taking into consideration the particular conditions in each Member State;

Whereas provision should be made for a five-year programme;

Whereas ECU 40 million is the amount estimated as necessary in order to implement the multiannual programme; whereas this amount is intended to fund the programme for the period 1993 to 1997 provided it is consistent with the Community's medium-term financial perspective in force as from 1 January 1993,

HAS ADOPTED THIS DECISION:

Article 1

Member States shall endeavour to contribute in their energy policies to the limitation of carbon dioxide emissions by taking account of the Community's indicative objectives relating to the renewable energy sources which are set out in Annex I.

Article 2

1.　The Community shall support a series of actions to promote renewable energy sources within the context of the Altener programme (specific actions for greater penetration of renewable energy sources), hereinafter referred to as 'the programme'.

2.　The programme shall last five years.

3.　The amount of Community funds estimated as necessary for implementation of the programme shall be ECU 40 million for the period 1993 to 1997, provided that amount is consistent with the Community's medium-term financial perspective in force as from 1 January 1993.

4.   The budget authority shall determine the appropriations available for each financial year, taking into account the principles of sound management referred to in Article 2 of the Financial Regulation of 21 December 1977 applicable to the general budget of the European Communities[1].

Article 3

Four categories of actions on renewable energy sources shall be financed under the programme, namely:

  a) studies and technical evaluations for defining technical standards or specifications;

  b) measures to support the Member States' initiatives for extending or creating infrastructures concerned with renewable energy sources. These initiatives shall include:

   - training and information activities with regard to renewable energy sources at a level as close as possible to operators and the final consumers of energy,

   - sectoral actions, as referred to in Annex II;

  c) measures to foster the creation of an information network aimed at promoting better coordination between national, Community and international activities through the establishment of appropriate means for exchanging information and at evaluating the impact of the various actions provided for in this Article;

  d) studies, evaluations and other appropriate measures aimed at assessing the technical feasibility and the advantages for the economy and the environment of the industrial exploitation of biomass for energy purposes, in particular heat and electricity production.

Article 4

1.   All costs relating to the actions referred to in Article 3 (a) shall be borne by the Community.

---

[1] OJ No L 356, 31. 12. 1977, p. 1. Financial Regulation as last amended by Regulation (Euratom, ECSC, EEC) No 610/90 (OJ No L 70, 16. 3. 1990, p. 1).

2.   The level of funding for the actions referred to in Article 3 (b) and (c) shall be between 30 and 50 % of their total cost.

In exceptional cases duly justified to the committee provided for in Article 7 (1) such funding may exceed the 50 % limit, while not, however, exceeding 60 %.

3.   The level of funding for the actions referred to in Article 3 (d) must not exceed 30 % of their total cost.

4.   The balance of the funding of the actions referred to in Article 3 (b), (c) and (d) may be made up from either public or private sources or from a contribution of the two.

Article 5

1.   The Commission shall establish guidelines for the support measures referred to in Article 3 (b), (c) and (d) each year, in consultation with the committee provided for in Article 7 (1).

2.   The proposed initiatives referred to in Article 3 (b) and the list of bodies which are to implement them shall be submitted annually by the Member States to the Commission, which shall decide on the level and conditions of Community funding according to the procedure provided for in Article 7 (1). The Commission shall sign contracts relating to the support measures with those bodies.

Article 6

1.   The Commission shall be responsible for the implementation of the programme.

2.   For the implementation of the actions referred to in Article 3 (a), (b) and (c), the Commission shall apply the procedure laid down in Article 7 (1).

3.   For the implementation of the actions referred to in Article 3 (d), the Commission shall apply the procedure laid down in Article 7 (2).

Article 7

1.   In carrying out the activities referred to in Article 6 (2), the Commission shall be assisted by an advisory committee composed of the representatives of the Member States and chaired by the representative of the Commission.

The representative of the Commission shall submit to the committee a draft of the measures to be taken. The Committee shall deliver its opinion on the draft within a time limit which the chairman may lay down according to the urgency of the matter, if necessary by taking a vote.

The opinion shall be recorded in the minutes; in addition, each Member State shall have the right to ask to have its position recorded in the minutes.

The Commission shall take the utmost account of the opinion delivered by the committee. It shall inform the committee of the manner in which its opinion has been taken into account.

2.   In carrying out the activities referred to in Article 6 (3), the Commission shall be assisted by a committee composed of the representatives of the Member States and chaired by the representative of the Commission.

The representative of the Commission shall submit to the committee a draft of the measures to be taken. The committee shall deliver its opinion on the draft within a time limit which the chairman may lay down according to the urgency of the matter. The opinion shall be delivered by the majority laid down in Article 148 (2) of the Treaty in the case of decisions which the Council is required to adopt on a proposal from the Commission. The votes of the representatives of the Member States within the committee shall be weighted in the manner set out in that Article. The chairman shall not vote.

The Commission shall adopt measures which shall apply immediately.

However, if these measures are not in accordance with the opinion of the committee, they shall be communicated by the Commission to the Council forthwith.

In that event, the Commission shall defer application of the measures which it has decided for a period of one month from the date of communication.

The Council, acting by a qualified majority, may take a different decision within the time limit referred to in the previous subparagraph.

Article 8

1.   During the third year of the programme, the Commission shall present a report to the European Parliament and to the Council on the results achieved. The report shall be accompanied by proposals for any amendments which might be necessary in the light of these results.

2.   On expiry of the programme, the Commission shall assess the results obtained, the application of this Decision and the consistency of national and Community actions. It shall present a report thereon to the European Parliament, the Council and the Economic and Social Committee.

Article 9

This Decision shall apply from 1 January 1993 to 31 December 1997.

Article 10

This Decision is addressed to the Member States.

Done at Brussels, 13 September 1993.

For the Council

The President

Ph. MAYSTADT

ANNEX I

Community indicative objectives for reducing carbon dioxide emissions by developing renewable energy sources

A 180-million tonne reduction in carbon dioxide emissions could be achieved in 2005 by:

a) increasing the contribution of renewable energy sources to the coverage of total energy demand from nearly 4 % in 1991 to 8 % in 2005[1].

   To achieve this objective, the production of renewable energy sources should rise from nearly 43 million toe in 1991 to approximately 109 million toe in 2005;

b) trebling the production of electricity from renewable energy sources (excluding large hydro-electric power stations).

   To achieve this objective, the capacity and electricity production of all power stations (excluding large hydro-electric power stations) using renewable energy sources should rise from 8 GW and 25 TWh in 1991 to 27 GW and 80 TWh in 2005;

c) securing for biofuels a market share of 5 % of total fuel consumption by motor vehicles.

   The production in 2005 of 11 million toe of biofuels is considered necessary in order to achieve this objective.

---

[1] In the energy balances on which the formulation of objective A is based, the electricity produced from the various alternative sources is accounted for in accordance with the conventions of the Statistical Office of the European Communities.

ANNEX II

Illustrative, non-restrictive list of sectoral actions, as referred to in the second indent of Article 3 (b)

1) Pilot actions aimed at introducing a 'guarantee of solar results' in the market for solar collectors and solar water heaters.

2) Pilot actions relating to vehicle fleets aimed at introducing biofuels in place of petroleum products in the transport sector.

3) Pilot studies on least-cost (integrated resource) planning and demand-side management.

4) Pilot projects on third-party financing within the framework of the European network for third-party financing (without direct Community funding).

5) Guarantee of financial risks arising from the geological uncertainties surrounding the development of geothermal resources.

6) Establishment of local plans for the development of renewable energy sources.

7) Establishment and development of infrastructures in the Member States for offering investors assistance with the drawing up of pre-feasibility studies.

8) Pilot actions involving the equipping of new or existing buildings with photovoltaic modules.

9) Pilot actions relating to the planning of windform projects.

10) Pilot actions to integrate bioclimatic systems into architecture.

COMMISSION DECISION 93/517/EEC[1]
of 15 September 1993
on a standard contract covering the terms of use of the Community eco-label

THE COMMISSION OF THE EUROPEAN COMMUNITIES,

Having regard to the Treaty establishing the European Economic Community,

Having regard to Council Regulation (EEC) No 880/92 of 23 March 1992 on a Community eco-label award scheme[2], and in particular Article 12 thereof,

Whereas Article 12 of Regulation (EEC) No 880/92 provides that the competent body shall conclude a contract, covering the terms of use of the label, with each applicant, and further provides that to that end a standard contract shall be adopted;

Whereas it is appropriate, in order not only to avoid distortions of competition but also to ensure that the interests of consumers and users are protected, that the terms of use of the label should be uniform throughout the Community;

Whereas, however, the competent bodies should be able, subject to compatibility with Regulation (EEC) No 880/92, to include additional provisions in the contract;

Whereas it is appropriate that the contract should include provisions for compliance monitoring which should allow the competent body to ensure that the label is used only for products which meet the objectives specified in Article 1 of Regulation (EEC) No 380/92 and the principles specified in Article 4 of the said Regulation and are in accordance with the terms of the contract; whereas it is further appropriate that, in cases of non-compliance with the objectives and principles of the said Regulation and the terms of the contract, provisions should be made for suspension or withdrawal of the award of the label;

Whereas the measures set out in this Decision are in accordance with the opinion of the Committee set up pursuant to Article 7 of Regulation (EEC) No 880/92,

HAS ADOPTED THIS DECISION:

---

[1] OJ No L 243, 29. 9. 1993, p. 13.
[2] OJ No L 99, 11. 4. 1992, p. 1.

Article 1

The contract which shall be concluded between the competent body and each applicant in accordance with Article 12 of Regulation (EEC) No 880/92 shall be in the form set out in the Annex to this Decision.

Article 2

Without prejudice to Article 1, the competent body may include in the contract additional provisions provided that such additional provisions are compatible with Regulation (EEC) No 880/92.

In that case, the competent body shall forward the text of the said contract to the Commission for examination as to its compatibility with Regulation (EEC) No 880/92.

Article 3

This Decision is addressed to the Member States.

Done at Brussels, 15 September 1993.

For the Commission

Yannis PALEOKRASSAS

Member of the Commission

ANNEX

STANDARD CONTRACT COVERING THE TERMS OF USE OF THE COMMUNITY ECO-LABEL

PREAMBLE

The Competent Body . . . . . . (full title) hereafter called 'the Competent Body', registered at . . . . . . (full address), which for the purposes of the signature of this contract is represented by . . . . . . (name of person responsible),

and

. . . . . . (full name of Holder), in his capacity as manufacturer or importer, whose official registered address in the European Community is . . . . . . (full address), hereafter called 'the Holder', represented by . . . . . . (name of person responsible),

have agreed the following with regard to the use of the Community eco-label:

Article 1   RIGHTS AND OBLIGATIONS

1.1.   The Competent Body grants the Holder the right to use the eco-label for his product . . . . . . registration number(s) . . . . . . and/or as described in the annexed product specifications, produced or imported at . . . . . . (premises), which conforms to the relevant product group criteria in force for the period . . . . . ., adopted by the Commission of the European Communities on . . . . . . (date), published in the *Official Journal of the European Communities* of . . . . . . (full reference), and annexed to this contract.

1.2.   The eco-label shall be used only in the form and colour laid down in the eco-label specifications provided by the Competent Body and annexed to this contract and shall be clearly visible. The right to use the eco-label does not extend to the use of the eco-label as a component of the trademark.

1.3.   The Holder shall ensure that the product to be labelled complies throughout the duration of this contract with all the terms of use and provisions set out in this contract and the product group criteria and eco-label specifications referred to in the Annexes to this contract which are applicable at the time in question.

Article 2 ADVERTISING

2.1. The Holder shall refer to the award of the eco-label only in relation to the product referred to in Article 1.1. of this contract.

2.2. The Holder shall not advertise or make any statement or use any label or logo in a way which is false or misleading or which results in confusion or calls into question the integrity of the eco-label.

2.3. The Holder shall be responsible under this contract for the manner in which the eco-label is used in relation to his product, especially in the context of advertising.

Article 3 COMPLIANCE MONITORING

3.1. The Competent Body, including its agents authorized for such purpose by the Competent Body, may undertake all or any necessary investigations to monitor the on-going compliance by the Holder with both the product group criteria and the terms of use and provisions of this contract. To this end, the Competent Body may request, and the Holder shall provide, any relevant documentation to prove such compliance.

3.2. Further, the Competent Body, including its agents authorized for such purpose by the Competent Body, may, at any reasonable time and without notice, request, and the Holder shall grant, access to the premises as stated in Article 1.1. or any part thereof, for the purposes mentioned in paragraph 1 of the present Article.

3.3. The Holder shall be liable for the reasonable costs incurred by the Competent Body under this Article.

Article 4 CONFIDENTIALITY

4.1. Except as required by Council Regulation (EEC) No 880/92, and in particular Articles 10 and 13 thereof, the Competent Body and any of its authorized agents may not disclose, or use for any purpose unconnected with this contract, information to which they have gained access in the course of assessing a product with a view to the award of the eco-label or in the course of monitoring compliance pursuant to Article 3 hereof.

4.2.   The Competent Body shall take all reasonable steps to secure the protection of the documents confided to it against falsification and misappropriation.

4.3.   Furthermore, the Competent Body shall take all reasonable steps to secure the protection of the documents entrusted to it from destruction, for a period of at least three years from the date of termination of this contract. At the end of this period the Competent Body may destroy the documentation.

Article 5   SUSPENSION AND WITHDRAWAL

5.1.   In a case where the Holder becomes aware that he fails to meet the terms of use or provisions contained in Articles 1, 2 and 3, the Holder shall notify the Competent Body and refrain from using the eco-label until those terms for use or provisions have been fulfilled and the Competent Body notified thereof.

5.2.   Where the Competent Body considers that the Holder has contravened any of the terms of use or provisions of this contract, the Competent Body shall be entitled to suspend or withdraw its authorization to the Holder to use the eco-label, and to take such measures as are necessary to prevent the Holder from using it further, including such measures as are provided for in Article 9.

Article 6   LIMITATION OF LIABILITY AND INDEMNITY

6.1.   The Holder shall not include the eco-label as part of any guarantee or warranty in relation to the product referred to in Article 1.1 of this contract.

6.2.   The Competent Body, including its authorized agents, shall not be liable for any loss or damage sustained by the Holder arising out of the award and/or use of the eco-label.

6.3.   The Competent Body, including its authorized agents, shall not be liable for any loss or damage sustained by a third party and arising out of the award and/or use, including advertising, of the eco-label.

6.4.   The Holder shall indemnify and keep indemnified the Competent Body and its authorized agents against any loss, damage or liability sustained by the Competent Body, or its authorized agents, as a result of a breach of this contract by the Holder or as a result of reliance by the Competent

Body on information or documentation provided by the Holder, including any claims by a third party.

Article 7 FEES

7.1. The Holder undertakes to pay to the Competent Body a fee, or fees, for use of the eco-label on the product referred to in Article 1.1, for the period of use as laid down in this contract, in accordance with the rules on fees in force at the time of the signature of the contract, made available by the Competent Body on . . . . . . (date und full reference), and as annexed to this contract. In the event of suspension or early termination by either the Competent Body or the Holder, the Holder shall not be entitled to repayment (of the fee(s)), either in whole or in part.

7.2. Use of the eco-label is conditional upon all relevant fees having been paid in due time.

Article 8 COMPLAINTS

8.1. The Competent Body may inform the Holder of any complaints made concerning the product bearing the eco-label, and may request the Holder to reply to those complaints. The Competent Body may withhold the identity of the complainant from the Holder.

8.2. Any reply made by the Holder in accordance with a request under Article 8.1 shall be without prejudice to the rights and/or obligations of the Competent Body under Articles 3 and 5 of this contract.

Article 9 CONTRACT DURATION AND APPLICABLE LAW

9.1. Except as provided for in Article 9.2, 9.3 and 9.4 hereof, this contract shall run from the date on which it is signed by the Holder and the Competent Body, for a period of (. . . . . .), save that, if the period specified in Article 1.1 is shorter than such period, that shorter period shall apply.

9.2. The Competent Body shall, by a registered letter to the Holder, terminate this contract at an earlier date than that specified in Article 9.1 where the Commission of the European Communities amends or withdraws the product group criteria referred to in Article 1.1 of this contract.

9.3. Where the Holder has contravened any of the terms of use or provisions of this contract within the meaning of Article 5.2, the Competent Body shall be entitled to treat this as a breach of contract entitling the

Competent Body, in addition to the provisions in Article 5.2, to terminate the contract, by registered letter to the Holder, at an earlier date than given in Article 9.1, within (a time period to be determined by the Competent Body).

9.4. The Holder may terminate the contract by giving the Competent Body one month's notice by registered letter.

9.5. If the product group criteria as stated in Article 1.1 are extended without amendments for any period, and if no written notice of termination from the Competent Body has been given at least two months before the expiry of the product group criteria and of this contract, the Competent Body shall inform the Holder at least two months in advance that the contract shall be automatically renewed for as long as the product group criteria remain in force.

9.6. After the termination of this contract the Holder may not use the eco-label in relation to the product specified in Article 1.1 of this contract, either as labelling or for advertising purposes, except that the display of the eco-label on exemplars of the product no longer held by the Holder in stock and placed on the market before the date of termination of this contract may remain on the market for a maximum period of six months after the termination date.

9.7. Any dispute between the Competent Body and the Holder or any claim by one party against the other based on this contract which has not been settled by amicable agreement between the Contracting Parties, shall be subject to the applicable law of the Member State/region of the Competent Body and to the jurisdiction of the courts of the Member State/region of the Competent Body.

The following Annexes shall form part of this contract:

- copy of Council Regulation (EEC) No 880/92 of 23 March 1992 on a Community eco-label award scheme, in (the relevant Community language(s)),

- product specifications,

- a copy of Commission Decision . . . . . . (on product group criteria),

- eco-label specifications,

- a copy of Commission Decision 93/326/EEC of 13 May 1993 establishing indicative guidelines for the fixing of costs and fees in connection with the Community eco-label, in (the relevant Community language(s)).

Done at ...., and date ....

....

Competent Body

Designated person ....

....

Legally binding signature

Competent
Body
seal

Done at ...., and date ....

....

Holder

Designated person ....

....

Legally binding signature

Company
seal

COMMISSION DIRECTIVE 93/80/EEC[1]
of 23 September 1993
amending Council Directive 90/656/EEC on the transitional measures applicable in Germany with regard to certain Community provisions relating to the protection of the environment

THE COMMISSION OF THE EUROPEAN COMMUNITIES,

Having regard to the Treaty establishing the European Economic Community,

Having regard to Council Directive 90/656/EEC of 4 December 1990 on the transitional measures applicable in Germany with regard to certain Community provisions relating to the protection of the environment[2], and in particular Article 18 (6) thereof,

Whereas Directive 90/656/EEC lays down various time limits for putting certain Community rules on the environment into effect in the territory of the former German Democratic Republic;

Whereas the time limits specified in the said Directive were based on information on the rules in force and the state of the environment in the territory of the former German Democratic Republic which was found to be incomplete, approximative, uncertain and unreliable;

Whereas this results in a situation which is exceptional in all respects;

Whereas neither the Federal Republic of Germany nor the institutions of the European Communities were able, at the time of adoption of the said Directive, to foresee sufficiently clearly how the state of the environment would change in the territory of the former German Democratic Republic;

Whereas the said Directive for this reason provides for a simplified procedure by which the Commission, after obtaining the opinion of an ad hoc Committee, may authorize the extension to 31 December 1995 at the latest of the deadlines for putting certain Community rules on the environment laid down in the said Directive into effect in the territory of the former German Democratic Republic;

---

[1] OJ No L 256, 14. 10. 1993, p. 32.
[2] OJ No L 353, 17. 12. 1990, p. 59.

Whereas the degree of obsolescence of the industrial production units situated in the territory of the former German Democratic Republic, which discharge dangerous substances into the surface water, and the severity of the environmental damage attributable to those discharges have been found to be far in excess of the evaluations on the basis of which the date of 31 December 1992 was laid down in Directive 90/656/EEC for putting the Directives into effect;

Whereas it is therefore necessary to extend the deadlines laid down for the application of the said Directives to installations which were situated in the territory of the former German Democratic Republic at the time of German unification, in order to allow time for making the necessary changes to the said installations;

Whereas the measures provided for in this Directive are in conformity with the opinion expressed by the Committee referred to in Article 18 (4) of Directive 90/656/EEC,

HAS ADOPTED THIS DIRECTIVE:

Article 1

Article 3 of Directive 90/656/EEC is hereby amended as follows:

1. Paragraph 1 is replaced by the following:

    '1. .... By way of derogation from Directive 76/464/CEE[1], Directive 82/176/CEE[2], Directive 83/513/CEE[3], Directive 84/156/CEE[4], Directive 84/491/CEE[5], Directive 86/280/CEE[6] and Directive 88/347/CEE[7], the Federal Republic of Germany shall be authorized to apply, in respect of the territory of the former German Democratic Republic, the

---

[1] OJ No L 129, 18. 5. 1976, p. 23.
   See also Community Legislation concerning the environment, volume 1, General Policy, first edition.

[2] OJ No L 81, 27. 3. 1982, p. 29.
   See also Community Legislation concerning the environment, volume 7, Water, first edition.

[3] OJ No L 291, 24. 10. 1983, p. 1.
   See also Community Legislation concerning the environment, volume 7, Water, first edition.

[4] OJ No L 74, 17. 3. 1984, p. 49.
   See also Community Legislation concerning the environment, volume 7, Water, first edition.

[5] OJ No L 274, 17. 10. 1984, p. 11.
   See also Community Legislation concerning the environment, volume 7, Water, first edition.

provisions laid down in the said Directives to industrial installations which, on the date of German unification, were located in that territory, from 31 December 1995 at the latest.'

2.   Paragraph 4 is replaced by the following:

'4. The special programmes provided for in Article 4 of Directive 84/156/EEC and Article 5 of Directive 86/280/EEC shall be drawn up and put into effect by 31 December 1995 at the latest.'

Article 2

This Directive is addressed to the Member States.

Done at Brussels, 23 September 1993.

For the Commission

Yannis PALEOKRASSAS

Member of the Commission

---

[6]   OJ No L 181, 4. 7. 1986, p. 16.
      See also Community Legislation concerning the environment, volume 7, Water, first edition.
[7]   OJ No L 158, 25. 6. 1988, p. 35.
      See also Community Legislation concerning the environment, volume 7, Water, first edition.

DECISION 93/C 323/01[1] taken by common agreement between THE REPRESENTATIVES OF THE GOVERNMENTS OF THE MEMBER STATES, MEETING AT HEAD OF STATE AND GOVERNMENT LEVEL,
On the location of the seats of certain bodies and departments of the European Communities and of Europol

THE REPRESENTATIVES OF THE MEMBER STATES, MEETING AT HEAD OF STATE AND GOVERNMENT LEVEL,

Having regard to Article 216 of the Treaty establishing the European Economic Community, Article 77 of the Treaty establishing the European Coal and Steel Community and Article 189 of the Treaty establishing the European Atomic Energy Community,

Having regard to Council Regulation (EEC) No 1210/90 of 7 May 1990 on the establishment of the European Environment Agency and the European environment information and observation network[2], and in particular Article 21 thereof,

Having regard to Council Regulation (EEC) No 1360/90 of 7 May 1990 establishing a European Training Foundation[3], and in particular Article 19 thereof,

Having regard to the Decision of 18 December 1991 under which the Commission approved the establishment of the Office for Veterinary and Plant-Health Inspection and Control,

Having regard to Council Regulation (EEC) No 302/93 of 8 February 1993 on the establishment of a European Monitoring Centre for Drugs and Drug Addiction[4], and in particular Article 19 thereof,

Having regard to Council Regulation (EEC) No 2309/93 of 22 July 1993 establishing inter alia a European Agency for the Evaluation of Medicinal Products[5], and in particular Article 74 thereof,

---

[1]   OJ No C 323, 30. 11. 1993, p. 1.
[2]   OJ No L 120, 11. 5. 1990, p. 1.
[3]   OJ No L 131, 23. 5. 1990, p. 1.
[4]   OJ No L 36, 12. 2. 1993, p. 1.
[5]   OJ No L 214, 24. 8. 1993, p. 1.

Whereas, further to the action programme adopted by the Commission on 20 November 1989 relating to the implementation of the Community Charter of the Fundamental Social Rights of Workers, the European Council made provision for creating the Agency for Health and Safety at Work;

Whereas the Treaty on European Union, which was signed on 7 February 1992 and will enter into force on 1 November 1993, provides for the establishment of the European Monetary Institute and the European Central Bank;

Whereas the institutions of the European Communities envisage the establishment of an Office for Harmonization in the Internal Market (trade marks, designs and models);

Whereas, further to the conclusions of the Maastricht European Council, the Member States envisage concluding a Convention on Europol (European Police Office), which will create Europol and also replace the Ministerial Agreement of 2 June 1993, which set up the Europol Drugs Unit;

Whereas the location of the seats of these different bodies and departments should be determined;

Recalling the Decisions of 8 April 1965 and 12 December 1992,

HAVE DECIDED AS FOLLOWS:

Article 1

a) The European Environment Agency shall have its seat in the area of Copenhagen.

b) The European Training Foundation shall have its seat at Turin.

c) The Office for Veterinary and Plant-Health Inspection and Control shall have its seat in a town in Ireland to be determined by the Irish Government.

d) The European Monitoring Centre for Drugs and Drug Addiction shall have its seat at Lisbon.

e) The European Agency for the Evaluation of Medicinal Products shall have its seat at London.

f) The Agency for Health and Safety at Work shall have its seat in Spain, in a town to be determined by the Spanish Government.

g) The European Monetary Institute and the future European Central Bank shall have their seat at Frankfurt.

h) The Office for Harmonization in the Internal Market (trade marks, designs and models), including its Boards of Appeal, shall have its seat in Spain, in a town to be determined by the Spanish Government.

i) Europol, and the Europol Drugs Unit, shall have their seat at The Hague.

Article 2

This Decision, which will be published in the *Official Journal of the European Communities*, shall enter into force on this day.

Done at Brussels on the twenty-ninth day of October in the year one thousand nine hundred and ninety-three.

DECLARATIONS

When adopting the above Decision on 29 October 1993, the Representatives of the Governments of the Member States adopted the following declarations by common agreement:

— Under Council Regulation (EEC) No 337/75 of 10 February 1975, which was adopted unanimously by the Council on a proposal from the Commission and after consulting the European Parliament, the seat of the European Centre for the Development of Vocational Training was located in Berlin. The Representatives of the Governments of the Member States call upon the institution of the European Community to provide that that seat shall be determined, as soon as possible, in Thessaloniki.

The Commission stated that it was willing to submit a proposal to that effect in the very near future.

— A Translation Centre for the bodies of the Union will be set up within the Commission's Translation Departments located in Luxembourg and will provide the necessary translation services for the operation of the bodies and departments whose seats have been determined by the above Decision of 29 October 1993, with the exception of the translators of the European Monetary Institute.

— The Member States undertake to support the candidacy of Luxembourg as seat of the Common Appeal Court for Community patents as provided for in the Protocol on the settlement of litigation concerning the infringement and validity of Community patents annexed to the Community Patent Agreement of 15 December 1989.

At the conference of the Representatives of the Governments of the Member States the Commission confirmed that it intends to consolidate the establishment of those of its departments that are located in Luxembourg.

Finally, the Member States noted that budgetary resources are available to enable the European Foundation for the Improvement of Living and Working Conditions in Dublin to perform a number of new tasks.

COMMISSION DECISION 93/701/EC[1]
of 7 December 1993
on the setting-up of a general consultative forum on the environment

THE COMMISSION OF THE EUROPEAN COMMUNITIES,

Having regard to the Treaty establishing the European Community,

Whereas in its resolution of 1 February 1993 on a Community programme of policy and action in relation to the environment and sustainable development[2], the Council approved the approach and general strategy of the programme 'Towards Sustainability' presented by the Commission;

Whereas the programme provides for the setting-up of a general consultative forum bringing together representatives from the sectors of production, the business world, regional and local authorities, professional associations, unions and environmental protection and consumer organizations;

Whereas the forum must be a place of consultation and dialogue between the representatives of the said sectors and the Commission;

Whereas the forum should contain a balanced number of representatives from the various sectors concerned; whereas its members should be appointed by the Commission in the light of recommendations from organizations representing each sector concerned at Community level,

HAS DECIDED AS FOLLOWS:

Article 1

1.   A consultative committee on the environment, to be known as the general consultative forum on the environment, hereinafter referred to as 'the forum', is hereby set up at the Commission.

2.   The forum shall consist of figures from the sectors of production, the business world, regional and local authorities, professional associations, unions and environmental protection and consumer organizations.

---

[1] OJ No L 328, 29. 12. 1993, p. 53.
[2] OJ No C 138, 17. 5. 1993, p. 5.
    See also Community Legislation concerning the environment, volume 1, General Policy, first edition.

Article 2

1.   The forum may be consulted by the Commission on any problem relating to the Community's environment policy.

2.   A vice-chairman of the forum may draw the Commission's attention to the expediency of consulting the forum on a matter within the latter's field of competence on which no opinion has been requested.

Article 3

The forum shall consist of 32 members. Seats shall be allocated as follows:

a)   seven to 12 seats for business figures;

b)   three to five seats for representatives from regional and local authorities;

c)   four to seven seats for representatives from environmental protection and consumer organizations;.

d)   one to three seats for union representatives;

e)   seven to 10 seats for figures with particular competence in the environmental field.

Article 4

Members of the forum shall be appointed by the Commission, which shall take account of the recommendations made to it by the parties referred to in Article 1 (1).

Article 5

1.   The term of office of a forum member shall be three years. It may be renewed.

2.   On expiry of the three-year period, forum members shall continue to perform theirs tasks until such time as they are replaced or reappointed.

3.   A member's term of office shall be termined before the end of the three-year period in the event of resignation or death. He shall be replaced for the remainder of his term of office in accordance with the procedure set out in Article 4.

4.   No remuneration shall be given in respect of the tasks performed by a forum member.

Article 6

The Commission shall publish the list of members in the *Official Journal of the European Communities*.

Article 7

1.   The forum shall be chaired by a representative of the Commission.

2.   The forum shall elect two vice-chairmen from among its members for a period of 18 months. This period may be renewed once. Election shall be by a two-thirds majority of members present.

3.   The chairman and the vice-chairmen shall constitute the bureau. The bureau shall prepare and organize the work of the forum.

Article 8

1.   The forum may, on a proposal from one of its members or the Commission, invite any person having a particular competence in a matter included in the agenda to participate in its work as an expert.

2.   Experts shall take part only in the deliberations on those items for which their presence is required.

Article 9

The forum may set up working parties.

Article 10

1.   The forum and the bureau shall meet at the seat of the Commission when convened by it.

2.   Representatives from the relevant Committee departments shall take part in the meetings of the forum, the bureau and the working parties.

1.   The Commission shall provide the secretariat for the forum, the bureau and the working parties.

Article 11

1.   The forum's deliberations shall deal with requests for opinions lodged by the Commission. They shall not be followed by a vote.

2.   When requesting an opinion from the forum, the Commission may set a deadline for delivery of the opinion.

3.   The positions adopted shall appear in a record sent to the Commission.

Article 12

Without prejudice to the provisions of Article 214 of the Treaty, forum members shall be required not to divulge information of which they become aware through the work of the forum or the working parties where the Commission informs the latter that an opinion requested or a question raised concerns a matter which is confidential.

In this event, only forum members and representatives of the Commission departments shall attend meetings.

Article 13

This Decision shall take effect on 7 December 1993.

Done at Brussels, 7 December 1993.

For the Commission

Yannis PALEOKRASSAS

Member of the Commission

CODE OF CONDUCT CONCERNING PUBLIC ACCESS TO COUNCIL AND COMMISSION DOCUMENTS (93/730/EC)[1]

THE COUNCIL AND THE COMMISSION,

HAVING REGARD to the declaration on the right of access to information annexed to the final act of the Treaty on European Union, which emphasizes that transparency of the decision-making process strengthens the democratic nature of the institutions and the public's confidence in the administration,

HAVING REGARD to the conclusions wherein the European Councils in Birmingham and Edinburgh agreed on a number of principles to promote a Community closer to its citizens,

HAVING REGARD to the conclusions of the European Council in Copenhagen, reaffirming the principle of giving citizens the greatest possible access to information and calling on the Council and the Commission to adopt at an early date the necessary measures for putting this principle into practice,

CONSIDERING it desirable to establish by common agreement the principles which will govern access to Commission and Council documents, it being understood that it is for each of them to implement these principles by means of specific regulations,

WHEREAS the said principles are without prejudice to the relevant provisions on access to files directly concerning persons with a specific interest in them;

WHEREAS these principles will have to be implemented in full compliance with the provisions concerning classified information;

WHEREAS this code of conduct is an additional element in their information and communication policy,

HAVE AGREED AS FOLLOWS:

---

[1]   OJ No L 340, 31. 12. 1993, P. 41.

General principle

The public will have the widest possible access to documents held by the Commission and the Council.

'Document' means any written text, whatever its medium, which contains existing data and is held by the Council or the Commission.

Processing of initial applications

An application for access to a document will have to be made in writing, in a sufficiently precise manner; it will have to contain information that will enable the document or documents concerned to be identified.

Where necessary, the institution concerned will ask the applicant for further details.

Where the document held by an institution was written by a natural or legal person, a Member State, another Community institution or body or any other national or international body, the application must be sent direct to the author.

In consultation with the applicants, the institution concerned will find a fair solution to comply with repeat applications and/or those which relate to very large documents.

The applicant will have access to documents either by consulting them on the spot or by having a copy sent at his own expense; the fee will not exceed a reasonable sum.

The institution concerned will be able to stipulate that a person to whom a document is released will not be allowed to reproduce or circulate the said document for commercial purposes through direct sale without its prior authorization.

Within one month the relevant departments of the institution concerned will inform the applicant either that his application has been approved or that they intend to advise the institution to reject it.

Processing of confirmatory applications

Where the relevant departments of the institution concerned intend to advise the institution to reject an application, they will inform the applicant thereof and tell him that he has one month to make a confirmatory application to the institution for that position to be reconsidered, failing which he will be deemed to have withdrawn his original application.

If a confirmatory application is submitted, and if the institution concerned decides to refuse to release the document, that decision, which must be made within a month of submission of the confirmatory application, will be notified in writing to the applicant as soon as possible. The grounds for the decision must be given, and the decision must indicate the means of redress that are available, i.e. judicial proceedings and complaints to the ombudsman under the conditions specified in, respectively, Articles 173 and 138e of the Treaty establishing the European Community.

Exceptions

The institutions will refuse access to any document whose disclosure could undermine:

—   the protection of the public interest (public security, international relations, monetary stability, court proceedings, inspections and investigations),

—   the protection of the individual and of privacy,

—   the protection of commercial and industrial secrecy,

—   the protection of the Community's financial interests,

—   the protection of confidentiality as requested by the natural or legal persons that supplied the information or as required by the legislation of the Member State that supplied the information.

They may also refuse access in order to protect the institution's interest in the confidentiality of its proceedings.

Implementation

The Commission and the Council will severally take steps to implement these principles before 1 January 1994.

Review

The Council and the Commission agree that the code of conduct will, after two years of operation, be reviewed on the basis of reports drawn up by the Secretaries-General of the Council and the Commission.

Council statement

This code of conduct and the decisions which the Council and the Commission will severally adopt on the basis thereof are intended to allow public access to Council and Commission documents.

They alter neither the existing practices nor the obligations of Member States' Governments toward their parliaments.

COUNCIL DECISION 93/731/EC[1]
of 20 December 1993
on public access to Council documents

THE COUNCIL,

Having regard to the Treaty establishing the European Community, and in particular Article 151 (3) thereof,

Having regard to its Rules of Procedure, and in particular Article 22 thereof,

Whereas on 6 December 1993 the Council and the Commission approved a code of conduct concerning public access to Council and Commission documents, reaching common agreement on the principles which must govern such access;

Whereas provisions should be adopted for the implementation of those principles by the Council;

Whereas these provisions are applicable to any document held by the Council, whatever its medium, excluding documents written by a person, body or institution outside the Council;

Whereas the principle of allowing the public wide access to Council documents, as part of greater transparency in the Council's work, must however be subject to exceptions, particularly as regards protection of the public interest, the individual and privacy;

Whereas, in the interests of rationalization and efficiency, the Secretary-General of the Council should sign on behalf of the Council and on its authorization replies to applications for access to documents, except in cases where the Council is called upon to reply to a confirmatory application;

Whereas this Decision must apply with due regard for provisions governing the protection of classified information,

HAS DECIDED AS FOLLOWS:

---

[1]   OJ No L 340, 31. 12. 1993, p. 43.

Article 1

1.   The public shall have access to Council documents under the conditions laid down in this Decision.

2.   'Council document' means any written text, whatever its medium, containing existing data and held by the Council, subject to Article 2 (2).

Article 2

1.   An application for access to a Council document shall be sent in writing to the Council[1]. It must be made in a sufficiently precise manner and must contain information enabling the document or documents requested to be identified. Where necessary, the applicant shall be asked for further details.

2.   Where the requested document was written by a natural or legal person, a Member State, another Community institution or body, or any other national or international body, the application must not be sent to the Council, but direct to the author.

Article 3

1.   The applicant shall have access to a Council document either by consulting it on the spot or by having a copy sent at his own expense. The fee shall be set by the Secretary-General.

2.   The relevant departments of the General Secretariat shall endeavour to find a fair solution to deal with repeat applications and/or those which relate to very large documents.

3.   3Anyone given access to a Council document may not reproduce or circulate the document for commercial purposes through direct sale without prior authorization from the Secretary-General.

Article 4

1.   Access to a Council document shall not be granted where its disclosure could undermine:

---

[1]   The Secretary-General of the Council of the European Union, 170 rue de la Loi, 1048 Brussels, Belgium.

— the protection of the public interest (public security, international relations, monetary stability, court proceedings, inspections and investigations),

— the protection of the individual and of privacy,

— the protection of commercial and industrial secrecy,

— the protection of the Community's financial interests,

— the protection of confidentiality as requested by the natural or legal person who supplied any of the information contained in the document or as required by the legislation of the Member State which supplied any of that information.

2.   Access to a Council document may be refused in order to protect the confidentiality of the Council's proceedings.

Article 5

The Secretary-General shall reply on behalf of the Council to applications for access to Council documents, except in the cases referred to in Article 7 (3), in which the reply shall come from the Council.

Article 6

Any application for access to a Council document shall be examined by the relevant departments of the General Secretariat, which shall suggest what action is to be taken on it.

Article 7

1.   The applicant shall be informed in writing within a month by the relevant departments of the General Secretariat either that his application has been approved or that the intention is to reject it. In the latter case, the applicant shall also be informed of the reasons for this intention and that he has one month to make a confirmatory application for that position to be reconsidered, failing which he will be deemed to have withdrawn his original application.

2.   Failure to reply to an application within a month of submission shall be equivalent to a refusal, except where the applicant makes a confirmatory application, as referred to above, within the following month.

3.   Any decision to reject a confirmatory application, which shall be taken within a month of submission of such application, shall state the grounds on

which it is based. The applicant shall be notified of the decision in writing as soon as possible and at the same time informed of the content of Articles 138e and 173 of the Treaty establishing the European Community, relating respectively to the conditions for referral to the Ombudsman by natural persons and review by the Court of Justice of the legality of Council acts.

4.   Failure to reply within a month of submission of the confirmatory application shall be equivalent to a refusal.

Article 8

This Decision shall apply with due regard for provisions governing the protection of classified information.

Article 9

This Decision shall be reviewed after two years of operation. In 1996 the Secretary-General shall submit a report on the implementation of this Decision in 1994 and 1995, in preparation for that review.

Article 10

This Decision shall take effect on 1 January 1994.

Done at Brussels, 20 December 1993.

For the Council

The President

W. CLAES

DECISION 94/1/ECSC, EC[1] OF THE COUNCIL AND THE COMMISSION
of 13 December 1993
on the conclusion of the Agreement on the European Economic Area between the European Communities, their Member States and the Republic of Austria, the Republic of Finland, the Republic of Iceland, the Principality of Liechtenstein, the Kingdom of Norway, the Kingdom of Sweden and the Swiss Confederation

THE COUNCIL OF THE EUROPEAN UNION,

THE COMMISSION OF THE EUROPEAN COMMUNITIES,

Having regard to the Treaty establishing the European Coal and Steel Community,

Having regard to the Treaty establishing the European Community, and in particular Article 238 in conjunction with Article 228 (3), second subparagraph thereof,

Having regard to the assent of the European Parliament[2],

Whereas the Agreement on the European Economic Area between the European Communities, their Member States and the Republic of Austria, the Republic of Finland, the Republic of Iceland, the Principality of Liechtenstein, the Kingdom of Norway, the Kingdom of Sweden and the Swiss Confederation, signed in Oporto on 2 May 1992 should be approved,

HAVE DECIDED AS FOLLOWS:

Article 1

The Agreement on the European Economic Area between the European Communities, their Member States and the Republic of Austria, the Republic of Finland, the Republic of Iceland, the Principality of Liechtenstein, the Kingdom of Norway, the Kingdom of Sweden and the Swiss Confederation, the Protocols, the Annexes annexed thereto and the Declarations, the Agreed Minutes and exchanges of letters attached to the Final Act are hereby approved

---

[1] OJ No L 1, 3. 1. 1994.
[2] OJ No C 305, 23. 11. 1992, p. 66.

on behalf of the European Community and the European Coal and Steel Community.

The texts of the acts referred to in the first paragraph are attached to this Decision.

Article 2

The act of approval provided for in Article 129 of the Agreement shall be deposited by the President of the Council on behalf of the European Community and by the President of the Commission on behalf of the European Coal and Steel Community[1].

Done at Brussels, 13 December 1993.

For the Council   *For the Commission*

The President   *The President*

Ph. MAYSTADT   J. DELORS

---

[1]   See page 606 of this Official Journal. (OJ No L 1, 3. 1. 1994)

AGREEMENT ON THE EUROPEAN ECONOMIC AREA

CHAPTER 3   ENVIRONMENT

Article 73

1) Action by the Contracting Parties relating to the environment shall have the following objectives:

   a) to preserve, protect and improve the quality of the environment;

   b) to contribute towards protecting human health;

   c) to ensure a prudent and rational utilization of natural resources.

2. Action by the Contracting Parties relating to the environment shall be based on the principles that preventive action should be taken, that environmental damage should as a priority be rectified at source, and that the polluter should pay. Environmental protection requirements shall be a component of the Contracting Parties' other policies.

Article 74

Annex XX contains the specific provisions on protective measures which shall apply pursuant to Article 73.

Article 75

The protective measures referred to in Article 74 shall not prevent any Contracting Party from maintaining or introducing more stringent protective measures compatible with this Agreement.

ANNEX XX

ENVIRONMENT

List provided for in Article 74

INTRODUCTION

When the acts referred to in this Annex contain notions or refer to procedures which are specific to the Community legal order, such as

- preambles;
- the addressees of the Community acts;
- references to territories or languages of the EC;
- references to rights and obligations of EC Member States, their public entities, undertakings or individuals in relation to each other; and
- references to information and notification procedures;

Protocol 1 on horizontal adaptations shall apply, unless otherwise provided for in this Annex.

SECTORAL ADAPTATION

For the purposes of this Annex and notwithstanding the provisions of Protocol 1, the term 'Member State(s)' contained in the acts referred to shall be understood to include, in addition to its meaning in the relevant EC acts, Austria, Finland, Iceland, Liechtenstein, Norway, Sweden and Switzerland.

ACTS REFERRED TO

I.   **General**

1)   **385 L 0337:** Council Directive 85/337/EEC of 27 June 1985 on the assessment of the effects of certain public and private projects on the environment (OJ No L 175, 5.7.1985, p. 40).

2)   **390 L 0313:** Council Directive 90/313/EEC of 7 June 1990 on freedom of access to information (OJ No L 158, 23.6.1990, p. 56).

II.   Water

3)   **375 L 0440:** Council Directive 75/440/EEC of 16 June 1975 concerning the quality required of surface water intended for the abstraction of drinking water in the Member States (OJ No L 194, 25.7.1975, p. 26), as amended by:

—   **379 L 0869:** Council Directive 79/869/EEC of 9 October 1979 (OJ No L 271, 29.10.1979, p. 44).

4)   **376 L 0464:** Council Directive 76/464/EEC of 4 May 1976 on pollution caused by certain dangerous substances discharged into the aquatic environment of the Community (OJ L 129, 18.5.1976, p. 23).

The provisions of the Directive shall, for the purposes of the Agreement, be read with the following adaptation:

Iceland shall put into effect the measures necessary for it to comply with the provisions of this Directive as from 1 January 1995.

5)   **379 L 0869:** Council Directive 79/869/EEC of 9 October 1979 concerning the methods of measurement and frequencies of sampling and analysis of surface water intended for the abstraction of drinking water in the Member States (OJ L 271, 29.10.1979, p. 44), as amended by:

—   **381 L 0855:** Council Directive 81/855/EEC of 19 October 1981 (OJ No L 319, 7.11.1981, p. 16),

—   **1 85 I:** Act concerning the Conditions of Accession and Adjustments to the Treaties — Accession to the European Communities of the Kingdom of Spain and the Portuguese Republic (OJ No L 302, 15.11.1985, p. 219).

6)   **380 L 0068:** Council Directive 80/68/EEC of 17 December 1979 on the protection of groundwater against pollution caused by certain dangerous substances (OJ No L 20, 26.1.1980, p. 43).

The provisions of the Directive shall, for the purposes of the Agreement, be read with the following adaptation:

the provisions of Article 14 shall not apply.

7)   **380 L 0778:** Council Directive 80/778/EEC of 15 July 1980 relating to the quality of water intended for human consumption (OJ No L 229, 30.8.1980, p. 11), as amended by:

—   **381 L 0858:** Council Directive 81/858/EEC of 19 October 1981 (OJ No L 319, 7.11.1981, p. 19).

—   **1 85 I:** Act concerning the Conditions of Accession and Adjustments to the Treaties — Accession to the European Communities of the

Kingdom of Spain and the Portuguese Republic
(OJ No L 302, 15.11.1985, pp. 219, 397).

The provisions of the Directive shall, for the purposes of the Agreement, be read with the following adaptation:

the provisions of Article 20 shall not apply.

8) **382 L 0176:** Council Directive 82/176/EEC of 22 March 1982 on limit values and quality objectives for mercury discharges by the chlor-alkali electrolysis industry (OJ No L 81, 27.3.1982, p. 29).

The provisions of the Directive shall, for the purposes of the present Agreement, be read with the following adaptation:

Iceland shall put into effect the measures necessary for it to comply with the provisions of this Directive as from 1 January 1995.

9) **383 L 0513:** Council Directive 83/513/EEC of 26 September 1983 on limit values and quality objectives for cadmium discharges
(OJ No L 291, 24.10.1983, p. 1).

The provisions of the Directive shall, for the purposes of the Agreement, be read with the following adaptation:

Iceland shall put into effect the measures necessary for it to comply with the provisions of this Directive as from 1 January 1995.

10) **384 L 0156:** Council Directive 84/156/EEC of 8 March 1984 on limit values and quality objectives for mercury discharges by sectors other than the chlor-alkali electrolysis industry
(OJ No L 74, 17.3.1984, p. 49).

The provisions of the Directive shall, for the purposes of the Agreement, be read with the following adaptation:

Iceland shall put into effect the measures necessary for it to comply with the provisions of this Directive as from 1 January 1995.

11) **384 L 0491**: Council Directive 84/491/EEC of 9 October 1984 on limit values and quality objectives for discharges of hexachlorocyclohexane (OJ No L 274, 17.10.1984, p. 11).

The provisions of the Directive shall, for the purposes of the Agreement, be read with the following adaptation:

Iceland shall put into effect the measures necessary for it to comply with the provisions of this Directive as from 1 January 1995.

12) **386 L 0280:** Council Directive 86/280/EEC of 12 June 1986 on limit values and quality objectives for discharges of certain dangerous substances included in List I of the Annex to Directive 76/464/EEC
(OJ No L 181, 4.7.1986, p. 16), as amended by:

— **388 L 0347:** Council Directive 88/347/EEC of 16 June 1988 amending Annex II to Directive 86/280/EEC (OJ No L 158, 25.6.1988, p. 35),

— **390 L 0415:** Council Directive 90/415/EEC of 27 July 1990 amending Annex II to Directive 86/280/EEC (OJ No L 219, 14.8.1990, p. 49).

The provisions of the Directive shall, for the purposes of the Agreement, be read with the following adaptation:

Iceland shall put into effect the measures necessary for it to comply with the provisions of this Directive as from 1 January 1995.

13) **391 L 0271:** Council Directive 91/271/EEC of 21 May 1991 concerning urban waste water treatment (OJ No L 135, 30.5.1991, p. 40).

The provisions of the Directive shall, for the purposes of the Agreement, be read with the following adaptation:

Iceland shall put into effect the measures necessary for it to comply with the provisions of this Directive as from 1 January 1995.

III. **Air**

14) **380 L 0779:** Council Directive 80/779/EEC of 15 July 1980 on air quality limit values and guide values for sulphur dioxide and suspended particulates (OJ No L 229, 30.8.1980, p. 30), as amended by:

— **381 L 0857:** Council Directive 81/857/EEC of 19 October 1981 (OJ No L 319, 7.11.1981, p. 18),

— **1 85 I:** Act concerning the Conditions of Accession and Adjustments to the Treaties — Accession to the European Communities of the Kingdom of Spain and the Portuguese Republic (OJ No L 302, 15.11.1985, p. 219),

— **389 L 0427:** Council Directive 89/427/EEC of 21 June 1989 (OJ No L 201, 14.7.1989, p. 53).

The provisions of the Directive shall, for the purposes of the Agreement, be read with the following adaptation:

Iceland shall put into effect the measures necessary for it to comply with the provisions of this Directive as from 1 January 1995.

15) **382 L 0884:** Council Directive 82/884/EEC of 3 December 1982 on a limit value for lead in the air (OJ No L 378, 31.12.1982, p. 15).

The provisions of the Directive shall, for the purposes of the Agreement, be read with the following adaptation:

Iceland shall put into effect the measures necessary for it to comply with the provisions of this Directive as from 1 January 1995.

16) **384 L 0360:** Council Directive 84/360/EEC of 28 June 1984 on the combating of air pollution from industrial plants (OJ No L 188, 16.7.1984, p. 20).

The provisions of the Directive shall, for the purposes of the Agreement, be read with the following adaptation:

Iceland shall put into effect the measures necessary for it to comply with the provisions of this Directive as from 1 January 1995.

17) **385 L 0203:** Council Directive 85/203/EEC of 7 March 1985 on air-quality standards for nitrogen dioxide (OJ No L 87, 27.3.1985, p. 1), as amended by:

—   **385 L 0580:** Council Directive 85/580/EEC of 20 December 1985 (OJ No L 372, 31.12.1985, p. 36).

The provisions of the Directive shall, for the purposes of the Agreement, be read with the following adaptation:

Iceland shall put into effect the measures necessary for it to comply with the provisions of this Directive as from 1 January 1995.

18) **387 L 0217:** Council Directive 87/217/EEC of 19 March 1987 on the prevention and reduction of environmental pollution by asbestos (OJ No L 85, 28.3.1987, p. 40).

The provisions of the Directive shall, for the purposes of the Agreement, be read with the following adaptations:

a) in Article 9 'the Treaty' shall read 'the EEA Agreement';

b) Iceland shall put into effect the measures necessary for it to comply with the provisions of this Directive as from 1 January 1995.

19) **388 L 0609:** Council Directive 88/609/EEC of 24 November 1988 on the limitation of emissions of certain pollutants into the air from large combustion plants (OJ No L 336, 7.12.1988, p. 1).

The provisions of the Directive shall, for the purposes of the Agreement, be read with the following adaptations:

a) Article 3(5) shall be replaced by the following:

' 5 (a) If a substantial and unexpected change in energy demand or in the availability of certain fuels or certain generating installations creates serious technical difficulties for the implementation by a Contracting Party of the emission ceilings, such a Contracting Party may request a modification of the emission ceilings and/or dates set out in Annexes I and II. The procedure set out in (b) shall apply.

(b) The Contracting Party shall immediately inform the other Contracting Parties through the EEA Joint Committee of such action and give reasons for its decision. If a Contracting Party so requires, consultations on the appropriateness of the measures taken shall take place in the EEA Joint Committee. Part VII of the Agreement shall apply.';

b) the following shall be added to the table for ceilings and reduction targets in Annex I:

	0	1	2	3	4	5	6	7	8	9
Austria	171	102	68	51	-40	-60	-70	-40	-60	-70
Finland	90	54	36	27	-40	-60	-70	-40	-60	-70
Sweden	112	67	45	34	-40	-60	-70	-40	60	-70
Switzerland	28	14	14	14	-50	-50	-50	-50	-50	-50

';

c) the following is added to the table for ceilings and reduction targets in Annex II:

	0	1	2	3	4	5	6
Austria	81	65	48	-20	-40	-20	-40
Finland	19	15	11	-20	-40	-20	-40
Sweden	31	25	19	-20	-40	-20	-40
Switzerland	9	8	5	-10	-40	-10	-40

';

d) at the time of entry into force of the Agreement, Iceland, Liechtenstein and Norway do not have any large combustion plants as defined in Article 1. These States will comply with the Directive if and when they acquire such plants.

20) **389 L 0369:** Council Directive 89/369/EEC of 8 June 1989 on the prevention of air pollution from new municipal waste-incineration plants (OJ No L 163, 14.6.1989, p. 32).

The provisions of the Directive shall, for the purposes of the Agreement, be read with the following adaptation:

Iceland shall put into effect the measures necessary for it to comply with the provisions of this Directive as from 1 January 1995.

21)   **389 L 0429:** Council Directive 89/429/EEC of 21 June 1989 on the reduction of air pollution from existing municipal waste-incineration plants (OJ No L 203, 15.7.1989, p. 50).

IV.   Chemicals, industrial risk and biotechnology

22)   **376 L 0403:** Council Directive 76/403/EEC of 6 April 1976 on the disposal of polychlorinated biphenyls and polychlorinated terphenyls (OJ No L 108, 26.4.1976, p. 41).

The provisions of the Directive shall, for the purposes of the Agreement, be read with the following adaptation:

The EFTA States shall put into effect the measures necessary for them to comply with the provisions of this Directive as from 1 January 1995, subject to a review before that date.

23)   **382 L 0501:** Council Directive 82/501/EEC of 24 June 1982 on the major accident hazards of certain industrial activities (OJ No L 230, 5.8.1982, p. 1), as amended by:

—   **1 85 I:** Act concerning the Conditions of Accession and Adjustments to the Treaties — Accession to the European Communities of the Kingdom of Spain and the Portuguese Republic (OJ No L 302, 15.11.1985, p. 219),

—   **387 L 0216:** Council Directive 87/216/EEC of 19 March 1987 (OJ No L 85, 28.3.1987, p. 36),

—   **388 L 0610**: Council Directive 88/610/EEC of 24 November 1988 (OJ No L 336, 7.12.1988, p. 14).

24)   **390 L 0219:** Council Directive 90/219/EEC of 23 April 1990 on the contained use of genetically modified micro-organisms (OJ No L 117, 8.5.1990, p. 1).

The provisions of the Directive shall, for the purposes of the Agreement, be read with the following adaptation:

Austria, Finland, Iceland, Liechtenstein, Norway and Sweden shall put into effect the measures necessary for them to comply with the provisions of this Directive as from 1 January 1995.

25)   **390 L 0220:** Council Directive 90/220/EEC of 23 April 1990 on the deliberate release into the environment of genetically modified organisms (OJ No L 117, 8.5.1990, p. 15).

The provisions of the Directive shall, for the purposes of the present Agreement, be read with the following adaptations:

a) Austria, Finland, Iceland, Liechtenstein, Norway and Sweden shall put into effect the measures necessary for them to comply with the provisions of this Directive as from 1 January 1995;

b) Article 16 shall be replaced by the following:

' 1. Where a Contracting Party has justifiable reasons to consider that a product which has been properly notified and has received written consent under this Directive constitutes a risk to human health or the environment, it may restrict or prohibit the use and/or sale of that product on its territory. It shall immediately inform the other Contracting Parties through the EEA Joint Committee of such action and give reasons for its decision.

2. If a Contracting Party so requires, consultations on the appropriateness of the measures taken shall take place in the EEA Joint Committee. Part VII of the Agreement shall apply.';

c) The Contracting Parties agree that the Directive only covers aspects relating to the potential risks to humans, plants, animals and the environment.

The EFTA States therefore reserve the right to apply their national legislation in this area in relation to other concerns than health and environment, in so far as it is compatible with this Agreement.

V.   Waste

26) **375 L 0439:** Council Directive 75/439/EEC of 16 June 1975 on the disposal of waste oils (OJ No L 194, 25.7.1975, p. 23), as amended by:

— **387 L 0101:** Council Directive 87/101/EEC of 22 December 1986 (OJ No L 42, 12.2.1987, p. 43).

27) **375 L 0442:** Council Directive 75/442/EEC of 15 July 1975 on waste (OJ No L 194, 25.7.1975, p. 39), as amended by:

— **391 L 0156:** Council Directive 91/156/EEC of 18 March 1991 (OJ No L 78, 26.3.1991, p. 32).

The provisions of the Directive shall, for the purposes of the Agreement, be read with the following adaptation:

Norway shall put into effect the measures necessary for it to comply with the provisions of this Directive as from 1 January 1995, subject to a review before that date.

28) **378 L 0176:** Council Directive 78/176/EEC of 20 February 1978 on waste from the titanium-dioxide industry (OJ No L 54, 25.2.1978, p. 19), as amended by:

— **382 L 0883:** Council Directive 82/883/EEC of 3 December 1982 on procedures for the surveillance and monitoring of environments concerned by waste from the titanium-dioxide industry
(OJ No L 378, 31.12.1982, p. 1),

— **383 L 0029:** Council Directive 83/29/EEC of 24 January 1983
(OJ No L 32, 3.2.1983, p. 28).

29) **378 L 0319:** Council Directive 78/319/EEC of 20 March 1978 on toxic and dangerous waste (OJ No L 84, 31.3.1978, p. 43), as amended by:

— **1 79 H:** Act concerning the Conditions of Accession and Adjustments to the Treaties — Accession to the European Communities of the Hellenic Republic (OJ No L 291, 19.11.1979, p. 111),

— **1 85 I:** Act concerning the Conditions of Accession and Adjustments to the Treaties — Accession to the European Communities of the Kingdom of Spain and the Portuguese Republic
(OJ No L 302, 15.11.1985, pp. 219, 397).

The provisions of the Directive shall, for the purposes of the Agreement, be read with the following adaptation:

the EFTA States shall put into effect the measures necessary for them to comply with the provisions of this Directive as from 1 January 1995, subject to a review before that date.

30) **382 L 0883:** Council Directive 82/883/EEC of 3 December 1982 on procedures for the surveillance and monitoring of environments concerned by waste from the titanium-dioxide industry
(OJ No L 378, 31.12.1982, p. 1), as amended by:

— **1 85 I:** Act concerning the Conditions of Accession and Adjustments to the Treaties — Accession to the European Communities of the Kingdom of Spain and the Portuguese Republic
(OJ No L 302, 15.11.1985, p. 219).

31) **384 L 0631:** Council Directive 84/631/EEC of 6 December 1984 on the supervision and control within the European Community of the transfrontier shipment of hazardous waste (OJ No L 326, 13.12.1984, p. 31), as amended by:

— **385 L 0469:** Commission Directive 85/469/EEC of 22 July 1985
(OJ No L 272, 12.10.1985, p. 1),

— **386 L 0121:** Council Directive 86/121/EEC of 8 April 1986
(OJ No L 100, 16.4.1986, p. 20),

— **386 L 0279:** Council Directive 86/279/EEC of 12 June 1986
(OJ No L 181, 4.7.1986, p. 13).

The provisions of the Directive shall, for the purposes of the Agreement, be read with the following adaptations:

the following shall be added to box 36 of Annex I:

'

ÍSLENSKA	duft	duftkennt	fast	lúmkennt	seigfl-jótandi	bunnfl-jótandi	vökvi	loftkennt
NORSK	pulver-formet	stov-formet	fast	pasta-formet	viskost (tyktfly-tende)	slam-formet	flytende	gass-formet
SUOMESKI	jauhe-mäinen	pöly-mäinen	kiinteä	tahna-mäinen	siirappi-mäinen	liete-mäinen	neste-mäinen	kaasu-mäinen
SVENSKA	pulver-formigt	stoft	fast	pastöst	visköst	slamfor-migt	flytande	gasfor-migt

•unnfljótandi

støvformetviskøstl

';

d) the following new entries shall be added to the last sentence of provision 6 of Annex III: 'AU for Austria, SF for Finland, IS for Iceland, LI for Liechtenstein, NO for Norway, SE for Sweden and CH for Switzerland.';

e) the EFTA States shall put into effect the measures necessary for them to comply with the provisions of this Directive as from 1 January 1995, subject to a review before that date.

32) **386 L 0278:** Council Directive 86/278/EEC of 12 June 1986 on the protection of the environment, and in particular of the soil, when sewage sludge is used in agriculture (OJ No L 181, 4.7.1986, p. 6).

ACTS OF WHICH THE CONTRACTING PARTIES SHALL TAKE NOTE

The Contracting Parties take note of the content of the following acts:

33) **375 X 0436:** Council Recommendation 75/436/Euratom, ECSC, EEC of 3 March 1975 regarding cost allocation by public authorities on environmental matters (OJ No L 194, 25.7.1975, p. 1).

34) **379 X 0003:** Council Recommendation 79/3/EEC of 19 December 1978 to the Member States regarding methods of evaluating the cost of pollution control to industry (OJ No L 5, 9.1.1979, p. 28).

35) **380 Y 0830(01):** Council Resolution of 15 July 1980 on transboundary air pollution by sulphur dioxide and suspended particulates (OJ No C 222, 30.8.1980, p. 1).

36) **389 Y 1026(01):** Council Resolution (89/C 273/01) of 16 October 1989 on guidelines to reduce technological and natural hazards (OJ No C 273, 26.10.1989, p. 1).

37) **390 Y 0518(01):** Council Resolution (90/C 122/02) of 7 May 1990 on waste policy (OJ No C 122, 18.5.1990, p. 2).

38) **SEC (89) 934 final:** Communication from the Commission to the Council and to Parliament of 18 September 1989. 'A Community strategy for waste management'.

COMMISSION DECISION 94/10/EC[1]
of 21 December 1993
on a standard summary form for the notification of a decision to award the Community eco-label

THE COMMISSION OF THE EUROPEAN COMMUNITIES,

Having regard to the Treaty establishing the European Community,

Having regard to Council Regulation (EEC) No 880/92 of 23 March 1992 on a Community eco-label award scheme[2], and in particular Article 10 (3) thereof,

Whereas Article 10 (3) of Regulation (EEC) No 880/92 provides that the decision to award an eco-label shall be made by the competent body of a Member State after assessment of the product; whereas it is further provided that such decision shall be notified to the Commission enclosing the full results of the said assessment together with a summary thereof;

Whereas a standard summary form should contribute to the transparency of the product assessment and award procedures;

Whereas the measures set out in this Decision are in accordance with the opinion of the Committee set up under Article 7 of Regulation (EEC) No 880/92,

HAS ADOPTED THIS DECISION:

---

[1] OJ No L 7, 11. 1. 1994, p. 17.
[2] OJ No L 99, 11. 4. 1992, p. 1.

Article 1

The standard summary form referred to in Article 10 (3) of Regulation (EEC) No 880/92 is hereby established, in the form set out in the Annex to this Decision.

Article 2

This Decision is addressed to the Member States.

Done at Brussels, 21 December 1993.

For the Commission

Yannis PALEOKRASSAS

Member of the Commission

ANNEX

Standard summary form to be completed by competent body for notification pursuant to Article 10 (3) or for information purposes in accordance with Article 10 (7) of Council Regulation (EEC) No 880/92

DATE OF SUBMISSION ☐☐☐

APPLICATION NUMBER[1] ☐

DECISION | APPROVE | REJECT | [2]

Objections from other competent bodies must reach the Commission by[3] ☐☐☐

39. DETAILS OF COMPETENT BODY

NAME AND FULL ADDRESS ....
....
....
TELEPHONE ....
FAX...
Contact person:..

40. DETAILS OF APPLICANT

NAME AND FULL ADDRESS ....
....
....
TELEPHONE ....
FAX...

❑ Manufacturer ❑ Importer ❑ Other (please specify)

Contact person:..
Location of plant(s): ....

41. DETAILS OF APPLICATION

❏ First application ❏ Renewal

— give Register number of original application[4] ☐

❏ Other (please specify - use a separate sheet if necessary) ....
....

42. PRODUCT DESCRIPTION

Product type: ....

Trade name(s): ....
....
....

43.   Which Commission/Council decision is applicable to this product?

           /   /CEE

44.   Does the product conform to Articles 1 and 4 of the Regulation?

Yes ❏   No ❏ → Application rejected

Have all the criteria laid down in the decision mentioned under 5 above been met?

Yes ❏   No ❏ → Application rejected

Has this product previously been rejected for the award of an eco-label?

No ❏   Yes ❏

— When? ☐☐☐

— By which competent body? ☐

— Register No[5] ☐

45.   This section need not to completed if the application is to be rejected.

Product assessment in accordance with Article 4 of the Regulation and the product group criteria as laid down in the decision mentioned under 6 above.

RESULTS OF PRODUCT ASSESSMENT[6]:

    Key criteria ....

    Best practice criteria (where relevant) ....

    Performance criteria (where relevant) ....

    Other criteria (where relevant) ....

CERTIFICATION / TESTING ORGANISATION:

    Name of person responsible: ....

    Name of organisation: ....

    Address of organisation: ....

Notes

[1]	Number allocated by competent body that appears on the application form for the use of the eco-label.
[2]	Delete whichever does not apply.
[3]	Deadline is 30 days after date of submission of standard summary form to Commission.
[4]	Number entered Register of successful applications.
[5]	Number entered in Register of unsuccessful applications.
[6]	Please use extra sheets if necessary.

Completed form should be submitted to the

Commission of the European Communities
Directorate-General XI/A/2
TRMF 4/111
rue de la Loi 200
B-1049 BRUXELLES
Tel.: (32 2) 299 03 85 — Fax: (32 2) 299 0313

For Commission use only

Date of receipt   [| |]

Noted in Register under No   [   ]

Copied | BE | DA | DE | EL | ES | FR | IR | IT | LU | NL | PT | UK |

Date   [| |]

COMMISSION DECISION 94/90/ECSC, EC, Euratom[1]
of 8 February 1994
on public access to Commission documents

THE COMMISSION OF THE EUROPEAN COMMUNITIES,

Having regard to the Treaties establishing the European Communities, and in particular Article 162 of the Treaty establishing the European Community,

Whereas, in accordance with the Declaration on the right of access to information annexed to the Final Act of the Treaty on European Union and with the conclusions of the Birmingham and Edinburgh European Councils on bringing the Community closer to its citizens, a code of conduct setting out the principles governing access to Commission and Council documents should be agreed upon with the Council;

Whereas these principles are based on the Commission's papers on public access to the institutions' documents of 5 May 1993 and openness in the Community of 2 June 1993;

Whereas specific provisions need to be adopted whereby the Commission can give effect to the code,

HAS DECIDED AS FOLLOWS:

Article 1

The code of conduct on public access to Commission documents set out in the Annex is adopted.

Article 2

In order to ensure that effect is given to the code referred to in Article 1, the following measures are adopted:

1)   All applications for access to documents shall be made in writing to the relevant Commission department at its headquarters, Commission Offices in the Member States or Commission Delegations in non-member countries.

---

[1]   OJ No L 46, 18. 2. 1994, p. 58.

2)   The relevant Director-General or Head of Department, the Director designated for the purpose in the Secretariat-General or an official acting on their behalf shall inform the applicant in writing, within one month, whether the application is granted or whether he intends to refuse access. In the latter case the applicant shall also be notified that he has one month in which to apply to the Secretary-General of the Commission for review of the intention to refuse access, failing which he shall be deemed to have withdrawn his initial application.

3)   The President shall be empowered to decide on applications for review in agreement with the relevant Member of the Commission. He may delegate this authority to the Secretary-General.

4)   Failure to reply to an application for access to a document within one month of application being made constitutes an intention to refuse access.

       Failure to reply within one month of an application for review being made constitutes a refusal.

5)   A fee of ECU 10, plus ECU 0.036 per sheet of paper, shall be charged for copies of printed documents exceeding 30 pages. Charges for information in other formats shall be set on a case-by-case basis but shall not exceed what is reasonable.

6)   If an applicant wishes to consult a document on Commission premises, the relevant department shall try to make arrangements to accommodate him. Where the department is unable to provide appropriate facilities, the documents shall be consulted in either of the Commission's central libraries in Brussels and Luxembourg in any of the Commission's Offices in the Member States or in any of its Delegations in non-member countries.

Article 3

This Decision will take effect from 15 February 1994. It will be published in the *Official Journal of the European Communities*.

Done at Brussels, 8 February 1994.

For the Commission

João PINHEIRO

Member of the Commission

ANNEX

Code of conduct concerning public access to Commission and Council documents

THE COMMISSION AND THE COUNCIL,

Having regard to the declaration on the right of access to information annexed to the final act of the Treaty on European Union, which emphasizes that transparency of the decision-making process strengthens the democratic nature of the institutions and the public's confidence in the administration,

Having regard to the conclusions wherein the European Councils in Birmingham and Edinburgh agreed on a number of principles to promote a Community closer to its citizens,

Having regard to the conclusions of the European Council in Copenhagen, reaffirming the principle of giving citizens the greatest possible access to information and calling on the Commission and the Council to adopt at an early date the necessary measures for putting this principle into practice,

Considering it desirable to establish by common agreement the principles which will govern access to Commission and Council documents, it being understood that it is for each of them to implement these principles by means of specific regulations,

Whereas the said principles are without prejudice to the relevant provisions on access to files directly concerning persons with a specific interest in them;

Whereas these principles will have to be implemented in full compliance with the provisions concerning classified information;

Whereas this code of conduct is an additional element in their information and communication policy,

HAVE AGREED AS FOLLOWS:

General principle

The public will have the widest possible access to documents held by the Commission and the Council.

'Document' means any written text, whatever its medium, which contains existing data and is held by the Commission or the Council.

Processing of initial applications

An application for access to a document will have to be made in writing, in a sufficiently precise manner; it will have to contain information that will enable the document or documents concerned to be identified.

Where necessary, the institution concerned will ask the applicant for further details.

Where the document held by an institution was written by a natural or legal person, a Member State, another Community institution or body of any other national or international body, the application must be sent direct to the author.

In consultation with the applicants, the institution concerned will find a fair solution to comply with repeat applications and/or those which relate to very large documents.

The applicant will have access to documents either by consulting them on the spot or by having a copy sent at his own expense; the fee will not exceed a reasonable sum.

The institution concerned will be able to stipulate that a person to whom a document is released will not be allowed to reproduce or circulate the said document for commercial purposes through direct sale without its prior authorization.

Within one month the relevant departments of the institution concerned will inform the applicant either that his application has been approved or that they intend to advise the institution to reject it.

Processing of confirmatory applications

Where the relevant departments of the institution concerned intend to advise the institution to reject an application, they will inform the applicant thereof and tell him that he has one month to make a confirmatory application to the institution for that position to be reconsidered, failing which he will be deemed to have withdrawn his original application.

If a confirmatory application is submitted, and if the institution concerned decides to refuse to release the document, that decision, which must be made within a month of submission of the confirmatory application, will be notified in writing to the applicant as soon as possible. The grounds for the decision must be given, and the decision must indicate the means of redress that are available, i.e. judicial proceedings and complaints to the ombudsman under the conditions specified in, respectively, Articles 173 and 138c of the Treaty establishing the European Community.

Exceptions

The institutions will refuse access to any document where disclosure could undermine:

— the protection of the public interest (public security), international relations, monetary stability, court proceedings, inspections and investigations),

— the protection of the individual and of privacy,

— the protection of commercial and industrial secrecy,

— the protection of the Community's financial interests,

— the protection of confidentiality as requested by the natural or legal persons that supplied the information or as required by the legislation of the Member State that supplied the information.

They may also refuse access in order to protect the institution's interest in the confidentiality of its proceedings.

Implementation

The Commission and the Council will severally take steps to implement these principles before 1 January 1994.

Review

The Council and the Commission agree that the code of conduct will, after two years of operation, be reviewed on the basis of reports drawn up by the Secretaries-General of the Council and the Commission.

COUNCIL REGULATION (EC) No 1164/94[1]
of 16 May 1994
establishing a Cohesion Fund

THE COUNCIL OF THE EUROPEAN UNION,

Having regard to the Treaty establishing the European Economic Community, and in particular the second subparagraph of Article 130d thereof,

Having regard to the proposal from the Commission[2],

Having regard to the assent of the European Parliament[3],

Having regard to the opinion of the Economic and Social Committee[4],

Having regard to the opinion of the Committee of the Regions[5],

Whereas Article 2 of the Treaty includes the task of promoting economic and social cohesion and solidarity among Member States as objectives essential to the Community's development and success; whereas the strengthening of such cohesion is referred to in point (j) of Article 3 of the Treaty as one of the activities of the Community for the purposes set out in Article 2 of the Treaty;

Whereas Article 130a of the Treaty provides for the Community to develop and pursue its actions leading to the strengthening of its economic and social cohesion, and provides in particular that it shall aim at reducing disparities between the levels of development of the various regions and the backwardness of the least-favoured regions; whereas Community action through the Cohesion Fund should support the achievement of the objectives set out in Article 130a;

Whereas the conclusions of the European Councils held in Lisbon on 26 and 27 June 1992 and in Edinburgh on 11 and 12 December 1992 concerning the establishment of the Cohesion Fund set out the principles governing it;

Whereas the promotion of economic and social cohesion requires action by the Cohesion Fund in addition to that taken through the Structural Funds, the European Investment Bank and the other financial instruments in the fields of the environment and transport infrastructure of common interest;

---

[1] OJ No L 130, 25. 5. 1994, p. 1.
[2] OJ No C 39, 9. 2. 1994, p. 6.
[3] Assent given on 5 May 1994 (not yet published in the Official Journal).
[4] OJ No C 133, 16. 5. 1994.
[5] Opinion delivered on 5 April 1994 (not yet published in the Official Journal).

Whereas the Protocol on economic and social cohesion annexed to the Treaty establishing the European Community reaffirms the Community's task of promoting economic and social cohesion and solidarity between Member States and specifies that a Cohesion Fund will provide a financial contribution to projects in the fields of the environment and transx-European networks in the Member States subject to two conditions: firstly that they have a per capita gross national product (GNP) of less than 90 % of the Community average and secondly that they have a programme leading to the fulfilment of the conditions of economic convergence as set out in Article 104c of the Treaty; whereas the relative prosperity of Member States is best assessed on the basis of per capita GNP, measured in purchasing power parities;

Whereas meeting the convergence criteria which are a precondition for moving to the third stage of economic and monetary union calls for a determined effort from the Member States concerned; whereas, in this context, all of the beneficiary Member States are to submit to the Council a convergence programme designed for that purpose and to avoid excessive government deficits;

Whereas the second subparagraph of Article 130d of the Treaty states that the Council is to set up a Cohesion Fund before 31 December 1993 to provide a financial contribution to projects in the fields of environment and trans-European networks in the area of transport infrastructure;

Whereas Article 129c (1) of the Treaty provides that the Community may contribute through the Cohesion Fund to the financing of specific projects in the Member States in the area of transport infrastructure, whilst taking into account the potential economic viability of the projects; whereas projects financed by the Fund should form part of trans-European network guidelines which have been adopted by the Council including those covered by the plans for trans-European networks approved by the Council or proposed by the Commission before the entry into force of the Treaty on European Union; whereas, however, other transport infrastructure projects contributing to the attainment of the objectives of Article 129b of the Treaty may be financed until the Council has adopted the appropriate guidelines;

Whereas Article 130r of the Treaty defines the objectives and principles of the Community in the field of the environment; whereas the Community may contribute, through the Cohesion Fund, to actions designed to achieve those objectives; whereas, in accordance with Article 130s (5) of the Treaty and without prejudice to the principle that the polluter should pay, the Council may decide on financial assistance from the Cohesion Fund where a measure based on paragraph 1 of that Article involves costs deemed disproportionate for the public authorities of a Member State;

Whereas the principles and objectives of sustainable development are established in the Community's programme of policy and action in relation to the environment and sustainable development as set out in the Council Resolution of 1 February 1993[1];

Whereas a suitable balance must be struck between financing for transport infrastructure projects and financing for environmental projects;

Whereas the Commission's Green Paper on the Impact of Transport on the Environment reiterates the need to develop a more environment-friendly transport system which takes into account the sustainable development needs of the Member States;

Whereas any calculation of the cost of transport infrastructure projects must encompass environmental costs;

Whereas, in the light of the undertaking by the Member States concerned not to decrease their investment efforts in the fields of environmental protection and transport infrastructure, the principle of additionality within the meaning of Article 9 of Council Regulation (EEC) No 4253/88 of 19 December 1988 laying down provisions for implementing Regulation (EEC) No 2052/88 as regards coordination of the activities of the different Structural Funds between themselves and with the operations of the European Investment Bank and the other existing financial instruments[2] will not apply to the Cohesion Fund;

Whereas, in accordance with Article 198e of the Treaty, the European Investment Bank (EIB) is to facilitate the financing of investments in conjunction with assistance from the other Community financial instruments;

Whereas it is necessary to coordinate action taken in the fields of the environment and of trans-European transport infrastructure networks through the Cohesion Fund, the Structural Funds, the EIB and the other financial instruments in order to enhance the effectiveness of Community assistance;

Whereas with a view, in particular, to helping Member States in the preparation of their projects, the Commission should be in a position to ensure that the necessary technical support is available to them, particularly in order to contribute to the preparation, implementation, monitoring and evaluation of projects;

---

[1] OJ No C 138, 17. 5. 1993, p. 1.
[2] OJ No L 374, 31. 12. 1988, p. 1. Regulation as amended by Regulation (EEC) No 2082/93 (OJ No L 193, 31. 7. 1993, p. 20).

Whereas, particularly in order to ensure value for money, a thorough appraisal should precede the commitment of Community resources in order to ensure that they yield socio-economic benefits in keeping with the resources deployed;

Whereas assistance from the Cohesion Fund must be consistent with Community policies, including environmental protection, transport, trans-European networks, competition and the award of public contracts; whereas environmental protection includes the assessment of environmental impact;

Whereas there should be provision for an indicative allocation of the global resources available for commitment between the Member States in order to facilitate the preparation of projects;

Whereas provision should be made, in conjunction with Article 104c (6) of the Treaty, for a form of conditionality in the granting of financial assistance;

Whereas it is necessary, given the requirements of economic and social cohesion, to provide a high rate of assistance;

Whereas, in order to facilitate the management of assistance from the Fund, there should be provision for identifying the stages of projects which may be be considered technically and financially separate and for grouping the projects together, if necessary;

Whereas it should be possible to opt for assistance from the Fund either by annual instalments or for the whole of the project; and whereas, in accordance with the principle laid down by the European Council meeting at Edinburgh on 11 and 12 December 1992, payment instalments following an initial advance should be closely and transparently linked with progress towards the completion of projects;

Whereas the respective powers and responsibilities of the Member States and the Commission concerning financial control over the Fund's operations should be specified;

Whereas, in the interests of the proper management of the Cohesion Fund, provision should be made for effective methods of evaluating, monitoring and checking Community operations, specifying the principles governing the evaluation, defining the nature of and the rules governing the monitoring, and laying down the action to be taken in response to irregularities or failure to comply with one of the conditions laid down when assistance from that Fund was approved;

Whereas adequate information should be provided, inter alia, in the form of an annual report;

Whereas provision should be made to give adequate publicity to Community assistance from the Cohesion Fund;

Whereas publication in the *Official Journal of the European Communities* of calls for public tenders concerning projects receiving assistance from the Fund should mention the assistance;

Whereas in order to facilitate the application of this Regulation, the implementing provisions should be defined in Annex II; whereas to ensure the necessary flexibility in their application, the Council, acting by a qualified majority on a proposal from the Commission, should be able, if necessary, in the light of experience gained, to amend those provisions;

Whereas this Regulation should, without interruption, replace Council Regulation (EEC) No 792/93 of 30 March 1993 establishing a cohesion financial instrument[1],

HAS ADOPTED THIS REGULATION:

Article 1   Definition and objective

1. A Cohesion Fund, hereinafter referred to as 'the Fund', is hereby established.

2. The Fund shall contribute to the strengthening of the economic and social cohesion of the Community and shall operate according to the provisions set out in this Regulation.

3. The Fund may contribute to the financing of:

— projects, or

— stages of a project which are technically and financially independent, or

— groups of projects linked to a visible strategy which form a coherent whole.

Article 2   Scope

1. The Fund shall provide financial contributions to projects, which contribute to achieving the objectives laid down in the Treaty on European Union, in the fields of the environment and trans-European transport infrastructure networks in Member States with a per capita gross national product (GNP),

---

[1]   OJ No L 79, 1. 4. 1993, p. 74.

measured in purchasing power parities, of less than 90 % of the Community average which have a programme leading to the fulfilment of the conditions of economic convergence referred to in Article 104c of the Treaty.

2.   Until the end of 1999, only the four Member States which currently meet the criterion regarding per capita GNP referred to in paragraph 1 shall be eligible for assistance from the Fund. Those Member States are Greece, Spain, Ireland and Portugal.

3.   With regard to the GNP criterion referred to in paragraph 1, the Member States referred to in paragraph 2 shall continue to be eligible for assistance from the Fund provided that, after a mid-term review in 1996, their GNP remains below 90 % of the Community average. Any eligible Member State whose GNP exceeds the 90 % threshold at that time shall lose its entitlement to assistance from the Fund for new projects or, in the case of important projects split into several technically and financially separate stages, for new stages of a project.

Article 3   *Eligible measures*

1.   The Fund may provide assistance for the following:

—   environmental projects contributing to the achievement of the objectives of Article 130r of the Treaty, including projects resulting from measures adopted pursuant to Article 130s of the Treaty and, in particular, projects in line with the priorities conferred on Community environmental policy by the Fifth Programme of Policy and Action in relation to the Environment and Sustainable Development,

—   transport infrastructure projects of common interest, financed by Member States, which are identified within the framework of the guidelines referred to in Article 129c of the Treaty; however, other transport infrastructure projects contributing to the achievement of the objectives of Article 129b of the Treaty may be financed until appropriate guidelines have been adopted by the Council.

2.   Assistance may also be granted for:

—   preliminary studies related to eligible projects, including those necessary for their implementation,

—   technical support measures, particularly:

a)   horizontal measures such as comparative studies to assess the impact of Community assistance;

b) measures and studies which contribute to the appraisal, monitoring or evaluation, of projects, and to strengthening and ensuring the coordination and consistency of projects, particularly their consistency with other Community policies;

c) measures and studies helping to make the necessary adjustments to the implementation of projects.

Article 4   Financial resources

For the period 1993 to 1999, the total resources available for commitment for the Fund under this Regulation and Regulation (EEC) No 792/93, as set out in the Interinstitutional Agreement of 29 October 1993, shall be ECU 15 150 million at 1992 prices.

The financial perspectives established with regard to the commitment appropriations available for each year of the period under the Regulations referred to in the first paragraph are as follows:

- 1993: ECU 1 500 million,

- 1994: ECU 1 750 million,

- 1995: ECU 2 000 million,

- 1996: ECU 2 250 million,

- 1997: ECU 2 500 million,

- 1998: ECU 2 550 million,

- 1999: ECU 2 600 million.

Article 5   Indicative allocation

An indicative allocation of the total resources of the Fund shall be made on the basis of precise and objective criteria, principally population, per capita GNP and surface area; it shall also take account of other socio-economic factors such as deficiencies in transport infrastructure.

The indicative allocation of the total resources resulting from the application of those criteria is set out in Annex I.

Article 6   Conditional assistance

1.   In the event of the Council deciding, in accordance with Article 104c (6) of the Treaty, that an excessive government deficit exists in a

Member State, and if that decision is not abrogated in accordance with Article 104c (12) of the Treaty within one year or any other period specified for correcting the deficit in a recommendation under Article 104c (7), no new projects or, in the case of large multi-stage projects, no new stages of a project shall be financed from the Fund for that Member State.

2.   Exceptionally, in the case of projects directly affecting more than one Member State, the Council, acting by a qualified majority on a recommendation from the Commission, may decide to defer suspension of financing.

3.   Suspension of financing shall not take effect less than two years after the entry into force of the Treaty on European Union.

4.   The suspension of financing shall cease when the Council, in accordance with Article 104c (12) of the Treaty, abrogates its decision adopted in accordance with Article 104c (6) of the Treaty.

Article 7   *Rate of assistance*

1.   The rate of Community assistance granted by the Fund shall be 80 % to 85 % of public or equivalent expenditure, including expenditure by bodies whose activities are undertaken within an administrative or legal framework by virtue of which they may be deemed to be equivalent to public bodies.

The actual rate of assistance shall be fixed according to the type of operation to be carried out.

2.   Where assistance is granted for a project which generates revenue, the amount of the expenditure on which the calculation of the assistance from the Fund is based shall be established by the Commission, taking account of revenue where it constitutes substantial net revenue for the promoters and in close collaboration with the beneficiary Member State.

'Project which generates revenue' means:

—   infrastructures the use of which involves fees borne directly by users,

—   productive investments in the environment sector.

3.   The beneficiary Member States may submit proposals for preparatory studies and technical support measures.

4.   Preliminary studies and technical support measures, including those undertaken at the Commission's initiative, may be financed exceptionally at 100 % of the total cost.

Total expenditure carried out pursuant to this paragraph may not exceed 0,5 % of the total allocation to the Fund.

Article 8 Coordination and compatibility with Community policies

1.   Projects financed by the Fund shall be in keeping with the provisions of the Treaties, with the instruments adopted pursuant thereto and with Community policies, including those concerning environmental protection, transport, trans-European networks, competition and the award of public contracts.

2.   The Commission shall ensure coordination and consistency between projects undertaken pursuant to this Regulation and measures undertaken with contributions from the Community budget, the European Investment Bank (EIB) and the other financial instruments of the Community.

Article 9 Cumulation and overlapping

1.   No item of expenditure may benefit both from the Fund and from the European Agricultural Guidance and Guarantee Fund, the European Social Fund, the European Regional Development Fund or the financial instrument of fisheries guidance.

2.   The combined assistance of the Fund and other Community aid for a project shall not exceed 90 % of the total expenditure relating to that project.

Article 10 Approval of projects

1.   The projects to be financed by the Fund shall be adopted by the Commission in agreement with the beneficiary Member State.

2.   A suitable balance shall be struck between projects in the field of the environment and projects relating to transport infrastructure. This balance shall take account of Article 130s (5) of the Treaty.

3.   Applications for assistance for projects under Article 3 (1) shall be submitted by the beneficiary Member State. Projects, including groups of related projects, shall be of a sufficient scale to have a significant impact in the field of environmental protection or in the improvement of trans-European transport infrastructure networks. In any event, the total cost of projects or groups of projects may in principle not be less than ECU 10 million. Projects or groups of projects costing less than this may be approved in duly justified cases.

4.   Applications shall contain the following information: the body responsible for implementation, the nature of the investment and a description
thereof, its costs and location, including, where applicable, an indication of
projects of common interest situated on the same transport axis, the timetable
for implementation of the work, a cost-benefit analysis, including the direct
and indirect effects on employment, information enabling possible impact on
the environment to be assessed, information on public contracts, the financing
plan including, where possible, information on the economic viability of the
project, and the total financing the Member State is seeking from the Fund and
any other Community source.

They shall also contain all relevant information providing the required proof
that the projects comply with the Regulation and with the criteria set out in paragraph 5, and particularly that there are medium-term economic and social
benefits commensurate with the resources deployed.

5.   The following criteria shall be applied to ensure the high quality of
projects:

—   their medium-term economic and social benefits, which shall be com-
       mensurate with the resources deployed; an assessment shall be made in
       the light of a cost-benefit analysis,

—   the priorities established by the beneficiary Member States,

—   the contribution which projects can make to the implementation of
       Community policies on the environment and trans-European networks,

—   the compatibility of projects with Community policies and their consist-
       ency with other Community structural measures,

—   the establishment of an appropriate balance between the fields of the
       environment and transport infrastructure.

6.   Subject to Article 6 and to the availability of commitment appropriations, the Commission shall decide on the grant of assistance from the Fund
provided that the requirements of this Article are fulfilled, as a general rule
within three months of receipt of the application. Commission decisions
approving projects, stages of projects or groups of related projects shall determine the amount of financial support and lay down a financing plan together
with all the provisions and conditions necessary for the implementation of the
projects.

7.   The key details of the Commission's decisions shall be published in the
Official Journal of the European Communities.

Article 11   Financial provisions

1.   The commitment appropriations entered in the budget shall be granted on the basis of the decisions approving the measures concerned, in accordance with Article 10.

2.   Assistance relating to the projects referred to in Article 3 (1) shall as a general rule be committed by annual instalments. However, in appropriate cases, the Commission may commit the total amount of the assistance granted when it adopts the decision granting the assistance.

3.   Expenditure within the meaning of Article 7 (1) shall not be deemed eligible for assistance from the Fund if incurred by the beneficiary Member State before the date on which the Commission receives the relevant application.

4.   Payments made after an initial advance must be closely and transparently linked to progress made in the implementation of the projects.

5.   Payments shall be made in ecus and shall be subject to the specific provisions set out in Annex II.

Article 12   Financial checks

1.   In order to guarantee successful completion of the projects financed by the Fund, Member States shall take the necessary measures:

—   to verify on a regular basis that operations financed by the Community have been properly carried out,

—   to prevent irregularities and take action against them,

—   to recover any amounts lost as a result of irregularity or negligence. Except where the Member State and/or the implementing authority provide proof that they were not responsible for the irregularity or negligence, the Member State shall be liable in the alternative for reimbursement of any sums unduly paid.

2.   Member States shall inform the Commission of the measures taken for those purposes and, in particular, shall notify the Commission of the description of the management and control systems established to ensure the efficient implementation of operations. They shall regularly inform the Commission of the progress of administrative and judicial proceedings. In that context, the Member States and the Commission shall take the necessary steps to ensure that the information exchanged remains confidential.

3.   Member States shall make available to the Commission any appropriate national control reports on the projects concerned.

4.   Without prejudice to checks carried out by Member States in accordance with national laws, regulations and administrative provisions and without prejudice to Article 188a of the Treaty or to any inspection arranged on the basis of Article 209 (c) of the Treaty, the Commission may, through its officials or agents, carry out on-the-spot checks, including sample checks, in respect of projects financed by the Fund, and may examine the control arrangements and measures established by the national authorities, which shall inform the Commission of measures taken to that end.

5.   As soon as this Regulation enters into force, the Commission shall adopt detailed rules for the application of this Article and shall inform the European Parliament thereof.

Article 13   Appraisal, monitoring and evaluation

1.   The Member States and the Commission shall ensure that the implementation of projects under this Regulation is effectively monitored and evaluated. Projects must be adjusted on the basis of the results of monitoring and evaluation.

2.   In order to ensure the effectiveness of Community assistance, the Commission and the beneficiary Member States shall, in cooperation with the EIB where appropriate, carry out a systematic appraisal and evaluation of projects.

3.   On receipt of a request for assistance and before approving a project, the Commission shall carry out a thorough appraisal in order to assess the project's consistency with the criteria laid down in Article 10 (5). The Commission shall invite the EIB to contribute to the assessment of projects as necessary.

4.   During the implementation of projects and after their completion, the Commission and the beneficiary Member States shall evaluate the manner in which they have been carried out and the potential and actual impact of their implementation in order to assess whether the original objectives can be, or have been, achieved. This evaluation shall, inter alia, address the environmental impact of the projects, in compliance with the existing Community rules.

5.   In vetting individual applications for assistance, the Commission shall take into account the findings of appraisals and evaluations made in accordance with this Article.

6.   The detailed rules for monitoring and evaluation, as provided for in paragraph 4, shall be laid down in the decisions approving projects.

Article 14   Information and publicity

1.   The Commission shall present an annual report on the activities of the Fund, for the purposes of examination and their opinion, to the European Parliament, the Council, the Economic and Social Committee and the Committee of the Regions.

The European Parliament shall deliver an opinion on the report as soon as possible. The Commission shall report on how it has applied the observations contained in the European Parliament's opinion.

The Commission shall ensure that Member States are informed of the activities of the Fund.

2.   The Member States responsible for implementing a measure receiving a financial contribution from the Fund shall ensure that adequate publicity is given to the measure with a view to:

—   making the general public aware of the role played by the Community in relation to the measure,

—   making potential beneficiaries and professional organizations aware of the possibilities afforded by the measure.

Member States shall ensure, in particular, that directly visible display panels are erected showing the percentage of the total cost of a given project which is being financed by the Community, together with the Community logo, and that representatives of the Community institutions are duly involved in the most important public activities connected with the Fund.

They shall inform the Commission of the initiatives taken under this paragraph.

3.   As soon as this Regulation enters into force, the Commission shall adopt detailed rules on information and publicity, shall inform the European Parliament thereof and shall publish them in the *Official Journal of the European Communities*.

Article 15   Implementation

The provisions for the implementation of this Regulation are set out in Annex II hereto.

Article 16   *Final and transitional provisions*

1.   The Council, acting on a proposal from the Commission in accordance with the procedure laid down in Article 130d of the Treaty, shall re-examine this Regulation before the end of 1999.

2.   As soon as it enters into force, this Regulation shall replace Regulation (EEC) No 792/93.

3.   This Regulation shall not affect the continuation of measures approved by the Commission on the basis of the provisions of Regulation (EEC) No 792/93 applicable before the entry into force of this Regulation, which shall consequently apply thereafter to those measures.

4.   Applications presented within the framework of Regulation (EEC) No 792/93 before the entry into force of this Regulation shall remain valid provided such applications are supplemented, where necessary, so as to comply with the requirements of this Regulation within not more than two months of the entry into force of this Regulation.

Article 17   *Entry into force*

This Regulation shall enter into force on the day following its publication in the *Official Journal of the European Communities*.

This Regulation shall be binding in its entirety and directly applicable in all Member States.

Done at Brussels, 16 May 1994.

For the Council

The President

Th. PANGALOS

ANNEX.I

INDICATIVE ALLOCATION OF THE TOTAL RESOURCES OF THE COHESION FUND AMONG THE BENEFICIARY MEMBER STATES

—	Spain:	52 % to 58 % of the total,
—	Greece:	16 % to 20 % of the total,
—	Portugal:	16 % to 20 % of the total,
—	Ireland:	7 % to 10 % of the total.

ANNEX II

IMPLEMENTING PROVISIONS

Article A   Designation of stages or groups of projects

1.   The Commission may, in agreement with the beneficiary Member State, group projects together and designate technically and financially separate stages of a project for the purpose of granting assistance.

2.   A stage may also cover preliminary, feasibility and technical studies needed for carrying out a project.

Article B   Ex-ante evaluation

1.   The Commission shall examine applications for assistance to verify in particular that the administrative and financial mechanisms are adequate for the effective implementation of the project.

2.   Pursuant to Article 13 (3), the Commission shall appraise projects to determine their anticipated impact in terms of the objectives of the Fund, quantified using appropriate indicators. The beneficiary Member States shall provide all necessary information, as set out in Article 10 (4), including the results of feasibility studies and ex-ante appraisals, to make this appraisal as effective as possible.

Article C   Commitments

1.   Budgetary commitments shall be made on the basis of the Commission decisions approving the measures concerned (project, stage of project, group of projects, study or technical support measure). Commitments shall be valid for a period determined by the nature of the measure and the specific conditions for its implementation.

2.   Budgetary commitments in respect of assistance granted to projects, stages of projects or groups of projects shall be carried out in one of two ways:

a)   commitments in respect of the projects referred to in Article 3 (1) to be carried out over a period of two or more years shall, as a general rule and subject to the provisions of subparagraph (b), be effected in annual instalments.

The commitments in respect of the first annual instalment shall be made when the decision granting Community assistance is adopted by the Commission. Commitments in respect of subsequent annual instalments shall be based on the initial or revised financing plan for the project and on the progress made in its implementation;

b) for projects to be carried out over a period of less than two years or where Community assistance is less than ECU 40 million, the total amount of assistance may be committed when the Commission adopts the decision to grant Community assistance.

3. In the case of the studies and technical support measures referred to in Article 3 (2), the assistance shall be committed when the Commission approves the measure concerned.

4. The arrangements for commitments shall be specified in the Commission decisions approving the measures concerned.

Article D   Payments

1. Payments of financial assistance shall be made in accordance with the corresponding budget commitments, to the authority or body designated for the purpose in the application submitted by the beneficiary Member State concerned. Payments may take the form either of advances or in intermediate payments or payments of balances in respect of expenditure actually incurred.

2. Where Community assistance is committed in accordance with Article C (2) (a), payments shall be made as follows:

a) an advance of up to 50 % of the amount of the first annual instalment committed shall be paid when the decision granting Community assistance is adopted;

b) intermediate payments may be paid provided that the project is progressing satisfactorily towards completion and that at least two-thirds of the expenditure relating to the previous payment have been made.

Subject to (c), each such payment may not exceed 50 % of the amount of each annual instalment committed;

c) the total amount of the payments made under (a) and (b) for all the instalments may not exceed 80 % of the total assistance granted. This percentage may be increased to 90 % for important projects and in justified cases;

d) the balance of Community assistance shall be paid provided that:

— the project, stage of the project, or group of projects, has been carried out according to its objectives;

— the designated authority or body referred to in paragraph 1 submits an application for payment to the Commission within six months of the physical completion of the project, stage of project or group of projects;

— the final report referred to in Article F (4) is submitted to the Commission;

— the Member State certifies to the Commission that the information given in the application for payment and in the report is correct.

3.   Where the commitment is made in accordance with Article C (2) (b), payment shall be made as follows:

a) the advance paid following the decision may be up to 50 % of the assistance relating to planned expenditure in the first year as shown in the financing plan approved by the Commission;

b) further intermediate payments may be made provided that the project is progressing satisfactorily towards completion and that at least two-thirds of the expenditure relating to the previous payment, and all expenditure relating to earlier payments, have been made.

Subject to subparagraph (c), each of those payments may amount to up to 50 % of the assistance relating to expenditure planned for the year in question, as shown in the initial or revised financing plan approved by the Commission;

c) the total amount of the payments referred to under subparagraphs (a) and (b) may not exceed 80 % of the total assistance granted;

d) the balance of Community assistance shall be paid provided that:

- the project, stage of the project, or group of projects, has been carried out according to its objectives;

- the designated authority or body referred to in paragraph 1 submits an application for payment to the Commission within six months of completion of the project, stage of project or group of projects;

- the final report referred to in Article F (4) is submitted to the Commission;

- the Member State certifies to the Commission that the information given in the application for payment and in the report is correct.

4.   Member States shall designate the authorities empowered to issue the certificates referred to in paragraphs 2 (d) and 3 (d).

5.   Payment shall be made to the authority or body designated by the Member State, as a general rule not later than two months after receipt of an admissible application for payment.

6.   In the case of the studies and other measures referred to in Article 3 (2), the Commission shall determine the appropriate payment procedures.

Article E   Use of the ecu

1.   Applications for assistance, together with the relevant financing plan, shall be submitted to the Commission in ecus or in national currency.

2.   The amounts of assistance and the financing plans approved by the Commission shall be expressed in ecus.

3.   Declarations of expenditure in support of the corresponding payment applications shall be expressed in ecus or in national currency.

4.   Payments of financial assistance by the Commission shall be made in ecus to the authority designated by the Member State to receive such payments.

Article F   Monitoring

1.   The Commission and the Member State shall ensure effective monitoring of implementation of Community projects part-financed by the Fund. Monitoring shall be carried out by way of jointly agreed reporting procedures, sample checks and the establishment of ad hoc committees.

2.   Monitoring shall be carried out by reference to physical and financial indicators. The indicators shall relate to the specific character of the project and its objectives. They shall be arranged in such a way as to show:

—   the stage reached in the receipt in relation to the plan and objectives originally laid down;

—   the progress achieved on the management side and any related problems.

3.   Monitoring committees shall be set up by arrangement between the Member State concerned and the Commission.

The authorities or bodies designated by the Member State, the Commission and, where appropriate, the EIB shall be represented on the committees.

Where regional and local authorities are competent for the execution of a project and, where appropriate, where they are directly concerned by a project they shall also be represented on such committees.

4. For each project, the authority or body designated for the purpose by the Member State shall submit progress reports to the Commission within three months of the end of each full year of implementation. A final report shall be submitted to the Commission within six months of completion of the project or stage of project.

5. On the basis of the results of monitoring, and taking account of the comments of the monitoring committee, the Commission shall adjust the amounts and conditions for granting assistance as initially approved, as well as the financing plan envisaged, if necessary on a proposal by the Member States.

6. For the greater effectiveness of the Fund, the Commission shall ensure that when the Fund is administered particular attention is paid to transparency of management.

7. The monitoring arrangements shall be laid down in the Commission decisions approving the projects.

Article G   Checks

1. Before carrying out an on-the-spot check, the Commission shall give notice to the Member State concerned with a view to obtaining all the assistance necessary. On-the-spot checks by the Commission without notice shall be subject to agreements reached in accordance with the Financial Regulation. Officials or agents of the Member State concerned may take part in checks.

The Commission may require the Member State concerned to carry out an on-the-spot check to verify the correctness of payment applications. Officials or agents of the Commission may take part in such checks, and must do so if the Member State concerned so requests.

The Commission shall ensure that any checks that it carries out are performed in a coordinated manner so as to avoid repeating checks in respect of the same subject matter during the same period. The Member State concerned and the Commission shall immediately exchange any relevant information concerning the results of the checks carried out.

2. The responsible body and authorities shall keep available for the Commission all the supporting documents regarding expenditure on any project for a period of three years following the last payment in respect of a project.

Article H   Reduction, suspension and cancellation of assistance

1.   If the implementation of a measure appears not to justify either a part, or the whole, of the assistance allocated, the Commission shall conduct an appropriate examination of the case, in particular requesting the Member State or authorities or bodies designated by it to implement the measure to submit their comments within a specified period of time.

2.   Following the examination referred to in paragraph 1, the Commission may reduce, suspend or cancel assistance in respect of the measures concerned if the examination reveals an irregularity or a failure to comply with one of the conditions in the decision to grant assistance, and in particular any significant change affecting the nature or conditions of implementation of the measure for which the Commission's approval has not been sought.

Any undue cumulation shall give rise to the recovery of sums unduly paid.

3.   Any sum to be recovered for want of due entitlement shall be repaid to the Commission. Interest on account of late repayment shall be charged in accordance with the rules to be adopted by the Commission.

Article I   Public contracts

In the context of the application of Community rules on the award of public contracts, notices sent for publication in the *Official Journal of the European Communities* shall specify those projects for which Community assistance has been applied for or granted.

Article J   Information

The information to be given in the annual report provided for in Article 14 shall be as set out in the Annex to this Annex.

The Commission shall be responsible for organizing an information meeting with the Member States every six months.

Article K   Review

If necessary, in the light of experience gained, the Council may, acting by a qualified majority on a proposal from the Commission and after consulting the European Parliament, amend the provisions of this Annex.

Annex to ANNEX II

The annual report shall provide information on the following:

1) financial assistance committed and paid by the Fund, with an annual breakdown by Member State and by type of project (environment or transport);

2) the economic and social impact of the Fund in the Member States and on economic and social cohesion in the Union;

3) summary of information on the programmes implemented in the beneficiary Member States to fulfil the conditions of economic convergence referred to in Article 104c of the Treaty and on the application of Article 6 of the Regulation;

4) information on the conclusions drawn by the Commission, with regard to the suspension of financing, from decisions taken by the Commission, such as those mentioned in Article 6 (1) and (2);

5) the contribution which the Fund has made to the efforts of the beneficiary Member States to implement Community environment policy and to strengthen trans-European transport infrastructure networks; the balance between projects in the field of the environment and projects relating to transport infrastructure;

6) assessment of the compatibility of operations of the Fund with Community policies, including those concerning environmental protection, transport, competition and the award of public contracts;

7) the measures taken to ensure coordination and consistency between projects financed by the Fund and measures financed with contributions from the Community budget, the European Investment Bank and the other financial instruments of the Community;

8) the investment efforts of the beneficiary Member States in the fields of environmental protection and transport infrastructure;

9) the preparatory studies and technical support measures financed, including a specification of the types of such studies and measures;

10) the results of appraisal, monitoring and evaluation of projects, including information on any adjustment of projects to accord with the results of appraisal, monitoring and evaluation;

11) the contribution of the EIB to the evaluation of projects;

12) summary of information on the results of checks carried out, irregularities found and administrative and judicial proceedings in progress.

Commission Communication 94/C 139/03[1]
in accordance with Council Regulation (EEC) No 1973/92 of 21 May 1992
establishing a financial instrument for the environment (LIFE), relating to priority actions to be implemented in 1995

I.   THE AIM OF LIFE - THE COMMUNITY FINANCIAL INSTRU-
       MENT FOR THE ENVIRONMENT

In accordance with Council Regulation (EEC) No 1973/92 of 21 May 1992 the principal objective of LIFE consists of:

— defining and promoting production models and behaviour consistent with the principles of sustainable development,

— demonstrating on a practical level the technical feasibility and economic effectiveness of the selected actions and models,

— supporting specific demonstration and pilot projects as well as horizontal information, education and training with the aim of exercising an influence on the economic actors by the implementation of practical examples,

— strenghtening of administrative structures.

II.   PRIORITY ACTIONS 1995

A.   ACTIONS IN THE COMMUNITY

1.   **Promotion of sustainable development and the quality of the environment**

Actions 1, 2, 3, 5 and 7 are priorities for 1995.

1) Establishing and development of new techniques and methods of measuring and monitoring the quality of the environment;

2) Establishing and development of new clean technologies, i.e. which create little or no pollution and make fewer demands on resources;

    The following three sectors are eligible: *the timber industry, the electronics industry, the paint, varnish and adhesive industry;*

---

[1] OJ No C 139, 21. 5. 1994, p. 3.

3) Devising and developing techniques for the collection, storage, recycling and disposal of waste, particularly toxic and dangerous waste and waste water;

4) Devising and developing techniques for locating and restoring sites contaminated by hazardous waste and/or hazardous substances: *Not a priority action in 1995*;

5) Establishment and development of models to integrate environmental factors into land-use planning and management, and socio-economic activities;

6) Reduction of discharges into the aquatic environment of nutritive substances and potentially bio-accumulative toxic, persistent pollutants: *Not a priority action in 1995*;

7) Improvement of the quality of environment in urban areas in both central and peripheral zones.

2.   Protection of habitats and nature

Actions 1, 2 and 3 are priorities for 1995.

1) Pursuant to Directive 79/409/EEC of 2 April 1979, to maintain or restore biotopes which are the habitat of endangered species or seriously threatened habitats which are of particular importance to the Community, or to implement measures to conserve or re-establish endangered species, with regard to:

a) conservation measures forming part of a programme drawn up or approved by the competent authorities and concerning special protection areas or areas recognized by Member States to be classified as such, providing a habitat for priority species or constituting sites of outstanding importance for abundant and diverse wild bird species or wetlands of international importance;

b) the drawing up of management plans or urgent actions relating to major special protection areas which overlap future special conservation areas under Council Directive 92/43/EEC and carried out under the responsibility or with the support of the competent authorities;

c) programmes drawn up or approved by the competent authorities and concerning the recovery of priority species.

2) To maintain or re-establish types of natural habitats of Community interest and the animal and plant species of Community interest listed in Annex I and Annex II respectively to Council Directive 92/43/EEC of 21 May 1992 on the conservation of natural habitats and of wild fauna and flora, with regard to:

   a) The establishment by the competent authorities of systems for the monitoring of NATURA 2000 sites and sites of importance to the Community and conditions which will make it possible to comply with the provisions of Article 6;

   b) The drawing up of management plants relating to future special conservation areas and carried out under the responsibility or with the support of the competent authorities;

   c) Emergency actions with immediate impact on future special conservation areas, forming part of a strategy drawn up or approved by the competent authorities, with the aim of halting the decline of priority natural habitats or priority species:

      - either by actions targeted at sites of strategic importance for these natural habitats or species,

      - or by programmes aimed at the regeneration or recovery of these habitats or species;

   d) Actions or initiatives conducted or supported jointly by two or more Member States aimed at:

      - the conservation or management of major ecosystems or groups of natural habitat types,

      - the conservation of the species listed in Annex IV.

3) To protect soil threatened or damaged by fire, desertification, coastal erosion or the disappearance of the dune belt.

4) To promote the conservation of marine life: *Not a priority action in 1995.*

5) To protect and conserve areas of fresh groundwater and fresh surface water: *Not a priority action in 1995.*

3.   Administrative structures and environment services

Action 1 is a priority for 1995.

1)   Actions to foster greater cooperation between the authorities of the Member States particularly with regard to the control of transboundary and global environmental problems.

2)   To equip, modernize or develop monitoring networks in the context of strengthening environmental legislation: *Not a priority action in 1995.*

4.   Education, training and information

Action 1 is a priority for 1995.

1)   Environmental training in administrative and professional circles.

2)   Environmental education, in particular through the provision of information, exchanges of experience, training and educational research: *Not a priority action in 1995.*

3)   To foster better understanding of problems and hence encourage behaviour models consistent with environmental objectives: *Not a priority action in 1995.*

4)   To disseminate knowledge concerning sound management of the environment: *Not a priority action in 1995.*

B.   ACTIONS OUTSIDE COMMUNITY TERRITORY

Action B.2 is a priority for 1995:

1)   To promote the establishment of the necessary administrative structures in the environmental field: *Not a priority action in 1995.*

2)   To provide the technical assistance needed for the establishment of environment policies and action programmes.

3)   To promote the transfer of appropriate environment-friendly technologies and to foster sustainable development: *Not a priority action in 1995.*

4)   To provide assistance to third countries faced with ecological emergencies: *Not a priority action in 1995.*

III. ARRANGEMENTS FOR PRESENTING A REQUEST FOR FINANCIAL SUPPORT FROM LIFE

Proposals should be submitted to the appropriate national administration, in six copies, by the date fixed and announced by each Member State. The list of addresses is attached. The national administration in question is responsible for transmitting to the Commission any proposals deemed eligible for LIFE in triplicate.

An information brochure will be available at the appropriate time from the offices in the attached list or from the Commission at the following address:

European Commission
Directorate-General XI
Environment, Nuclear Safety and Civil Protection
Unit XI-C-2
5, avenue de Beaulieu
B-1160 Brussels
Fax: No: (32-2) 296 95 61

ANNEX

COMPETENT NATIONAL AUTHORITIES FOR LIFE

Member State	Priority actions	
	All actions except 2.1 and 2.2	Nature protection actions 2.1 and 2.2
Belgique / België (B)	Ministère de la santé publique et de l'environnement, direction de l'environnement (LIFE), Quartier Vésale 2/3, Cité administrative de l'Etat, B-1010 Bruxelles Ministerie van Volksgezondheid en Leefmilieu, Directie Leefmilieu (LIFE), Vesaliusgebouw 2/3, Rijksadministratie Centrum, B-1010 Brussel	
Deutschland (D)	Landesumweltministerien (see List)	
Danmark (DK)	Miljøstyrelsen (LIFE), Strangade 29, DK-1401 København K	Skov- og Naturstyrelsen (LIFE), Haraldsgade 53, DK-2100 København Ø
España (E)	Secretaria de Estado para la política del agua y del medio ambiente (LIFE), Ministerio de Obras Públicas y Transportes, Paseo de la Castellana, 67, E-28046 Madrid	ICONA, Subdirección General de Espacio Naturales (LIFE), Gran Via de San Francisco, 35, E-28005 Madrid
France (F)	Ministère de l'environnement (LIFE), 20, avenue de Ségur, F-75302 Paris 07 SP	
Ellas (GR)	Ministry of Environment, Physical Planning and Public Works (LIFE), Patission, 147, GR-11251 Athens	
Ireland (IRL)	Environmental Control Section (LIFE), Department of the Environment, Custom House, IRL-Dublin 1	National Parks and Wildlife Service (LIFE), Office of Public Works, 51 St Stephen's Green, IRL-Dublin 2
Italia (I)	Ministerio dell'ambiente - Gabinetto del ministro (LIFE), Piazza Venezia, 11, I-00187 Roma	
Luxembourg (L)	Ministère de l'environnement (LIFE), 18, Montée de la Pétrusse, L - 2918 Luxembourg	
Nederland (NL)	Ministerie van Volkshisvesting, ruimtelijke Ordening en Milieubeheer, Directie bestuurszaken, Afdeling milieutechnologie (LIFE), Rijnstraat 8 - Postbus 30945, NL-2500 GX Den Haag	Ministerie van Landbouw, Natuurbeheer en Visserij, Directie natuur, bos, landschap en fauna, Hoofdsector natuur (LIFE) - Postbus 20401, NL-2500 EK Den Haag

Member State	Priority actions	
	All actions except 2.1 and 2.2	Nature protection actions 2.1 and 2.2
Portugal (P)	Ministério do Ambiente e dos Recursos Naturais (LIFE), Direcção Geral da Qualidade Ambiente, Avenida Almirante Gago Coutinho, 30, P-1000 Lisboa	Direcção de Serviço da Conservação da Natureza (LIFE), Rua Filipe Folque, 46 - 1°, P-1000 Lisboa
United Kingdom (UK)	EPC Division (Life), Department of Environment, Romney House, 43 Marsham Street, UK-London SW1P 3PY	

Landesumweltministerien

Ministerium für Umwelt Baden-Württemberg (LIFE)
Kernerplatz 9
D-70182 Stuttgart

Bayrisches Staatsministerium für Landesentwicklung und Umweltfragen (LIFE)
Rosenkavalierplatz 2
D-81925 München

Senatsverwaltung für Stadtentwicklung und Umweltschutz (LIFE)
Lindenstraße 20-25
D-10958 Berlin

Ministerium für Umwelt, Naturschutz und Raumordnung des Landes Brandenburg (LIFE)
Albert-Einstein-Straße 42-46
D-14473 Potsdam

Der Senator fur Umweltschutz und Stadtentwicklung (LIFE)
Hanseatenhof 5
D-28195 Bremen

Umweltbehörde der Freien und Hansestadt Hamburg (LIFE)
Steindamm 22
D-20099 Hamburg

Hessisches Ministerium für Umwelt, Energie und Bundesangelegenheiten (LIFE)
Mainzer Straße 80
D-65189 Wiesbaden

Umweltministerium des Landes Mecklenburg-Vorpommern (LIFE)
Schloßstraße 6-8
D-19053 Schwerin

Niedersächsisches Umweltministerium (LIFE)
Archivstraße 2
D-30169 Hannover

Ministerium für Umwelt, Raumordnung und Landwirtschaft des Landes Nord-rhein-Westfalen (LIFE)
Schwannstraße 3
D-40190 Düsseldorf

Thüringer Ministerium für Umwelt und Landesplanung (LIFE)
Richard-Breslau-Straße 11a
D-99094 Erfurt

Ministerium für Umwelt des Landes Rheinland-Pfalz (LIFE)
Kaiser-Friedrich-Straße 7
D-55116 Mainz

Ministerium für Umwelt des Saarlandes (LIFE)
Hardenbergstraße 8
D-661 19 Saarbrücken

Sächsisches Staatsministerium für Umwelt und Landesentwicklung (LIFE)
Ostra-Allee 23
D-01067 Dresden

Ministerium für Umwelt und Naturschutz des Landes Sachsen-Anhalt (LIFE)
Pfälzer Straße
D-39106 Magdeburg

Ministerium für Natur und Umwelt des Landes Schleswig-Holstein (LIFE)
Grenzstraße 1-5
D-24149 Kiel

COMMISSION 94/C 154/01[1]
Eleventh annual report to the European Parliament on monitoring the application of Community law — 1993

G. ENVIRONMENT

1.   ·INTRODUCTION

1.1.   General situation

The main new Community initiatives were the adoption of the Fifth Environmental Action Programme[2] and Directive 91/692/EEC on the harmonization of national reports on the implementation of directives by means of periodic questionnaires to simplify the task of the Member States. These instruments reflect the new trend in environmental policy and usefully reinforce the facilities for monitoring the application of Community law in terms of its efficiency and of the concept that all are responsible.

The Fifth Action Programme (towards sustainable development) provides for new instruments to improve the practical implementation of Community environmental law. In support of the activities of the Community institutions, forums are set up for dialogue to improve the preparation of measures and coordinate and monitor their application (a general consultative body, a network of those responsible for practical application and a general monitoring group).

The functions of these various bodies will be to generate awareness of responsibilities borne by those in charge of these things in a framework of partnership and to ensure that Community environmental measures are applied correctly and transparently.

The harmonization of national reports offers hop for the future; the questionnaires designed with the Member States will give the Community access to comparable data on the implementation of environmental directives, enabling it to proceed from information supplied from official sources instead of relying on complaints from individuals and questions from Members of the European Parliament.

---

[1]   OJ No C 154, 6. 1. 1994, p. 42.
[2]   COM(92) 23 final; Council Resolution of 1 February 1993;
      OJ No C 138, 17. 5. 1993, p. 1.

If the number of complaints received by the Commission appears to have fallen, this is partly because the Commission is now merging cases for treatment together where the nature of the problem or the legal instrument infringed is identical.

1.2. Failure to notify national implementing measures

As previous reports already stated, there is a problem with the time taken to enact national measures implementing directives. In most cases the delays are attributable to problems of administrative coordination.

Action taken on cases of failure to notify in 1993 breaks down as follows:

- 90 Article 169 letters (95 in 1992);
- 26 reasoned opinions (18 in 1992);
- 7 cases referred to the Court of Justice (4 in 1992);
- 53 cases were terminated (63 in 1992).

During the report period fourteen directives fell due for transposal.

The full list of environmental directives is given at point 3 and progress in implementing them is summed up at Annex IV.

1.3. Conformity of national measures implementing directives with Community law

The number of proceedings commenced for incorrect transposal has remained broadly stable since 1988. In 1993 the Court of Justice gave judgment in four such cases, the Commission issued twelve reasoned opinions (two of them for failure to give effect to earlier judgments) and one new Article 169 letter, relating to an Article 171 proceeding. Four proceedings were terminated when the infringement was remedied.

The distribution of powers between Belgium's component regions is still a source of difficulty. Problems of compatibility of Belgian national implementing measures concern in particular waste, water and nature conservation.

No infringement proceedings were commenced against Denmark for incorrect transposal. The rare cases where there is cause to object are usually cleared up with the rapid adoption of measures that comply with Community law without any need for infringement proceedings. The Commission would stress here the excellent cooperation from the Danish authorities, who virtually always supply concordance tables to highlight the practical effect given to individual articles of directives in Danish law; its task is all the easier as a result.

In Germany, there is still a serious problem of conformity in the transposal of directives by circular. The planned legislation to replace circulars has yet to be enacted. The area chiefly concerned is water quality; measures to solve air quality problems have now been taken.

Although Greece often takes over the full text of the Community directive and incorporates it into national law, some directives are not properly transposed. The Commission is pursuing its bilateral talks with the Greek authorities with a view to resolving the difficulties.

There has been a number of infringement proceedings for incorrect or incomplete transposal in France relating to waste, water and nature conservation.

In 1993, the Commission notified four reasoned opinions to Ireland for failure to fully and properly implement certain environmental directives, relating to impact assessment, waste, protection of wildlife and radiation protection.

By and large, Luxembourg national implementing measures display a good conformity rating. But Directive 85/337/EEC (impact assessment) is one of the rare exceptions.

The Dutch legislation tends to impose more stringent requirements than those imposed by the directives, as is allowed under Article 130t of the Treaty. The few problems of conformity that arise are concentrated in a limited number of areas (wild birds and drinking water).

There are problems of non-conformity in Portugal (air quality, waste and water), Spain (environmental impact assessment, waste and nature conservation) and Italy (water, waste, laboratory animals and wild birds).

In the United Kingdom the problem areas are impact assessment, wild birds and air quality.

1.4. Incorrect application of directives

Incorrect application of environmental law in various parts of the Community is most commonly detected through complaints from Community citizens and through questions put by Members of the European Parliament.

The directives that create the greatest difficulties are those relating to waste, discharges into the aquatic environment, the protection of wild birds and environmental impact assessment.

The Commission issued fourteen reasoned opinions to Member States and sent an Article 171 letter to Italy concerning the dumping of waste in Campania (Case C-33/90 Commission v Italy).

The Court of Justice gave two judgments for the Commission on 2 August 1993.

The main problems of practical application in Belgium arose from the water Directives.

No cases of incorrect application of Community law in Denmark were brought to the Commission's attention. The Commission's informations is that Community environmental law is being applied in a generally satisfactory manner there.

In Germany the main problem areas as regards practical application were the waste directives and water quality in the new Länder.

In Greece, there has been no substantial change in the position since last year's report, the chief difficulties concerning wild birds, waste and air quality. The number of complaints about the impact assessment directive is still rising.

The main issues covered by complaints in Spain are nature conservation, impact assessments, water and waste.

In France, problems chiefly concern the application of the wild birds and impact assessment directives.

In both Ireland and the United Kingdom, problems of application of directives are encountered primarily in matters of water quality (bathing waters, shellfish waters, drinking water).

Specific problems arise in Italy with the application of the impact assessment and wild birds directives.

The difficulties encountered in the application of the waste and water Directives in Luxembourg flow from the fact that these Directives impose the same obligations on the smallest of the Member States as on the largest, where they are already found difficult to perform.

The main problems of practical application being scrutinized by the Commission in the Netherlands relate to wild bird protection and the designation of special protection areas and wetlands.

Problems in Portugal cover a range of environmental directives, but waste and water account for the bulk.

1.5. Structural Funds and other sources of Community finance

The Community's 5th Environmental Programme, adopted on 1 February 1993, envisages financial support mechanisms as one of four categories of instrument that will be used to further environment policy. There are now several such mechanisms.

LIFE — the financial instrument for the environment — entered its second year of application[1].

The Commission was notified of the plans and programmes implementing Regulation No 2078/92 on agricultural production methods compatible with the requirements for the protection of the environment and the countryside. This regulation aims to reinforce Community legislation on water pollution and habitat protection.

Article 130d of the Treaty on European Union provides for the creation of a Cohesion Fund to benefit four Member States — Spain, Portugal, Greece and Ireland. It is to be devoted to environmental investments and trans-European transport networks. Pending ratification of the Treaty, the Community adopted Regulation No 792/93 on 30 March 1993 establishing a cohesion financial instrument. Under Article 2 of this Regulation, Cohesion Fund assistance may be granted for, among other things, environmental projects contributing to the achievement of the objectives of Article 130r of the EC Treaty. In 1993 approximately 300 environmental projects, covering waste disposal facilities, sewage treatment plants, water supply and nature conservation measures, were submitted for approval.

The integration of environmental concerns has been reinforced by new provisions in the Structural Funds Regulations, which were formally adopted in July[2]. They provide for the inclusion in national and regional funding plans of a national or regional environmental appraisal, an evaluation of the sustainability of the proposed development strategy and details of the consultation arrangements with the competent environmental authorities.

Through these various instruments the Commission is contributing to the application of Community law. It is to be hoped that the Member States will use a significant proportion of their new Structural Fund allocations to finance projects aimed at protecting and rehabilitating the environment.

---

[1]   OJ No L 206, 22. 7. 1992, p. 1.
[2]   OJ No L 215, 30. 7. 1992, p. 85.

1.6. Freedom of access to information on the environment

I January 1993 was the date appointed for full transposal in all Member States of Directive 90/313/EEC on freedom of access to information on the environment. Three Member States — Germany, Greece and Italy — have yet to notify their national implementing measures (even though in Italy, transposal was provided for in the 1991 Community Act). In Germany, pending the enactment of federal legislation, the Länder are giving direct effect to the Directive.

All the instruments notified by the Member States are now undergoing detailed scrutiny for conformity with the provisions of Directive 90/313/EEC[1].

Practical implementation has given rise to complaints which have brought problems of both incorrect implementation and incorrect application to light. The bulk of the complaints are received from Belgium, Germany, Greece, Ireland, Spain and the United Kingdom. Most cases of incorrect application relate to the definition of 'environmental information' or to the categories exempted by the Directive so that information is withheld.

In the absence of national implementing measures enacted within the time allowed, the citizen enjoys a direct right of access under the provisions of the Directive which are directly applicable.

1.7. Environmental impact assessment

The lion's share of infringements of Community environmental directives relate to Directive 85/337/EEC, which is a comprehensive instrument applying at all levels of responsibility. Failure to assess the impact of specific projects is the commonest subject of complaints to the Commission.

The Commission is concentrating on securing greater conformity of national legislation with the Directive; contacts continue with Spain, and reasoned opinions were addressed to Ireland, Italy and the United Kingdom.

But Luxembourg has still not notified its measures, and the Commission referred the case to the Court of Justice in June (Case C-313/93). The existing Luxembourg measures fall short of the Directive's requirements, notably as regards road infrastructure projects.

An action has been commenced against Germany in the Court of Justice (Case C-431/92) for omitting to undertake a proper impact assessment before constructing an waste oils incineration facility.

All but three projects covered by Annex II to Directive 85/337/EEC (environmental impact assessment) are excluded from the Spanish legislation, contrary to Articles 2 and 4. Given the frequency of complaints, the Spanish authorities have informed the Commission of their intention to remedy the matter, but the complexity of the procedure is such that this will only be done in 1994.

The Commission addressed a reasoned opinion to Italy for failure to transpose Annex II properly. But in December 1992 the Italian authorities issued a circular reproducing the Commission's interpretation of the concept of high-speed road, this being the subject of many of the complaints received by the Commission.

---

1 *Belgium*: Décret du 13 juin 1991 concernant la liberté d'accès des citoyens à l'information relative à l'environnement dans la Région Wallonne (Decree on freedom of access to environmental information in the Walloon Region) (Moniteur belge 11. 10. 1991, p. 22559); Ordonnance du 29 août 1991 sur l'accès à l'information relative à l'environnement dans la Région de Bruxelles-Capitale (Order on access to environmental information in the Brussels-Capital Region) (Moniteur belge 1. 10. 1991, p. 21505); Besluit van de Vlaamse Executieve houdende vaststelling van het vlaams reglement betreffende de milieuvergunning (Decree of the Flemish Executive of 6 February 1991 on Flemish regulations governing authorizations in environmental matters) (Belgisch Staatsblad, 26. 6. 1991, p. 14269);
Denmark: Lov om offentlighed i forvaltningen (Freedom of Administrative Information Act) (No 572 of 19 December 1985);
Spain: Ley de Régimen Jurídico de las Administraciones Públicas y del Procedimiento de Administración Común (Legal Status of Public Administration and General Administrative Procedure Act) (No 30/1992 of 26. 11. 1992: BOE 285, 27. 11. 1992);
France: Loi portant diverses mesures d'amélioration des relations entre l'administration et le public et diverses dispositions d'ordre administratif, social et fiscal (Administration, Social and Revenue Procedures (Miscellaneous Provisions) Act (No 78-753 of 17. 11. 1978: JO 18. 11. 1978, p. 2851); Décret relatif à la procédure d'accès aux documents administratifs (Administrative Documents (Access) Decree) (No 88-465 of 28. 4. 1988: JO 30. 11. 1988, p. 5900);
Ireland: Section 110 of the Environmental Protection Agency Act 1992; Access to Information on the Environment Regulations, SI No 133 of 1993;
Luxembourg: Loi concernant la liberté d'accès à l'information en matière d'environnement (Freedom of Environmental Information Act), 10. août 1992; Règlement Grand-Ducal déterminant la taxe à percevoir lors de la présentation d'une demande en obtention d'une information relative à l'information (Environmental Information (Charges for Supply) Regulations, 10 août 1992 (JO A No 71, 28. 9. 1992, p. 2204);
Netherlands: Wet Openbaarheid Bestuur — WOB (Freedom of Administrative Information Act), Staatsblad 1991, 703; Wet Administratieve Rechtspraak Overheidsbeschikkingen (Administrative Decisions (Appeals) Act), Staatsblad 1975, 284; Wet Milieugevaarlijke Stoffen — WMS (Environmentally Dangerous Substances Act), Staatsblad 1985, 639; Wet Milieubeheer (Environment Act), Staatsblad 1992, 551; Regeling Uitvoering WOB (WOB (Implementation) Regulations, Staatscourant 118, 23. 6. 1992; Aanwijzingen inzake Openbaarheid van Bestuur (Freedom of Information Circular), Staatscourant 84, 1. 5. 1991;
Portugal: Lei No 65/93: Regula o acesso aos documentos da Administração (Administrative Documents (Access) Act): Diàrio da República I Series A No 200, 26. 8. 1993, p. 4524);
United Kingdom: Environment Information Regulations SI 1992 No 3240; Environment Information Regulations, Northern Ireland, SI 1993 No 45.

The Commission considered that Irish legislation is insufficiently stringent in regard to determining the need for impact assessment for certain types of project (for example, initial afforestation and peat extraction) and the sort of information which a developer should provide. It also considered that inadequate provision had been made for consultation of the public and other Member States. The Irish authorities have indicated a willingness to make certain legislative changes.

The United Kingdom was sent a reasoned opinion for failing to apply Directive 85/337/EEC to projects which were submitted for approval before the Directive became due for transposal but were not granted authorization until after that date. The reasoned opinion helped to persuade the UK authorities to abandon the East London River Crossing project.

The national courts are more and more fully involved in enforcing Community law in environmental matters, as earlier reports suggested. To take the example of the Somport tunnel in France, the Pau Administrative Court gave judgment on 2 December 1992 annulling the Order of the Préfet of the Pyrénées-Atlantiques declaring the construction of the tunnel and its access roads to be a public-interest project, on the ground that Directive 85/337/EEC had been wrongly applied. The principle that the citizen may rely on an environment directive in an action against a Member State in the courts was thus translated into reality.

1.8. Measures needed

The Commission intends to concentrate on the prevention of infringements, in particular through:

— action to be taken in response to new thinking generated by the Green Paper on civil liability;

— the integration of environmental considerations in other Community policies (Article 130r (2)); first steps in this direction were taken in relation to agricultural production techniques and rural conservation measures by Council Regulation (EEC) No 2078/92 of 30 June 1992[1];

— practical development of dialogue forums for the improvement of Community environment law and monitoring facilities.

---

[1] OJ No L 215, 30. 7. 1992, p. 85.

2. THE SITUATION SECTOR BY SECTOR

2.1. Waste

The Commission is still awaiting national measures implementing the Directive on batteries containing dangerous substances (91/157/EEC) from most Member States, only Denmark, Luxembourg and the Netherlands having notified. Article 169 letters have been sent to all the Member States for failure to notify national measures implementing the Directive on batteries and accumulators containing dangerous substances (93/86/EEC).

The Commission was able to terminate the proceeding against Belgium for non-conformity of national measures implementing the titanium dioxide Directive, and there is progress in complying with the judgment given in 1988 concerning incorrect transposal of the Directive on disposal of PCBs[1]. But no effect has yet been given to the judgment given in December 1986 for incorrect transposal of the Directive on cross-border shipments of waste, and the Article 171 proceedings are in motion.

Belgium, Denmark and Portugal have transposed Directive 91/156/EEC on waste. The Commission is awaiting notifications from the other Member States.

At the end of 1992 the Commission commenced an action in the Court of Justice to have the German legislation implementing Directives 75/442/EEC, 78/319/EEC and 84/361/EEC (waste, toxic waste and cross-border shipments) declared ou of order on the ground that it excluded waste for recycling and gave priority to treatment of waste within Germany. The Commission also criticized the inadequacy of the dangerous waste disposal programmes produced to give effect to Directive 78/319/EEC.

In Greece the problems regarding waste are the same as before — waste is dumped in various places without concrete environmental and human health protection measures. These problems were highlighted by the judgment given by the Court of Justice for failure to comply with Directives 75/442/EEC (waste) and 78/319/EEC (toxic waste) in relation specifically to the dump at Kouroupitos in Crete[2].

Proceedings are also in hand against Portugal for failure to notify the programmes to cut the volume of containers of liquids for human consumption required by Directive 85/339/EEC.

---

[1] Case C-230/85.
[2] Case C-45/91 [1992] ECR I-2509.

The implementation of regional and local waste treatment plans in Spain is behind schedule, and numerous complaints have been received about waste being dumped in open wells at various places. The outcome is a serious public health hazard of the kind that Directive 75/442/EEC seeks to outlaw. As the previous report stated, the Commission has no information on the programme to reduce the tonnage and volume of packagings for liquids for human consumption (Directive 85/339/EEC). The Court of Justice has given judgment against Spain[1], but the Commission has still not been notified of a programme. And where programmes have been notified, as in the case of the national toxic waste treatment programme, the information they contain is not in accordance with Directive 78/319/EEC.

The programmes required by Directive 85/339/EEC (containers of liquids for human consumption) have still not been adopted and notified by France, despite the judgment given by the Court of Justice in Case C-252/89 (against Luxembourg) to the effect that there is an obligation to prepare and notify such programmes[2].

A reasoned opinion was addressed to Ireland concerning Directives 75/442/EEC on waste and 78/319/EEC on toxic and dangerous waste. The Commission has challenged the fact that, contrary to those Directives, Irish local authorities have been given exemptions from the need for authorizations for their waste facilities (complete in respect of the first Directive, partial in respect of the second). The Irish authorities have accepted the Commission's arguments, and are committed to regularising the position in comprehensive new waste legislation.

2.2.   Water

There are relatively few delays in notification of measures to transpose the water directives falling due in 1993. National measures implementing Directive 91/217/EEC (urban waste water) are still awaited from Greece, Luxembourg, the Netherlands, Portugal, Spain and the United Kingdom and measures implementing Directive 90/415/EEC (dangerous discharges into the aquatic environment) are awaited from Greece.

The qualitative progress reported for 1992 in the conformity of national legislation continued in 1993.

The problem of legislation implementing the groundwater Directive (80/68/EEC) has been settled in Spain and is on the way to a solution in France,

---

[1]   Case C-192/90 [1991] ECR I-5933.
[2]   Case C-252/89 Commission v Luxembourg.

but a second judgment has been given in the Court of Justice against Belgium (Walloon Region and to some extent the Brussels Region) (Case C-174/91).

The position in relation to Directive 80/778/EEC (drinking water) has improved in Luxembourg and Germany, which has now given effect to the judgment given against it by the Court of Justice in November 1992[1]. But reasoned opinions have been addressed to Italy and the Netherlands regarding the conformity of their legislation.

Problems of correct application are rare, but they often take time to settle.

After receiving a reasoned opinion in 1993, the United Kingdom authorities have announced measures, to be introduced gradually over a period extending until 1995, to comply with the judgment given by the Court of Justice regarding conformity with the drinking-water Directive (80/778/EEC)[2].

The quality of drinking water in the new Länder has not yet reached the desired level despite the German authorities' efforts (but Directive 90/656/EEC does allow them until 1995). The Council was obliged to agree to extension of the deadline for application in the new Länder of the Directives governing discharges into the aquatic environment as facilities in use there turned out to be even more obsolete than was thought at the time of unification.

A reasoned opinion was addressed to France on the subject of the excessive levels of pesticide residues in drinking water permitted by two administrative circulars.

A French Ministerial Order of 26 April 1993 amends the Order of 10 July 1990 prohibiting discharges of certain substances from industrial plant into groundwater. The result is an improvement in the implementation of Directive 80/68/EEC (protection of groundwater against pollution by certain dangerous substances), which should have been transposed by December 1981.

The position regarding bathing waters (Directive 76/610/EEC) is improving: Spain has sent in quality improvement plans, which are under scrutiny, and the Commission has been able to terminate its proceeding against Luxembourg.

Ireland's lack of implementation in Bantry Bay of Directives 79/923/EEC on the qualities required of shellfish waters and 76/160/EEC concerning the quality of bathing water was the subject of a reasoned opinion. The reasoned opinion also challenged Ireland's failure to provide a proper statutory basis for implementing Directive 79/923/EEC and its failure to fully transpose the

---

[1]   Case C-237/90 [1992] ECR I-5973.
[2]   Case C-337/89 [1992] ECR I-6103.

criteria of Directive 76/160/EEC for identifying bathing waters which must be protected under the Directive.

The Court of Justice gave judgment against the United Kingdom in July for failure to preserve the quality of bathing water at Blackpool and neighbouring areas of Southport, contrary to Directive 76/610/EEC[1].

There are problems with the conformity of Italian legislation designating shell-fish waters (Directive 79/923/EEC; a reasoned opinion has been sent) and fish waters (78/659/EEC; a second action has been commenced in the Court of Justice (Case C-291/93)).

No Member States have complied with their obligation under Article 7 of Directive 76/464/EEC to adopt and notify programmes to reduce pollution of the aquatic environment by discharges of dangerous substances. The Commission has addressed reasoned opinions to France, Germany, Italy, Luxembourg and Portugal.

The water pollution controls introduced in France by Act No 92-3 on 3 January 1992 will have considerable implications for the application of Community directives since new schemes such as the SAGE (water use and management schemes) will be grafted on to the measures already in place to give effect to the directives.

Infringement proceedings for incorrect application of the Directive are in motion against Portugal.

2.3.   Air

There are no serious problems either of transposal or of conformity. But there are a few exceptions. The Court of Justice gave judgment against Belgium for non-conformity of national implementing measures with Directives 85/207/EEC (nitrogen dioxide)[2], and the Commission has referred Luxembourg's national measures implementing Directive 84/360/EEC (industrial plant) to the Court. The British legislation on air quality standards (nitrogen dioxide — 85/203/EEC) makes inadequate provision for sampling techniques and observation stations in relation to the country's surface area. But the Commission is glad to report that the authorities have responded to a reasoned opinion by amending the offending legislation in line with the Directive's requirements.

---

[1]   Case C-56/90, judgment given on 14 July 1993, not yet reported.
[2]   Case C-186/91, judgment given on 10 March 1993, not yet reported.

The Commission is not satisfied with the efforts by government departments in the Member States to discharge their obligation to insist that new industrial plant use the best available technologies not imposing excessive cost burdens (Directive 84/360/EEC). For existing plant, the situation is even worse. There are widely divergent interpretations of the concept of best available technologies not imposing excessive cost burdens in the Member States, whohave not always notified the Commission of the policies and strategies they have adopted for the gradual adaptation of existing plant. But the situation has improved in comparison with earlier years, thanks to the BATNEEC notes prepared by the Commission with the assistance of the Member States for a number of industries.

The situation regarding information on effect given to obligations imposed by the air quality directives (80/779/EEC on SO_2 and suspended particulates; 82/884/EEC on lead; 85/203/EEC on No_x) has not evolved. The main air quality problems concerning pollution in Athens subsist. The situation is not apparently improving, despite the efforts made by the Greek authorities. The solution would not seem to lie in a series of individual measures but rather in a detailed air quality improvement programme of the kind required by Directive 80/779/EEC (sulphur dioxide); Greece should have notified this by October 1981. The Commission is actively looking into the matter.

Work done in 1993 under Directive 91/692/EEC (rationalization and harmonization of reports) for the elaboration of questionnaires for the transmission of information required by the air quality directives should improve the situation in the near future.

Two Member States (Belgium and Ireland) have yet to notify the Commission of their programmes to cut pollution from large combustion plants as required by Directive 88/609/EEC. The Commission is working on comparisons of programmes, though the information supplied by the Member States is of uneven quality. The Member States are behind schedule with the transmission of emission data for 1993.

2.4.   Noise

A Bill to implement the aircraft noise Directive (92/14/EEC) in Germany has been presented, but no date has been stated for its enactment. Implementing measures are still outstanding in France, Italy and Luxembourg.

Confirming the trend described in previous reports, the application of the noise directives raised no significant problems in 1993. The directives set emission standards for newly marketed products but contain no provisions regulating ambient noise from a diversity of combined sources. Consequently the Community has no power to tackle problems of urban noise such as that generated by traffic jams or industrial plant. No problems of noteworthy importance are to be reported for this area in 1993.

2.5.   Nature protection

On 2 August the Court of Justice gave a significant judgment against Spain concerning the status and protection of the Santoña marshes, an important bird habitat in northern Spain[1]. The Court accepted the Commission's argument that the area should be recognized as requiring protection under the wild birds Directive (79/409/EEC) since it hosted large numbers of certain vulnerable species, and that the Spanish authorities had failed to provide an adequate level of protection. The Case served to clarify several points of interpretation of the Directive's bird habitat protection provisions.

In some cases satisfactory solutions have been found. The proceeding concerning application of Directive 79/409/EEC to the Bay of Cadiz, for instance, was terminated when pollution control measures were taken, the authorities having commenced the procedure for designation as an Article 4 special protection area.

Many of the French cases brought to the Commission's attention reveal combined infringements of Directives 79/409/EEC and 85/337/EEC.

The Nantes Administrative Court has applied to the Court of Justice under Article 177 for a preliminary ruling on the interpretation of Article 7 (4) of Directive 79/409/EEC (wild birds) as regards the close season for shooting certain species.

In Belgium, problems of conformity of legislation with the wild birds Directive (79/409/EEC) continue to arise in both Wallonia and Flanders. In Flanders, insufficient protection measures have been taken for the designated areas, whereas in Wallonia there are problems with the shooting rules despite

---

[1]   Case C-355/90, not yet reported.

a judgment given by the Court of Justice[1]. The Commission issued a reasoned opinion under Article 171 on 25 May. Belgium has yet to notify the Commission of measures to give effect to the Directive on conservation of wild birds (91/244/EEC).

Denmark, Greece, Luxembourg and the Netherlands are still behind schedule with the transposal of Directive 91/244/EEC amending Directive 79/409/EEC on wild birds.

Greece has still not designated a sufficient number of special protection zones for the conservation of wild birds (Directive 79/409/EEC), and it has not demarcated the designated zones with adequate precision or taken practical protection measures for them.

In Italy problems subsist with the application of Article 4 (special protection areas).

In the Netherlands there is a problem with the wild birds Directive (79/409/EEC), on which the Court of Justice gave a second judgment in 1992[2]. Despite Commission pressure to have the relevant clauses of the Flora and Fauna Bill 1989 brought into line with the Directive, there is no evidence of progress here and the Article 171 proceedings are continuing. The Commission is pursuing its talks with the Dutch authorities to have several special protection areas and wetlands designated for the purposes of Directives 79/409/EEC and 85/411/EEC.

2.6.   Chemicals

Discussions are in progress with several Member States regarding Directives 82/501/EEC and 88/610/EEC on major industrial accident hazards.

Emergency plans and other measures prescribed by the former are to be established by the Member States, but their application in many specific industries is not yet secured.

The Commission, in cooperation with the Greek authorities, is using all the means at its disposal to have this Directive properly applied; it hopes thereby to avoid recurrences of accidents such as that which occured at the Petrolla-Ellas refinery in September 1992.

A reasoned opinion was addressed to Ireland for incorrect transposal of the laboratory animals Directive (86/609/EEC) and the case against Luxembourg for

---

[1]   Case C-247/85 [1987] ECR 3029.
[2]   Case C-75/91 [1992] ECR I-549.

failure to notify the full set of national implementing measures was referred to the Court of Justice. Talks are continuing with Italy and the United Kingdom to seek solutions to some outstanding problems of conformity.

Italy has still not notified national measures implementing the asbestos Directive (87/217/EEC) and there are problems of conformity in several other Member States. The adaptation of Dutch law to the asbestos Directive (87/217/EEC) requires the enactment of six separate instruments; the Commission is supporting the Dutch authorities.

Greece, Luxembourg and Spain have not notified national measures implementing Directives 90/219/EEC and 90/220/EEC on genetically modified organisms, and reasoned opinions were issued. Problems of conformity of legislation enacted in France and Germany are under discussion with the Commission.

All Member States have notified national measures implementing the Directives on good laboratory practice (87/18/EEC and 88/320/EEC).

2.7.   Radiation protection

Italy is still behind schedule in implementing the radiation protection directives, notably the basic Directive (80/836/Euratom, deadline December 1982) and the amending Directive (84/467/Euratom, deadline April 1986). It has not complied with the judgment given by the Court of Justice on 7 May 1991[1] and the Commission has issued a reasoned opinion under Article 171.

By and large directives are correctly transposed, the exception being Luxembourg. Infringement proceedings commenced against Ireland were terminated when national legislation was amended to transpose the directives correctly. When scrutinizing national implementing measures for conformity with the directives, the Commission had regard to the draft instrument to revise standards and to the ruling by the Court of Justice that the Member States were entitled to set stricter standards than those allowed by the Directive[2].

Despite the vital importance of informing the population about radiation emergency risks, pointed up by the Chernobyl accident, only five Member States (Belgium, Denmark, Ireland, Spain and the United Kingdom) have notified full measures giving effect to Directive 89/619/Euratom. France and Germany have notified some measures, but they are incomplete. Article 169 letters have been sent to Luxembourg and the Netherlands and reasoned opinions have been addressed to Italy and Portugal. The Commission is particularly attentive to the

---

[1]   Case C-246/88 [1991] ECR I-2049.
[2]   Case C-376/90 [1992] ECR I-6153.

tendency of the Member States to put a restrictive interpretation on the Directive's scope. The Directive is not confined to protection of people living in the neighbourhood of a nuclear power-station but seeks also to protect those who are exposed to the risk of an emergency arising from other uses of nuclear energy. Germany is the only Member State that has notified the Commission of measures to give full effect to Directive 90/641/Euratom on the radiation protection of outside workers (deadline 31 December 1993); the United Kingdom has simply notified a draft set of standards by the procedure of Euratom Treaty Article 33.

The Directive on the radiation protection of medical patients (84/466/Euratom) has turned out to be difficult to transpose on account of its very broad-ranging subject-matter (notably involving training of doctors and paramedical staff, inventories and acceptability criteria for treatment facilities, and the monitoring and replacement of facilities) and of the fact that it is drafted in general terms. The Commission pursued its infringement proceedings against six Member States for incorrect transposal; reasoned opinions were addressed to Belgium, Ireland, the Netherlands, Portugal and Spain. In June the Court of Justice held that Italy was in breach of its obligations to implement the Directive, since its unpublished circular, having no mandatory status, did not properly transpose it into national legislation[1].

---

[1] Case C-195/92

3.   PROGRESS IN IMPLEMENTING DIRECTIVES APPLICABLE TO
THE ENVIRONMENT

The results obtained by the Member States in 1993 are satisfactory, though
Greece, Ireland and Italy 'could do better'.

Member States	Directives applicable on 31.12.1993	Directives for which measures have been notified	%
Belgium	117	107	91
Denmark	117	115	98
Germany	119	108	91
Greece	119	100	84
Spain	117	106	90
France	117	111	95
Ireland	117	103	88
Italy	117	95	81
Luxembourg	117	108	92
Netherlands	117	108	92
Portugal	117	106	90
United Kingdom	117	106	90

Note: this table concerns the following Directives:
General matters: 85/337, 90/313, 90/656, 90/660.
Waste: 75/439, 75/442, 76/403, 78/319, 84/631, 85/339, 85/469, 86/121, 86/278,
86/279, 87/101, 87/112, 91/156, 91/157, 92/112, 93/86.
Water: 75/440, 76/160, 76/464, 78/176, 78/659, 79/869, 79/923, 80/68, 80/778,
81/855, 81/858, 82/176, 82/883, 83/29, 83/513, 84/156, 84/491, 86/280,
88/347, 90/415.
Air: 75/716, 80/779, 81/857, 82/884, 84/360, 85/203, 85/210, 85/580, 85/581,
87/219, 87/416, 88/609, 89/369, 89/427, 89/429.
Noise: 79/113, 80/51, 81/1051, 83/206, 84/533, 84/534, 84/535, 84/536, 84/537,
84/538, 85/405, 85/406, 85/407, 85/408, 85/409, 86/594, 86/662, 87/252,
88/180, 88/181, 89/514, 89/629, 92/14.
Nature: 79/409, 81/854, 83/129, 85/411, 85/444, 86/122, 89/370, 91/244, 91/271.
Chemicals: 79/831, 80/1189, 81/957, 82/232, 82/501, 83/467, 84/449, 86/431, 86/609,
87/18, 87/216, 87/217, 87/432, 88/302, 88/490, 88/610, 90/219, 90/220,
90/517, 91/325, 91/326, 91/410, 91/632, 92/32, 92/37, 92/69, 93/67, 93/90,
93/105.
Radiation protection: 80/836, 84/466, 84/467, 89/618, 90/641.

European Commission

European Community environment legislation
Volume 1 — General policy

Luxembourg: Office for Official Publications of the European Communities

1996 — lx, 260 pp. — 16.2 x 22.9 cm

ISBN 92-827-6835-X (Volume 1)
ISBN 92-827-6828-7 (Volumes 1-7)

Price (excluding VAT) in Luxembourg: ECU 13 (Volume 1)
                                     ECU 74 (Volumes 1-7)